Heroin

Living and Dying with an Addict You Love

How to Survive When Everyone Dies

Robert L. Hobbs Jr.

Disclaimer

This is the author's recollection of events, which have been related to the best of his knowledge. Some identities have been changed or are composites.

The author of this book does not dispense medical advice or prescribe the use of any technique as a form of treatment for physical, emotional, or medical problems without the advice of a physician, directly or indirectly. The intent of the author is only to offer information of a general nature to help in your quest for well-being. In the event you use any of the information in this book, the author and publisher assumes no responsibility for your actions.

Published by

 PADUKA PRESS

Copyediting and formatting by Joni Wilson

Printed in the United States of America

Paperback
ISBN: 978-0-9989008-1-0

Dedication

To Little Boy Blue

You were dressed in blue on your very first day
You were my pride and joy I was proud to say
The day you turned blue, I knew you lost your way
When they saved you I hoped you'd be ok
When the doctors said it might happen again
I said not to a boy like him, man
Never to a boy like him

"And the cat's in the cradle and the silver spoon
Little boy blue and the man in the moon
When you comin' home son
I don't know when, but we'll get together then, Dad
We're gonna have a good time then."
~Harry F. Chapin, Sandy Chapin

Come home, Little Boy Blue, I'm waiting.

Love,
Dad

Contents

Foreword

There is something astonishing when you look into the eyes of someone addicted to drugs and/or alcohol, and they finally understand the driving forces behind the pain, misery, suffering, hurt, and degradation that consist of their present lives, as a result of their addiction. Then there is the look of the ever-tormenting fear, depicted by the parents or loved ones who have gone through this journey of addiction, almost relieved to see new life in the addict, after being so affected by the lies, dishonesty, deceit, betrayal, and the theft of material things (some with no real value except they belong to the parents, families, or loved ones, and some with immeasurable value that they will never get back).

Along with the theft of dreams, well-being, education, family, prosperous life, retirement, and a host of other lost elements, depending on who the survivor happens to be, parents and loved ones are paralyzed by love and hate, unable to distinguish which emotions are appropriate to feel toward their child or loved one. Most times, loved ones are not able to discern the difference between love for the addict and hate for the addiction. A kaleidoscope of emotions bombards the lives of the individuals who do not have problems with addiction, but, are living the life of an addict with all the uncertainty of the addicted.

This book captures the essence of the addiction of an opiate addict from the eyes of his father. It depicts the full spectrum of emotions that he lives with every day, not knowing whether his son is going to live or die. Imagine what it is like to be drained daily of your life force from a drug addiction, while your only interest is the life of someone you love. While your life deteriorates, the addict's life goes on, as he or she watches how the addiction affects you, with no consequence to him or her.

I commend this father for being so transparent in his storytelling and wanting to share his experience with the many parents and loved ones of addicts all around the world. First, I think the greatest gift to others is the act of self-expression. This parent has conceptualized a truly life-changing experience. Second, I think the most damaging part of addiction is the intense secrecy, kept by the addicts and their loved ones, because of its potential for embarrassment and judgment. Last, there is something comforting about identifying with others' personal pain, knowing they too understand your struggle. This is an immensely healing process. Because the addiction is no longer personal, it is the nature of addiction that your loved one has undertaken and not a personal attack on you.

Enjoy the reading and, most important, let the knowledge of addiction from the experience of a parent set you free.

—Gerald Rhett, LCSW, CADCII, CCS, SAP

Acknowledgments

I cannot describe how hard it is to write a book. Until you try it yourself, you will never understand. I have now done it and I still do not know how this happened, where the inspiration came from, or why so many people have come back into my life. This section is supposed to be short, and it will be, but only if I use well-worn clichés in thanking those of you who were here with me for the past 100 days. Please know that in my heart, there is far more love and gratitude than can be expressed here.

Wendy Elisabeth, I have no idea where we are going or how we will get there, but I know I will only go with you by my side. Thank you, with all my love always.

I apologize for everything that my four children have had to endure—you have suffered as much as anyone, and my truest wish is that you each find joy and happiness.

My greatest cheerleaders have always been my mom and dad. I could lose my legs and they would still encourage me to win a gold medal at the Olympics. They only see the good in people; a trait I hope to find in myself. I am sorry this isn't a gold medal, but...

There is nothing in the world like a brother; I have been overly blessed. My brothers Myron, Tom, Kevin, Bucky, Joe, and Ray have each inspired and supported me throughout a rather tumultuous lifetime. I appreciate and love you all and especially Ray, Tom, and Kevin for your help on this project.

The artwork, produced by my niece Trinity, has overwhelmed me emotionally since she created it. I still cannot believe how a few simple words resulted in her capturing the essence of my story. The paintings are so beautiful. I wish I could share how deeply they touch me.

My Aunt Ursula and my Aunt JoAnn have never turned their backs on me—despite some fairly horrible behavior. They stood by me as I produced this book—with prayers, loving guidance, and excellent feedback.

My father-in-law, Ron Saczalski, has been one of my closest friends for more than ten years. I am so grateful, Ron, that you are still here with me and I am grateful for your support of this book.

Writing is a long and lonely experience sometimes. I did do a few twenty-three-hour days, and when I did, my best friends in the world were right beside me. Berkeley and Fitzgerald, thanks for your unconditional love. Belle, thanks for your perfectly timed interruptions—I needed a break.

I have a huge family with more than forty first cousins. I have second cousins and in-laws all around the world, and I often wonder how they are faring and if they know how fondly I think of them and the times we spent together as kids. Inspiration comes in many forms,

There is no finer place in the world to grow up than in my hometown of McDonald, Ohio. I am grateful to my fellow Blue Devils everywhere, but on this project especially Marie J Carkido, Lori Backlund, Lori Babik, and Karen Delon. I also wish to thank Tammy Parteleno, Mike Kochera, Christy O'Donnell, Missy O'Connell, Lisa Jordan, Dave Nagy, and Beth Vannoy.

I have many lifelong friends who have joined me on this journey at various times. I would like to thank from The Morgue at Ohio University—Keith Kaple, Dave Zwolenik, and Brock Onat; from Knolls Atomic Power Laboratory—Karl Pritchard; from IBBS—Dave Keil and Effie Chin; and from the 324th MP Company—Eddie Yuhas.

I would like to thank those who taught me about addiction and contributed directly to this book: Dr. Walter Brooks, Dr. (ABD) Gerald Rhett, and Robert Jordan.

Much of what I have come to understand came when helping others. I'd like to thank Kim Pelligrini and her entire family for giving me what I needed to move on.

I am fortunate to be alive and for that I thank my doctors: Jeff Stone, Pat Skellie, and Elizabeth Licalzi.

There were times when I believed there was only one way. Thank you to my teachers Adam Funderburk, Mark and Magali

Peysha, and Geshe Phende, for showing me over and over that there is more than one. I am never trapped.

To my brothers and sisters in recovery everywhere, especially Bryan B., Bill D., and Cliff T., there are not enough pages to contain the debt of gratitude I hold for the privilege of having you in my life. I hope that today you get what you asked for and that tonight you are grateful for whatever you got.

No book would ever be complete without a talented and dedicated editor. *Heroin—Living and Dying with an Addict You Love* enabled me to not just work with a truly wonderful editor but to also make a new friend who probably feels as though she has known me her entire life. Thank you, Joni Wilson, for making the end of this process memorable.

And before I forget, to all those men and women out there day and night battling this enemy face to face, I, and everyone involved in this effort, express deepest gratitude to you for protecting and saving lives when you can, and delivering bad news when you must. When I was a young boy, everyone wanted to be a police officer, a firefighter, or an emergency medical technician, because we wanted to be heroes. You men and women did it—you became real-life heroes. Thank you!

To the readers of this book who I have not yet met—thank you for trusting me with an important part of your learning. I wish I could personally walk with each of you as your journey unfolds. Wherever you are, please know that you are not alone, you are never alone.

May we all be together as one.

—Bob

Preface

Why This Is Important

For Family Members

In February 2014, I found myself in a situation that was completely foreign to me. I was in a life-threatening circumstance, and I didn't know what to do. Making matters worse was the fact that the threat was intravenous heroin; not something you can casually discuss with your friends and neighbors. The shame and embarrassment associated with heroin is a powerful deterrent from seeking help through the normal channels. I ended up searching online for answers about what to do and where to go. I had to research heroin, recovery, detox, and withdrawal. There was so much I didn't know; it was a difficult time.

I vowed then that I would eventually do whatever was in my power to ensure no other parent or loved one of a heroin addict would need to suffer through the lonely discovery process the way I did. I wish I could have written this book sooner, but the side effects of being related to a heroin addict were having their way with me. Partly due to my son's heroin addiction, I have battled PTSD, anxiety, and major depressive disorder for three years. These illnesses have sidelined me from most of life's playing field. Only just recently have I been able to put aside my thoughts sufficiently to focus on a project of the scale and magnitude of publishing a book.

My truest desire is to provide parents and loved ones of heroin addicts with two primary gifts from my harrowing experiences. First, a how-to guide about heroin addiction. I want to help all parents and loved ones of addicts find the best possible outcomes available to them, based on their personal situation. These people should not have to search online for answers about heroin, what's happening to them, and where to rehab their addicted family member.

Second, I hope to provide parents and loved ones with solace, security, and confidence in knowing that whatever they are feeling or thinking as they go through this process—it's okay. Their feelings, however obscene, are not their fault. Feelings come and go like a fresh breeze on a spring morning. You can't latch onto the breeze and keep it—and we shouldn't latch onto the feelings we experience either. No one should feel guilty, abnormal, bad, immoral, or unloving because of the thoughts and feelings they have toward an addicted loved one. Whatever the feeling is, it's acceptable. Whatever the feeling is, it has been felt before. You're not alone—it's okay.

To all the parents and loved ones reading this, I hope you find the information you need and that while going through this process, you'll have the confidence you need, knowing you're not alone.

For Addicts

I've come to believe that from time to time addicts believe that their parents and loved ones are actively working against them and their best interest. This was never true in my personal experience, and I doubt it's true in any case. We always want what's best for our kids. As parents, we often feel responsible when our children go astray. We always feel a need to help and never lose the feeling of control that we had when our kids were young. If one of our kids needs fixing, dammit, we would go to any length to fix them. It takes a long time to realize that we can't control our children.

I think it's important for addicts to come to understand what parents might think and feel at various times during the addiction process. We are human. We are hurting. There is nothing we wouldn't do to save you. We don't blame you. We don't resent you. We just want you back—the real you.

Maybe by reading this book, some addicts will learn to empathize with their parents a little bit more—cut them a little slack. I promise we parents are doing our best, even though at times we have no idea what we're doing. This isn't meant to be a guilt trip. It is meant to share what I often believe children miss in their parents, and that is humanity—the imperfect beauty of being human.

For Mental Health Professionals

With the opioid epidemic in full swing, I'm sure that mental health professionals are getting much experience with the impact that addiction has on families, especially parents. I don't believe that the feelings I have had on this journey are unique to me. I think that many parents have had exactly the same types of thoughts and feelings that I have had; that they have felt much guilt and shame for what they have thought and felt.

Parents need help in processing the emotions, the feelings, and the thoughts that they have with respect to their child and their child's addiction. There is obviously much guilt, shame, fear, and anger involved because of the addiction. But there is another layer, maybe more than one layer, that goes beyond the obvious guilt, shame, anger, and fear of addiction in the first layer.

This is the guilt and shame the parent might hold because of what they think about the addict—not the addiction, but the person. These feelings might tilt toward hate, the loss of love, a desire that this all end in any possible way, in some escape, some eject handle. These are not easy things to communicate, even in private therapy. They are thoughts and feelings the parents and loved ones regret deeply.

This area should be explored, because the parent and loved ones will never find peace, as long as this guilt and shame is not openly dealt with. It is so vile, so obscene, to have some of these thoughts and feelings—no parent will utter any of these deeply held secrets. It is up to the professionals to understand that these thoughts and feelings do arise, but the parent is trying to bury them and will not discuss them.

Professionals should explore these emotions and help their clients understand that it is okay to have these thoughts and feelings. There should be no shame, no guilt, no anger, and no regret for feeling anything as a human. Professionals should help their clients understand that feelings and thoughts are just part of the human experience and not a definition of any single individual.

Battling the Heroin Epidemic

There *is* hope for heroin addicts and those who love them. It is a difficult journey, as told through my experiences in this book. I invite you to learn from what I've been through. Educate yourself about what is best for you and the addict in your life. Know that you are not alone, and there is help available from professionals.

As the country becomes more aware of the heroin epidemic, resources are being added to assist affected families. There is a way to end the recovery and relapse lifecycle, as related in this book. I remain optimistic that this epidemic will be eliminated soon and no longer disrupt the sacredness of our human lives.

Introduction

Why I Wrote This Book

Imagine being kidnapped and taken to the middle of the ocean on a stolen sailboat. Your abductor is picked up by accomplices on a yacht. He leaves you alone—you have never sailed—never even been on the water—there is a storm coming, and other sailors know your boat is stolen. They do not want to associate with you—they sail toward safety—and leave you out in the storm. You have nowhere to go—no one to ask—except the radio—and the person on the other side wants to charge you hundreds of thousands of dollars to help you out.

When you ask what you can do while you wait, the individual discusses jibs, genoas, reefing, halyards, and rode. You sit there stumped; you have no idea what the person is talking about. You're floating in the ocean, watching a storm roll-up on you, and you're wondering what the hell Jenny and reefer has to do with it.

You look behind you, and you can see the storm battering the horizon where the ocean and sky meet. It's almost on you, and there is nothing you can do.

This was my situation in late February 2014. I found out that my son was a heroin addict. Without my consent, I was tossed into the chaos of addiction, with no preparation, no training, and no understanding. I quickly called for help, but before help came, the storm of overdose washed over my life. As I tried to survive, there were many things I had to learn. The learning didn't come easy for me. The purpose of this book is to serve as a guide for those learning to deal with the addiction of a loved one.

There are many complex areas of learning that are necessary, and I could never describe all of them. For me, I had to learn the clinical nature of heroin addiction, the emotional trauma it would have on me and other family members, and the impact it would have on every relationship in our lives. In these pages, I attempt to introduce the clinical process, my emotional journey, and how my relationships have evolved.

Every journey is unique. Yours will be yours. My deepest wish is that with this book, you will find your way through the storm toward calm waters, fair winds, and sunny skies. May you be one with all.

Chapter 1

Crashing into Reality

The more real you get the more unreal the world gets.
~John Lennon

February 24, 2014, 5:00 PM

I couldn't believe what he just did; he passed by me as I waited for him on the side of the road. He knew I was there—he saw me, but he drove by as if I were invisible. My truck is huge; it stands out. There was no traffic, and he was right behind me in his Cadillac.

I pulled back onto the main road and got right behind him; at least he was still heading in the right direction. As soon as he noticed I was there, he began to accelerate.

He is fucking nuts, I thought.

We were on narrow, two-lane roads with a speed limit of 35 mph. He was pushing 55 mph and was tailgating the car in front of him.

What the hell is he doing?

He had always been a terrible driver; his passengers experienced what was at best a thrill ride, and at worst a death wish. All his siblings made fun of how he was always all over the road, and, though obvious to us, he seemed oblivious to his inability to keep a steady track or maintain a lane.

We approached an intersection where, coincidentally, he had totaled his previous car, another Cadillac, in addition to the brand new pick-up truck he pulled in front of. That accident—one of many to come—was at least $50,000. Thank goodness for insurance. As we got to the intersection, I wondered if he was thinking about that crash . . .

He continued his erratic and evasive driving. It appeared he was trying to get away from me. That would make no sense—I had just bailed him out of jail, for Chrissake.

Why is he doing this now?

I was getting frustrated; but I had not yet witnessed the extent that he was willing to go to evade me.

The next intersection, on our short drive home from a nearby county jail, was a T intersection. From our position, we could turn left, or turn right onto yet another two-lane road that was heavily traveled by commuters at this time of day. We were to turn left onto Mars Hill Road and go less than 3 miles to the entrance to our subdivision and our home—where his mother was waiting.

Mars Hill Road was especially congested, as people were arriving back in the suburbs following a typical Monday afternoon fighting with Atlanta rush-hour traffic. To our right, roughly 800 yards, was a traffic light that controlled the flow of traffic at the intersection of Mars Hill Road and Due West Road. This was a popular turning point for the many commuters who lived nearby.

The Mars Hill/Due West intersection was where both two-lane roads expanded to three lanes, to allow for a left-turning lane at each of the four stops. Traffic flow was controlled by the signal, where each of the left-turning lanes had an arrow light, and each of the straight-ahead lanes had a typical green light that went active after the left arrow went red.

We were at a stop sign, waiting to turn left onto Mars Hill Road. He was in front of me and would turn first, and then I would turn left when traffic permitted. I had my left signal on; he, of course, did not.

I'll talk to him about that too, I thought.

As his car finally arrived at the front of the line, I eased up, and took my spot as second in line. What happened next is still hard to believe.

He aggressively made a right turn and started to accelerate to an extremely high speed. I am sure he redlined the Northstar V8 engine and easily reached 85 mph as he approached the Due West intersection. In disbelief, I reached for my phone, as I turned right to follow him. He swerved left into the now empty left-turning lane, just as the arrow went red. Then he crossed into the intersection and quickly swerved back to the right, in front of the traffic just starting to edge forward as the straightaway light turned green.

There were at least six cars waiting to go straight; he passed them all on their left, in the turning lane, and then cut in front of them and flew down Mars Hill Road toward the city of Powder Springs. No way could, or would, I try to replicate his maneuver. He was flying down Mars Hill Road, at 85 mph or more, at least six cars ahead of me. He was gone.

Wow. What is he doing; what in the hell is he doing?

My thoughts were flying through my mind. They were moving so fast I couldn't seem to grasp any of them. I had never seen anything like his maneuver before. It was far and away the most reckless and dangerous driving I had ever witnessed. Hell, not just the most reckless driving; it was the most reckless behavior of any kind.

What is going on with him?

I thought back to what had been transpiring during the past few days.

Three Days Earlier

February 21, 2014, 10:30 PM

He usually called by now—just to let us know that he was ok and would be coming home from work soon. He was twenty-two years old, but part of the agreement we made before letting him move back home included some unusual restrictions. He had to let us know where he was always, and before he left one location, he had to let us know where his next location was. He also had to be home by midnight—no exceptions.

"Nothing good happens to a twenty-two year old in a Cadillac after midnight," I told him. "Especially on a Friday night."

He had been back at our place for quite some time. Eight months, which for him was a long time to not be in any known serious trouble. From my perspective, him not being in any known trouble had become a major accomplishment. Long ago, I had given up on all the typical hopes and dreams a father has for his son—his oldest child. Now, just staying out of trouble was more than enough for me. Hell, I was proud that he wasn't in any trouble.

Little did I know that soon my expectations would drop even lower. In fact, they would drop so low, that I would be more than grateful if he were just alive. He could be in jail, out of jail, homeless, anything. I wouldn't care. If I could talk to him—that would become good enough— that would become GOOD.

Had things changed so much? I thought.

They had.

He had been slipping lately. His calls after work were getting later and later, and his arrival home from work was trending more and more toward midnight. There were plenty of indicators that it wasn't just his lack of respect for our agreement that was emerging. Something else was wrong; something else was going on, but I didn't know what. If I were to accuse him, I would be met with lies and cover-ups. General hate and discontent would soon follow for everyone around us. Trying to prove he was up to something was an equally bad idea. The only real proof would come from a drug test; asking him to incriminate himself had never worked in the past. Why fight for that terrain again? That kind of argument disrupted the entire family—all six of us. It was not worth it.

It was about 11:00 PM when I got a text from him explaining that he was giving a buddy a ride home from work, and then from home to another buddy's house. It didn't sit well with me, but he texted that he would be home on time. What was I going to say? He was twenty-two, driving his car, telling me where he was, and where he was going, and that he would be home on time. I didn't have any justification to complain to him, other than that uneasy feeling I get in my gut when something bad is about to happen.

I responded to his text: "I will see you soon."

Fuck, I thought.

I waited up for him; I usually did. I was still a control freak and was convinced that whatever was wrong with him I could fix it. I would fix it—eventually—I would fix everything. After all, I was smart, educated, religious, successful, and had plenty of money and influence. I truly believed, with all my being, that I could fix his problems, whatever they were. I just hadn't figured out the right solution. But I would; eventually, I would.

Sometime after midnight, he still wasn't home, and I was pissed. I knew it! I knew he wasn't upfront with me. I texted him and got no response. I called and got his voicemail. I called again and got his voicemail again.

Then I got a text from him: "I am going to jail."

"What? When? Where?" I responded.

"Right now, Paulding County, I think."

"Why?" I asked.

"My buddy has drugs in the car, and they just called the K9 unit to bring the dogs, because I won't let them search."

"Where is your buddy?" I texted.

"Arrested. Back of a cop car. DUI."

"What did you do?"

No response.

"Jack."

Nothing.

"What did you do?"

No response.

"Jack?"

He was gone. Paulding County Jail. Possession of who knows what. He had already been to jail—well—several actually. He had multiple stays in juvenile detention—drug related and disobedience. As an adult, after multiple arrests, he had been charged with possession of prescription pills, possession of marijuana, possession of marijuana with intent to distribute, possession of methamphetamine, possession of a firearm, first-degree forgery, and second-degree forgery. The forgeries were of a physician's prescription pad. He forged prescriptions for pain pills and presented them to a pharmacist.

He was guilty of all the charges. But his felony convictions were from one arrest. He pleaded guilty to two forgeries and possession of meth. He was sentenced to ten years in prison, with credit for time served (one year), with the balance served on probation, of which at least two years were reporting to a probation officer. He had been out of jail for twenty months or so. He was on probation and reporting until just recently, when his status changed to nonreporting. We were all quite relieved; him most of all.

I was scared. Really scared. If the police officers discovered he was on probation, they would likely revoke it and send him to prison. Because he was already convicted of the forgeries and the possession of meth, the sentencing judge simply had to revoke his probation and send him to prison. There is no trial, no defense, no argument. Probation conditions are clear, and a felony arrest is obviously a violation of probation. Quick math in my head led me to believe he was going to prison for seven years. That seemed to be how much time was left on the ten-year sentence. I was convinced he was headed to state prison. I could not fathom it. I was overwhelmed with despair. My only son, my pride and joy, was going to prison for seven years. He was all of 5'7" tall and weighed maybe 145 pounds. Prison would not be kind to him; he might not survive it. I was terrified; I had no plan; I had no idea what to do. I kept asking, no one in particular, "Now what? Now, what do I do?"

I lay awake all night long, hoping for some creative solution to arise in my mind. None did. I had no answers.

The coming shame and humiliation that I would suffer, my wife would suffer, and, most important, my daughters would suffer started to weigh on me. How do I answer a question such as, "Hey, how is your son? How is Jack?"

I was not well practiced in the art of answering such well-meaning people with conversations about state prisons and felony convictions. Fuck.

He had been in and out of trouble for eight years, and everyone knew it. He was dealing drugs on and off, in and out of jail, in and out of school, and people talk. They might not let us know that they know—but they know. It never really felt right, but we tried to make the best of it. We tried to integrate with the community, knowing full well that our son was probably pitching weed to their kids—or even worse. There is no playbook for this kind of thing. We were stuck. All we could do was try to keep up a good image for our girls. Everyone probably knew it was fake. But what else could we do? It was lonely; we were isolated by our shame and humiliation, by our judgment of ourselves, and by our inability to express exactly what we were going through.

His behavior and track record up until this point were bad enough. Prison was going to take this to a whole new level. I could not imagine the pain my daughters might experience if their high school classmates found out that their brother was in prison. How would the parents of those classmates react toward our daughters and us, once they find out he was in prison? Hell, high school was hard enough on a girl. Carrying this burden was going to make it all the worse. I couldn't blame others for how they might treat us—because I know how I would react if I were in their shoes. No way would my kids be allowed to hang out with the siblings of someone like my son—and for no reason other than what was probable, what potentially could happen. Is my kid more likely to get in trouble at the prisoner's house or some other house? I don't like that I think that way—but I do—or I did. It was unnerving. All of it was unnerving.

"I'm going to jail."

Like many things I have seen, heard, and said during the course of the past eleven years, this is one that just stuck in my mind—branded into the forefront of my consciousness.

"I'm going to jail."

Somehow, this one was different. It wasn't like the other six or seven times he went to jail. I could sense a feeling of relief that he had in writing this text. As if—"Finally, I don't have to do this anymore; I don't have to run around hiding all the time . . . I am going to jail."

This bothered me too.

I couldn't sleep. But being awake hurt—not just emotionally, but physically. My whole body had a painful tension, a nervous anxiety. It felt as if I were in serious trouble myself. It was an overwhelming sense of dread. I could not get rid of it. It persisted.

I signed into my MacBook and started searching the county website for information about his arrests. I knew from previous experience that his arrest information would not be available until he was booked-in. That could take quite a while in rural Georgia on a Friday night. At some point, in the early morning hours, I read his charges:

Possession of marijuana, less than 1 oz

Possession of marijuana with intent to distribute

Possession of methamphetamine

Fuck. Fuck, fuck, fuck. He is totally screwed; two fucking felonies! Prison! My son is going to fucking Georgia State Prison.

I cried. No, I sobbed. There was no way he could escape this one. None. All his plea wild cards were used up on his previous arrests. He was already a convicted felon with two or three counts. Eventually, they would find out that he was on probation and that charge would be added to the list too.

He is gone. Done. I was the only person awake in the house. I sobbed—alone. I was so terribly sad; partly because of what he had coming to him and partly because of my failure to control the situation. I let him down. I let his mother down. I let his sisters down. I was supposed to fix this; somehow, someway, I was supposed to prevent this from getting to this point, and I failed. My son was going to prison. Somehow, I had to learn how to cope with this as much as he would have to. It would not be easy telling his mom. Fuck.

At 10:00 AM on Saturday, I called the jail and asked about bail. They didn't exactly laugh at me— though I half expected them to. Clearly, they didn't yet know that he was a convicted felon and on probation. I sure as hell wasn't going to mention it. I was told that he had a probable cause and bail hearing on Monday morning, and that I should attend that.

I didn't want to go. Seeing him in a prisoner jumper with cuffs, shackles, and waist chains is not easy. However, I was also uncertain if I would see him again. At any time, he could be shipped to Candler County to face his probation violation, and be sent directly to State Prison.

Now what am I supposed to do?

Saturday was hard. I couldn't focus on anything. I had been up all night and had tied myself in knots. As much as I tried to put all this out of my mind—I couldn't. My brain just kept replaying last night's events; then it would rewind all the way back to 2006. Every mistake I had made as a father was highlighted in the playback. My whole body was in pain—debilitating, deep, constant pain. The odd thing about this pain was—it was also at the forefront of my consciousness. It was the first thing I was aware of—ALL THE TIME! Hard to focus on anything productive or meaningful when your mind is focused on some physical pain that it had created itself.

I didn't wake up Sunday morning, so much as I got out of bed. It was hard to find enough peace to fall asleep when pain and prison were so prevalent in my thoughts. Maybe it was an illegal search; maybe it was the other kid's drugs; he was driving and did get a driving under the influence (DUI); maybe they didn't read him his rights—all that television drama stuff was pouring out. I was looking for a loophole. The "not my kid" loophole, or the "this doesn't happen to guys like me" loophole, or the "I don't deserve this bullshit" loophole.

Nothing. Besides, he was already convicted in Candler County. So, once they learned of his arrest, and its circumstances, it wouldn't matter if he was "technically" guilty or not in the Paulding County case. What matters was his probation could be revoked—no trial required, and the Candler County judge could put him in prison.

I was fairly sure I was going to lose my mind. Friends at work had been predicting a nervous breakdown for years. But, I had three daughters, a wife, a good job, and other responsibilities. I had to stay strong and maintain an edge for their sake. It wasn't easy to "suck it up," but I did—on the outside anyway. One more time—suck it up— figure it out, and deal with it, so no one else has to. That was always my goal—and despite my best intentions, it never seemed to work out.

Monday came. I don't remember if I called off work or not. I didn't want to burden my employer and coworkers with more of my ridiculously intense and seemingly perpetual family crisis. They were always great about it—but to me it was humiliating and—it seemed so over-the-top dramatic. Seriously, if I were listening to my story—I wouldn't believe it. I wasn't quite yet to the "I don't give a fuck" level of disregard for my career, but I was getting there. Little did I know.

February 24, 2014, 9:00 AM

I arrived at the Paulding County courthouse and found my way to the courtroom where he would have his hearing. It turned out that the inmates would be "in court" via closed circuit television from the jail. So, I was not going to see him after all. The only reason for being there was so that I could see him, just in case he was leaving for prison. I stayed and waited anyway. Monday morning bail hearings are quite busy due to the arrests made during the weekend; especially those on Friday and Saturday nights after the bars close.

Despite the overly full docket, the judge, Tex Farr, who wore a cowboy hat and cowboy boots on the bench, moved quickly through his cases. When Jack's case came up, it was fairly straightforward; there was probable cause that a felony was committed, and despite the fact that his prior convictions were not yet known, the judge set bail at a hefty $7,800. We did not live in this county, so I could not use a property bond. I hesitated to use cash, because I had convinced myself he was going to prison, and he might freak out and run.

The judge was kind and asked the courtroom if any family or friends had come to court to support Jack. I raised my hand and answered a few questions about who I was and how I knew Jack. The judge then asked if I had any questions. I didn't. He then told me to call him later if I did. He told the courtroom that he thought it was important that family members come to court, and that he appreciated us. He also explained his willingness to help families out if they needed help. I didn't know what that meant, but I thanked him before leaving the courthouse.

I arrived home a little after noon on Monday. I texted my assistant and let her know that I would be working from home and that we had another issue with Jack. She knew what that meant, and she was understanding, as always. She got a lot of joy out of taking care of me. She would deal with work on my behalf. I didn't need to worry about it anymore.

I checked my email and called one of my managers to make sure everything was ok with my projects. Then, I checked online to figure out how much "time" he might be facing in prison. I knew that I wouldn't find anything useful, but somehow checking made me feel useful; as if I was helping him in some way.

It was 1:30 PM or so when I received a phone call from a strange number. I picked it up and was shocked to hear it was Judge Tex Farr.

He told me to come down to the jail in about an hour. He was going to let me bail Jack out on my signature. I was stunned. I had never heard of such a thing. Certainly, I never expected to hear from a superior court judge. I asked him some questions, and, in hindsight, his answers were not revealing. He said this happens sometimes, and that he hoped I could get my son some help before it was too late. He ended the call by telling me it would take an hour to get the paperwork filed, and that I should bring $20 cash for the administration fee. I thanked him and ended the call. It all seemed strange. Not divinely strange but something-was-missing-here strange. Jack was the luckiest criminal to ever live. He skated justice with such ease. I waited an hour and arrived at the jail with $20.

I went into the reception area and filled out some forms, paid the $20, and signed my name as required. The officer told me it might be a few minutes, so I went outside and waited in my truck. As I sat behind the steering wheel, waiting for him to come out, I reflected on many of the times he sat in this front seat next to me. It was a 2006 Silverado that I had bought when he was a hockey player. Many times, we traveled to hockey tournaments listening to rap music and talking about his future. It all seemed so distant; he had gone from jail to the front seat of this truck a few other times. The most vivid moment was on September 1, 2006, when he sat in this truck and told me explicitly that he did not want or need me in his life. I should just leave him the fuck alone. That was more than ten years ago, and it still stings today as much as it did then.

I thought about what I would say when I saw him. There were not many things to say that had not already been said many times. We were both tired of my speeches. I figured I would be compassionate and see where he wanted to take any conversation we might have.

It was fifteen minutes before he came out of the front door. The bright sun caused him to squint and shade his eyes as he looked for the truck. Once he spotted me, he made his way through the parked cars to the passenger door. He was carrying some papers and a clear, ziplock bag that contained his personal items. He looked like shit. He was dirty and greasy; his color was off, and he looked sick—flu-like sick.

"Hey, Jack."

"What the fuck are you doing here?"

"What do you mean? I just bailed you out of jail."

"I didn't fuckin' need your help! I have this all under control."

"Really, how's that? How do you have it under control?"

"I worked it out with them so that all of this will go away. I have to meet them tomorrow and do what they tell me, and if I do, then all this will disappear."

The strange circumstances surrounding the judge's earlier call started to make a little more sense. Maybe the prosecutors called the judge and told them to let Jack go.

This was heavy stuff, I thought. Scary stuff.

I didn't have to ask what he meant; I knew enough. I didn't want to know anymore. My recurring nightmare ran through my head: <u>Is this why I am shot in the chest at the front door</u>?

I squeezed my eyes shut, then opened them and looked over at him. He was looking at me—but it didn't seem that he was using his eyes. They were dark, gloomy.

"Well, I don't know what you are talking about, but when a superior court judge calls me at home and tells me to come to the jail and pick up my son—I do it."

"Can we go get my car out of the impound?"

"They won't let you have your car; it is evidence. They probably haven't even finished searching it yet."

"They told me to go down there and get it—they are giving it back to me."

This was odd. Really odd.

He gave me directions and guided me to where he thought his car was impounded. It took a little time, and we had to turn around once or twice, but we eventually found the impound lot. While we were driving, I asked him about the charges and the drugs.

He told me the whole story, and as I could have guessed—the drugs were not his. He didn't know about them—they belonged to the other guy—he was a dealer. According to this story, Jack did not know there were drugs in the car until the cops told him. The weed was in the kid's duffle bag.

Man! I wanted to believe him. But I didn't. How could I? It would be so foolish of me to buy into yet another of his stories. He was, at the least, a pathological liar.

"Why was he driving your car?"

"Because I was passed out."

"On meth?"

"No, I don't do meth; and they didn't find any meth either. They found a piece of cellophane with residue on it. They think the residue was meth."

"What was it?"

"Heroin."

"What?"

"Heroin."

"Heroin? You mean like needles in your arm? What the fuck is heroin?"

"It is what I have been on. I was passed out because I had just shot up."

Oh, my. I had never—ever—spoken to anyone who had put a needle in their arm before. I never knew any drug addict, let alone a heroin addict. And now, as I talked to one for the first time in my life, I am looking into the eyes of my son. My boy. My pride and joy.

My mind was racing again. Heroin is really heavy stuff—it's not the rat poison, is it? No . . . that's PCP, I think. I know what LSD is. What the hell is heroin? It was a ghetto drug in the '70s—Harlem and New York City subway type of thing . . . right? How the hell did he get on this stuff?

It was 2014. Despite the fact that an opiate epidemic was gripping the entire nation, and that I lived with an addict, this was the first time the thought of heroin ever entered my mind. My fear became so strong, so overwhelming, in that moment, that I had a hard time drawing in a breath.

Now what. Now, what do I do? *I thought.*

I collected myself as best I could.

"How long have you been using heroin? Needles dude, needles? You stick fucking needles in your arm?"

"Yeah. And other places. I started when I was eighteen. I took pills for a couple of years after I broke my collarbone. Pills are expensive. I tried to quit using Suboxone, but it didn't work. Heroin was all I could afford—and it is a lot stronger than pills."

I had never connected pain pills to heroin. Of course, I didn't even know what heroin was yet. Holy shit. This was fucked up! Now, what was I supposed to do? I had no idea. I was paralyzed by a mind that could not answer my question.

"Whatever this is, we will figure it out. We will figure it out somehow. Just stop using and let me think it through."

We arrived at the impound. The car had been there since Friday night/Saturday morning. Thankfully, the lot took credit cards. I didn't have enough cash to pay for the tow and three days of impound. It took some time to get the car released to us, because we had no proof of ownership. As usual with Jack, none of the required paperwork was in the car. No registration, no insurance card. It's never easy. Luckily, I could pull up the insurance card on my phone. The impound manager was kind and willing to accept it as proof of ownership.

"Ok, you are going to follow me home, right?"

"Yeah, I am coming home."

"All right, cool. I will let your mom know."

I got in the truck and pulled out of the gated parking area and onto the access road. It felt like I was making a movie, and this wasn't going to be the last time I felt that way. Everything was so surreal, so made up, so dramatic. And—this kind of thing doesn't happen to people I know, and it certainly never happens to me. I am just a vanilla, suburban professional. Maybe I was overexaggerating what was happening during the past few days. I thought it through: I had just learned that my son was a heroin addict; that he has been using for four years, and that he took Suboxone and pain killers for two years before that. He was a convicted felon, arrested again while on felony probation. Somehow, he was let out of jail on a signature bond just hours after bail was set at $7,800. And it felt as though he told me he was going to do some deal with the Georgia Bureau of Investigation (GBI) to get this latest arrest to disappear.

No, I told myself, no, you are not exaggerating this. You don't know a single person who has ever done heroin, you don't know anything about the GBI, and you don't know anyone you can call to talk this through with. This is a really scary situation. And there is the dream— getting shot at the front door dream.

How did I not know any of this? How could I be so deep in his business, and not even know what he was addicted to? How could I not know what it is or how it works?

I was angry. In fact, I was feeling many emotions, and none of them was the good kind. I was entering a dark place—I just didn't know it yet. I cried again as we started the drive home. He was right behind me.

Now what. Now, what do I do?

I let my thoughts just do what they were gonna do. I was getting tight in my hips. I knew that the nervous anxiety that always followed would soon physically overwhelm me. The pain that I felt in my body from these emotions was indescribable.

Is this normal? I'll have to check on this pain in my body at some point. But first, I must learn what heroin is. And what the hell is Suboxone? I also need to find a rehab or somebody who can tell me what to do.

Right now, I just want to get him home. I want him to be safe. One more night, try to get him through one more night.

For some reason, he started to fall behind. Car trouble maybe? I figured I'd pull over and wait for him. Just wanna make sure he was ok.

Chapter 1 Concepts

1. If you think a loved one is hiding something from you that might be drug related, the depth of the problem might be far greater than you can imagine.
2. A heroin addict in withdrawal will go to almost any length to get a fix.
3. There is a tremendous difference in appearance, demeanor, and personality between a withdrawing heroin addict just before a fix and just after a fix.
4. The realization of heroin addiction will have a huge impact on you physically, emotionally, and mentally. It has the potential to affect your life, until there is seemingly nothing of value left.
5. Few, if any, heroin addicts start off with heroin. It takes time and other addictions to get there.
6. Abuse of pain pills leads to heroin abuse.
7. Suboxone use is an indicator of heroin (and other narcotic opiates) abuse.

Chapter 2

Heroin

If you change the way you look at things, the things you look at change.
~Wayne Dyer

Deadly Impact

In 2015, heroin killed 13,000 people in the United States (Figure 1)[1]; that is roughly the same as the average number of Americans killed annually in the three deadliest years (1967–1969) of the Vietnam War. The heroin death rate continues to rise, and soon we will face the prospect of losing 100,000 American lives in less than a decade—nearly twice the total of Vietnam deaths.

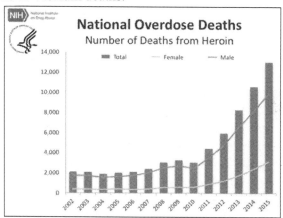

Figure 1: Number of Deaths from Heroin. Source: National Institute on Drug Abuse; National Institutes of Health, U.S. Department of Health and Human Services.

These numbers are staggering, shocking, and scary, and if this were a war, and we were losing so much for so little gain—there would be an uprising like the country has never seen. Though this epidemic continues to grow in numbers and spread geographically, I would wager that more Americans know that 58,000 military personnel were killed in Vietnam, fifty years ago, than know how many lives were taken by heroin last year. Somehow, these drug deaths go mostly unnoticed, unrecognized. I

---

1 Full-color files from this book are available free at www.heroinlivinganddying.com.

would never demean the service of an American service person—especially those who fought and died for us. My point is the loss of life in Vietnam brought tremendous social uprising and civil protest; today, we lose lives at a similar rate and hardly a sound is made. Maybe if deaths due to heroin overdose were announced on the news every evening—the youth would get the message, that a needle in their arm is the first shovel full of dirt dug from the hole of their grave. As important, heroin kills the addict's nonusing family members too; they just happen to continue living.

I cannot explain why this epidemic is shrouded in such secrecy, not completely anyway. What I do know is that family members of addicts, fathers like me, are so ashamed and humiliated by the stigma of heroin in the household that we would take the truth to our graves. The embarrassment is not just surrounding our child's addiction to a nasty, needle-administered narcotic, but also the guilt associated with our failure as a parent, as a member of the community, and a contributing member of society.

I have maintained for some time that heroin's greatest ally is the secrecy that surrounds it. Addicts and dealers certainly are not going to share their stories. Parents, siblings, spouses, partners, and other family members are shamed into silence. In many jurisdictions, even law enforcement and medical examiners are resistant or unable to publicize the cause of death accurately as heroin or opioid related.

I do not know the solution to the problems we face with heroin addiction and overdose. However, I have come to believe that shining a light through the shroud of secrecy, and illuminating the issue, can only aid in destroying heroin's grip on our people. There are hundreds of thousands of families dealing with this exact problem as I write this, and as many as 50 percent might not even know yet that heroin is the problem. A majority of these families and family members are living in a lonely, frightening, and dark place. Few realize that there is help—they try to fight alone—only to realize they cannot win. Others lose before they even realize there is a fight. I want to reach out to all of them now and offer my love and assistance—and I would like to ask others to do the same.

Why Is a Heroin Epidemic Occurring Now?

Several occurrences came together almost perfectly to help drive the heroin epidemic, as we know it today. In his book, *Dreamland*, Sam Quinones[2] explains, in great detail, the rapid growth and distribution of prescription painkillers in the United States, beginning in the 1990s and continuing until recently. One stunning statistic is that there are currently enough prescription painkiller scripts written in the United States to provide every adult with a bottle of pills.[3] Quinones also describes the cheap production of high potency, Mexican, black tar heroin and its pizza delivery distribution system developed by Mexicans from the town of Xalisco. High-quality, low-cost heroin, delivered like pizza to individuals who have been overprescribed pills is certainly one set of drivers of this epidemic.

Another driver of heroin's rise in popularity is the potency of what is on the street today. In the 1970s, the purity of heroin was about 10 percent, and it cost $3,260 per gram (1981). In 2017, the purity ranges from 30 to 40 percent,[4] and it costs roughly $200 per gram.[5] At one time, the requirement of injecting heroin with a syringe provided a rather high barrier for many first-time users. The high concentration of modern-day heroin provides a potential first-time user an extremely euphoric experience by smoking or snorting the drug, thereby removing the stigma of using needles. For many, the pursuit of stronger and stronger highs results in less and less resistance to using needles.

The perfect storm, if you will, which has culminated over more than two decades, consists of the convergence of high availability of prescription pain pills; high-potency, low-cost heroin; convenient distribution; and the elimination of the stigma associated with needles in first-time users. Additionally, the Mexican distribution system is well

---

[2] Quinones, Sam. (2015). *Dreamland: The True Tale of America's Opiate Epidemic*. New York: Bloomsbury Press.

[3] American Society of Addiction Medicine. (2016). Opioid Addiction 2016 Facts and Figures. Retrieved February 2017 from http://www.asam.org/docs/default-source/advocacy/opioid-addiction-disease-facts-figures.pdf

[4] Drug Enforcement Administration—DEA. (2016). National Heroin Threat Assessment Summary—Updated (DEA-DCT-DIR-031-16). Retrieved February 2017 from https://www.dea.gov/divisions/hq/2016/hq062716_attach.pdf

[5] Retrieved from various online sources.

suited to attack obvious and traditional markets, and new markets, in suburban areas of middle-sized towns.

What Is Heroin?

Heroin is an extremely addictive and dangerous derivative of morphine, a compound produced by the seeds of poppy plants. The compound is processed into a white or brown powder, or sometimes a sticky, dark, tar-like substance. Most of the world's heroin is produced in South Asia, Mexico, and Colombia. Eighty percent of all heroin in the United States crossed the southern border from Mexico,[6] regardless of the country of origin.

Heroin has many street names, including boy, boi, H, smack, horse, black tar, and others. It is often "cut," or diluted, or "stepped-on" with substances such as starch, sugar, and more dangerously fentanyl, a synthetic opioid that can be 100 times more potent than heroin. Many overdose deaths in 2016, and so far in 2017, are credited to heroin cut with fentanyl (Figure 2). Heroin is usually dissolved into a heated liquid and then smoked or injected. It can also be snorted into the nasal passages while in powder form, similar to cocaine.

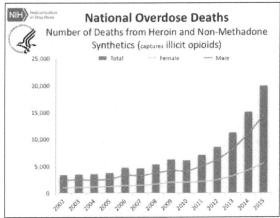

Figure 2: Number of Deaths from Heroin and Non-Methadone Synthetics. Source National Institute on Drug Abuse; National Institutes of Health, U.S. Department of Health and Human Services.

---

[6] DEA. (2016). National Heroin Threat Assessment Summary—Updated (DEA-DCT-DIR-031-16). Retrieved February 2017 from https://www.dea.gov/divisions/hq/2016/hq062716_attach.pdf

Injection is by far the most potent method of administering heroin. However, all three methods rapidly introduce the drug to the brain. As it enters the brain, the drug quickly causes a strong euphoria or "rush," which is sometimes compared to a sexual orgasm. The feeling of euphoria is followed by an overall sense of relaxation, like the sensation one experiences when on the threshold between being awake and being asleep. This feeling might last several hours and is often accompanied by nausea, overall warmth, dry mouth, heavy limbs, constricted (pinpoint) pupils, drowsiness, and depressed breathing and heart rate.

Depression of respiration is what kills an addict during an overdose. The effect of the drug so overwhelms the nervous system that the nonvoluntary reflex activity of breathing simply stops. If not reversed, coma, brain damage, and death can occur. This cause of death is the same for all opioids—and more than 33,000 Americans died due to opioid overdose in 2015.

How It Works

Perhaps you have heard of runners experiencing a "runner's high" or an "endorphin rush." Endorphins are neurotransmitters that are naturally produced in the body to reduce or block pain. Endorphins attach to certain receptors in the brain and nervous system and result in pain regulation, hormone release, and an overall feeling of well-being. Some receptors are located in the brain's reward center, and when endorphins attach there, another neurotransmitter, dopamine, is released. Dopamine produces an overall sensation of pleasure and achievement.

Endorphin is the combination of two words "endo" meaning of the body, and "morphine" meaning like morphine. Externally administered opioids behave similarly to endorphins—except that the body does not control the number, potency, rate of introduction, or half-life of morphine molecules introduced to the brain. In fact, because the users have no real knowledge of the exact contents of the powder or tar they consume—they can't control how much they are putting in their body.

As stated earlier, when the morphine molecules reach the brain and nervous system, they quickly attach to the opioid receptors and generate a powerful euphoria or rush, followed by an overall sense of relaxation and wellness. This feeling leads to repeated usage as the addict tries to replicate the sensations. The body begins to "defend itself" by building a tolerance to the morphine molecule. As the tolerance grows, the effect of the user's "normal" dose diminishes—so more heroin per dose is needed to satisfy the urge to experience the euphoric sensation. As the dose is increased, the tolerance increases, so the dose increases again. Though the overall tolerance of the body increases at a given rate—the respiratory system's tolerance is thought to lag. The respiratory system's lower overall tolerance to a relatively higher dose is one theory of accidental overdose.

The buildup of tolerance is primarily due to substantial physiological and physical changes in the brain and nervous system, which are difficult to reverse. If the addict attempts to abruptly quit using at this juncture, he will suffer great pain and other withdrawal symptoms. Essentially, the body has adjusted to the presence of the morphine molecule—abruptly taking it away, without giving the body time to compensate, results in withdrawal. This is physical dependence. The user is at a seemingly lose-lose fork in the road. If he doesn't use, he will become sick; if he does use, he takes a considerable risk with his life. It is difficult to quit when suffering through withdrawal, and many, many addicts choose to use, rather than to suffer. Unfortunately, the physical pain is not the worst of the addiction problem. If it were, we could detox every addict, and they would never choose to experience the pain of stopping a second time—therefore they wouldn't relapse.

Unfortunately, there is a psychological side to the addiction. I am not qualified to describe it—but you must have some idea of the struggle. So, consider this—many addicts become "infatuated" with heroin and the euphoric rush that it provides. Remember, the rush is often compared to a sexual orgasm and the craving is often compared to the urge for sexual intercourse. For many addicts, the pursuit of the next high becomes their life's primary purpose. Everything else takes a backseat. In fact, everything the addict has is now at risk of being lost—money, belongings, cars, houses, jobs, relationships, spouses, partners, children, all of it. Some addicts will sacrifice all for just one more encounter with their *seductive lover*. For a few of the least fortunate, there is nothing they will not sacrifice for heroin—nothing.

So How Has This Affected Us?

As I put this chapter together, it is February 2017. The most recent available statistics are from 2015. The 2016 statistics have not been released. Additionally, there are multiple sources of information that take common data and interpret it differently. Small variations in definitions of terms can result in wide variations in reported numbers. With that said, almost every number comes with the caveat that these numbers are likely understated, as not all jurisdictions, law enforcement agencies, and medical examiners report consistently. Therefore, the numbers that I will share in this section are my gross estimates, unless a source is cited in the footnotes. With that said, consider the following:

There are as many as one million heroin users in the United States, with half of those using in the last month. Historically, 25 percent of all users are addicted; that would imply that 1 in 1,000 adult Americans are heroin addicts.

In real numbers, it reads like this: Annually, there are one million heroin users, 500,000 are active (used in the last month), 250,000 are addicted, and 15,000 die.

Let's consider another angle. There are five million prescription pain pill users using without a prescription.[7] The government estimates that 4 percent of this population will become heroin addicts.[8] The quick math shows that 4 percent of five million is 200,000 heroin addicts who started as prescription pill users.

The government also estimates that 80 percent of heroin addicts[9] started using heroin after using prescription painkillers. If my estimate of 200,000 heroin addicts who started with pills represents 80 percent of all addicts, then 100 percent of all heroin addicts is 250,000. These numbers seem to correlate. One more—the government also reported that in 2013, 300,000[10] people were admitted to a public treatment center for heroin addiction.

A Question for the Curious

"What about the heroin users who are not using?"

---

[7] DEA. (2016). National Heroin Threat Assessment Summary—Updated (DEA-DCT-DIR-031-16). Retrieved February 2017 from
https://www.dea.gov/divisions/hq/2016/hq062716_attach.pdf
[8] National Institute on Drug Abuse—NIDA. (2017). Heroin. Retrieved March 16, 2017, from https://www.drugabuse.gov/publications/drugfacts/heroin
[9] NIDA. (2017). Heroin. Retrieved March 16, 2017, from
https://www.drugabuse.gov/publications/drugfacts/heroin
[10] DEA. (2016). National Heroin Threat Assessment Summary—Updated (DEA-DCT-DIR-031-16). Retrieved February 2017 from
https://www.dea.gov/divisions/hq/2016/hq062716_attach.pdf

Again, the numbers I am stating are rough and at least thirteen months old. If there are one million users, 500,000 actives, and 250,000 addicted, then we can infer that there are 500,000 nonactive users (clean more than one month), and 250,000 active users who are not addicted.

Let's first examine the 500,000 nonactives who have at least one month clean. Remember, in 2013, 300,000 heroin users sought public treatment. We should assume that a fair number of the nonactive population is either in treatment or recovery. It is also likely that a fair number of this population is in jail or prison. Finally, it is possible that some number have been using something other than heroin for the past month. Regardless, studying the 500,000 nonactive users could lead to a solution or a path to solving the addiction epidemic in which we are currently ensnared.

Of the 500,000 active users, 250,000 are not addicted. I cannot say whether they ever will become addicted or not, but I have learned to never bet against heroin. Between 2012 and 2015, it is estimated that the annual number of new heroin users was between 150,000 and 200,000 Americans.[11] That is an extremely high number of new users, and certainly many of them would fall into the active nonaddicted classification. Where they end up remains to be seen.

How Deadly Is Heroin Compared to Other Drugs?

Heroin is by far the deadliest drug in use in the United States today. Of the five million prescription pill users, 22,000 died from an overdose. There are 1.5 million cocaine users in the United States, less than 6,000 died from an overdose. Heroin has one-third the users of cocaine and one-tenth the users of prescription pills, yet it has twice the deaths of coke and one-half the deaths of prescription pain pills[12] (Figure 3).

	Prescription Pain Pills	Cocaine	Heroin
Deaths	22,000	6,000	13,000
Users	5,000,000	1,500,000	500,000
Death Rate (%)	0.44	0.40	2.60

Figure 3: Deaths and Death Rates for Narcotics.

[11] NIDA. (2014). Heroin. Retrieved March 16, 2017, from
https://www.drugabuse.gov/publications/research-reports/heroin
[12] DEA. (2016). National Heroin Threat Assessment Summary—Updated (DEA-DCT-DIR-031-16). Retrieved February 2017 from
https://www.dea.gov/divisions/hq/2016/hq062716_attach.pdf

What Do We Need to Know?

Heroin is an extremely addictive narcotic that is highly potent, relatively cheap, and easy to obtain. The acceptance and availability of prescription pain pills as recreational drugs create a large potential market of heroin users. This population is directly targeted by heroin distribution networks that deliver heroin directly to the addict. The addict does not need to go to a sketchy location to get dope. The high potency eliminates the stigma associated with needles, making first-time users less fearful to try it. The convergence of these phenomena results in a large and growing user base and a growing number of overdose deaths.

For those of us who have not used and would like to protect our children from using—consider this: The safest mind is one that has never heard or answered the seductive voice of heroin. Parents and caretakers of potential heroin users/addicts would do well to prevent knowledge of heroin's euphoria. Once a potential user becomes a user, I am afraid that the power of influence rapidly shifts, from your love for them to their love for heroin. It is a sick infatuation. And as much as you or the user would like to "unknow" the feeling—it cannot be unknown. How a sexual orgasm feels during intercourse cannot be unfelt. This is the nature of things. This is the evil nature of heroin. Like a hurricane, destruction and ruin are soon to follow.

So once the genie is out of the lamp, a person who loves a potential heroin addict, or an active user, has only one other course, and that is to begin planning for the inevitable. The inevitability of addiction, overdose, and the need for treatment. By the end of this book, you should have a good understanding of what your plan should look like. For now, here is a summary of what will be included (Figure 4).

Phase	Primary Professional Service	Medication
Overdose Survival	Emergency Services	Narcan
Detoxification	Hospitalization	Subutex/Benzos
Rehabilitation	Therapy/Counseling/Group	Benzos, Vivitrol
Intensive Outpatient Program	Life Skills Development Twelve-Step Group	Vivitrol
Long-Term Well-Being	Life Coaching	Vivitrol Supplements
Relapse Planning	Therapy/Counseling	Supplements
Adjusted Long-Term Well-Being	Success Coaching	Supplements
Life's Purpose/Meaning	Spiritual Teaching	Supplements

Figure 4: Highlights of Your Plan for after an Overdose.

Here are medications and how they are referred to in this book.

Common Name	Trade Name	Synonym	Referred to in Book
Narcan	Naloxone & Evzio		Narcan
Suboxone	Buprenorphine/Naloxone Bunavail & Zubsolv		Suboxone
Subutex	Buprenorphine		Suboxone
Methadone	Methadose & Dolophine		Methadone
Benzos	Benzodiazepine	Xanax, Klonopin, many others	Benzos
Revia	Naltrexone (oral) & Vivitrol		Vivitrol
Vivitrol	Naltrexone (injected) & Revia		Vivitrol

Figure 5: Medication Names.

The goal is to help the addict achieve a belief in a purpose for living that is so overwhelmingly important, that heroin becomes repulsive, due to its interference in the objective. As long as heroin has a purpose recognized by the addicts, they are likely to relapse; they are likely to answer heroin's seductive call.

"Just once more, one more time."

Chapter 2 Concepts

1. Heroin's biggest ally is secrecy.
2. Heroin is deadlier than the Vietnam War.
3. There are a variety of medications to help heroin addiction.
4. The vast majority of heroin crosses into the United States through Mexico.
5. Heroin is delivered like pizza.
6. Heroin works on opiate receptors, like naturally occurring neurotransmitters.
7. Plan how you will deal with the progression of addiction.

Chapter 3

Neither Die, Neither Live

There is a voice that doesn't use words. Listen.
~ Rumi

February 24, 7:00 PM

I was still in disbelief at what I had watched him do to evade me. It was clear that he had made a decision, to either make that maneuver work—or die. He was willing to die to get away from me.

What the hell?

He had just told me he was a heroin addict. I didn't even know what that meant. He told me that I didn't need to bail him out of jail because he had taken care of everything. When I probed what that meant, he said that it was a secret between him and the GBI. I was still assuming it was some sting operation where he would help the cops bust somebody. Maybe that was it. Maybe he was afraid of ratting someone out, so he was going to warn them about what was coming tomorrow.

Then, of course, the doubt about that whole thing entered my mind—I am just a plain ol' suburbanite. Drama like this doesn't happen in my world. Again, the thought of being on a TV show flew through my head—*This is not real—this is not happening.*

He had just taken off at 85 mph down Mars Hill Road. I didn't even try to stay with him. I started calling him. Voicemail. I called again. Voicemail. Repeatedly for fifteen minutes, I pushed the redial button after getting his voicemail. I pulled over into a parking lot and sent him several texts. Their tone ranged from anger and frustration to sympathy, guilt, and regret.

"Please, just come home. We can work it out; whatever it is, we can work it out."

Fifteen minutes of dialing and redialing and then a dozen or so texts and no response. I was angry, sad, and frightened all simultaneously. I had no idea what I was dealing with.

What was heroin?

I didn't even know. I think it was melted in spoons and injected with a needle. That is all I knew.

It can't be that. We live in the suburbs—we are upper-middle class. Heroin can't exist where we live, can it?

I sat in the parking lot and stared at the passing traffic. Cars had their lights on now, and I noticed the glare on my contacts from my tears. I didn't know what to do. What I just witnessed was the most reckless and dangerous action I had ever seen another person take—and that person was my son. Whatever he was up to—he was either going to be successful, or he was going to die trying. I couldn't figure that part out—he was willing to die to get where he was going.

He is willing to die. He is willing to die.

Today was so dramatic that it almost seemed imaginary. And I kept challenging myself.

You are making this a bigger deal than it is, man. Stop making mountains out of molehills—this is ok. Everything is ok.

No sooner did those thoughts go through my head than my whole body shuttered with a nervous seizure. Just a short shake. My body was intervening. This was a big deal—a really big deal. And I had better not underestimate it.

I called his mom and had difficulty maintaining my composure. I was charged with a ton of negative energy, and it was going to find its way out eventually. If I lost control, she would get scared, and I did not want to scare her. I got on and off the phone, as quickly as I could; I told her he took off and I was on my way home. She knew I was upset. Hopefully, she thought I was mad or sad. I didn't want her to know I was terrified. My plan was to get home and learn as much about heroin as I could—and then tell her what was going on from a more informed point of view.

As soon as I got off the phone with her, I got a text from him.

"I was sick as fuck and had to get me some, be home in 20 min."

I thought about the two teenage daughters who were still at home. I wondered how much danger they were in; how much danger we were all in. Of course, the nightmare flashed through my consciousness again,

Does that gunshot kill me?

Heroin, jails, high-speed recklessness, GBI, heroin dealers, drug busts. This is not normal stuff to be worrying about. This is crazy shit. I have an active heroin addict on his way home from his dealer—a dealer he is probably going to rat out tomorrow. A dealer who might show up at the front door tonight and blow a hole through my torso and then do who knows what with my family. Fuck.

I texted back: "No. Don't come home. Stay away from us."

As soon as I hit send, I regretted it. I didn't know what it might mean to him. I started having terrible thoughts about him dying in the streets—cold, lonely, hungry, sick from drugs, using drugs.

Fuck. Did I just seal his fate too?

This was crazy. Save his life and jeopardize my girls? Let him go? Stuff like this doesn't happen to guys like me for a reason—we have no idea how to handle it. I do not know anyone who knows anything about this. What am I going to do? Knock on my neighbor's door and say, "Hey man, when your son was shooting heroin—how did you deal with it?"

There is no place to go—nowhere to turn. I have no idea what to do or who to call. I have never heard another live human talk about heroin—not in conversation, not in a joke, not on the news. I was totally humiliated and embarrassed. I was clueless and helpless. I felt so alone; totally and completely isolated from all other humans. Caged by this stigma, imprisoned by my fear, paralyzed by my dread.

Now what do I do? Where do I start?

I left the parking lot and was making the 6-mile drive home. I texted my wife and reminded her again I was coming. I don't know why she needed to know twice.

What am I going to say to her? What if he dies and I don't tell her what happened?

I was going to lose my mind. I made another quick mental scan of every person I knew: Who can I call, who can I ask?

NOTHING, NO ONE. I was isolated from every single person I knew. I could never tell anyone about this. It would ruin me; it would ruin my girls—thought after thought kept rolling through my mind as I drove home—all the while wondering and worrying about him.

February 24, 2014, 7:30 PM

When I got home, I explained everything to Wendy. I could never predict how she might react on the outside. But I always knew how she felt on the inside. She had a deep love for her kids; and right, wrong, or indifferent, she would protect and nurture them at all costs. It took her a little time—but she would eventually get to protect and nurture.

I write *eventually* because sometimes protection and nurturing are not exactly what is needed to protect and nurture a young life. I know that sounds like a paradox, and it is. As I described what had happened—she took a look of disbelief. That would be the look you would expect. But though the story is hard to believe—I did witness it—all of it.

Her disbelief did not seem to be in the story itself, but the person presenting it. She didn't believe me. I was not believable. Some of what I was saying was so extremely dramatic that it had to be made up; it had to be exaggerated. I couldn't blame her for not believing me—because even as I told the story—I didn't believe it myself. It could not have happened that way, could it?

I told her about his last text. In fact, I showed it to her. "I am sick as fuck and needed to get some. Be home in 20 min."

She stared at it for a minute and asked, "What does that mean?"

"I don't know," I shrugged.

Then I showed her my text back to him: "No. Don't come home. Stay away from us."

I went on to explain how much I regretted that I had sent it. But then explained to her my rationale. "Listen," I said, "I have no idea what heroin is, I'm afraid of the danger he puts us in; that he puts the girls in. I don't know what he is doing with the GBI; I don't know what his state of mind will be later; I know that what I saw him do in that car was extremely desperate and dangerous and honestly, I don't want to get shot in the chest the next time I open the front door."

She listened intently. She knew about the dream. She had woken me from it a time or two, and I had woken her while in it more than once. She didn't say anything yet, because she knew if she let me talk long enough, I would become rational and reasonable.

Then I went on to describe all the fear and regret that I had. "I am worried about him. He has nowhere to go; he knows he is facing prison; he is sick. Obviously, he is crazy; I mean he is willing to die for whatever he is after. That thing he did in the car—it was either going to work, or he was going to die. He is willing—was willing to die and take other people with him."

I paused, took a breath, and continued, "He is going to be cold, hungry, frustrated. I don't want him driving. I want to get him back here so we can talk to him."

She said, "Well, why don't you quickly find out what heroin is and find out if it causes violence or puts others in danger and then decide what's best? I don't want anyone to get hurt either."

I reached for my laptop and started some online searches: heroin violence, effects of heroin. Does heroin make you violent? Do heroin addicts hurt others?

The searches all returned results, but none of them seemed to indicate that he would be a danger to any of us while he was high. There were some results that indicated that an addict in withdrawal might do some extraordinary things when desperate for a hit, but an active addict seemed harmless.

"Text him, please. Text him and ask him if you can meet him; if he agrees, go get him and bring him home. Tell him to stop driving."

She was already on her phone punching out a text. We waited a few moments until he responded, "Dad doesn't want me around."

"I am with Dad; he wants me to come get you."

"Ok. Meet me at McDonald's on Mars Hill and 120."

"10 min." she texted back.

She gave me a hug and kiss—and then left to get him. I don't remember where the girls were—but they were not at home; at least not yet. It was a school night—so I will assume that the seventeen year old was with her boyfriend, and the thirteen year old was at soccer practice.

Fifteen minutes later, I got a text from Wendy: "We are leaving the car at McD; he wants to make sure we can get it for him before tomorrow."

"We will get it tonight," I responded

"Ok. OMW home."

"Cool."

I did not have a plan for how we would get the car back. But that was the least of my worries right now.

What was I going to do with him?

Ten minutes later, I heard her car pull into the driveway. I had looked up heroin addiction, heroin rehab, and heroin recovery while I was waiting. What I learned in twenty-five minutes was not good. Recovery rates were low, relapse rates were high, death and incarceration were likely, and it was a long and expensive process. There was only time to read headlines and scan articles before they got back. All I knew was that we had to talk about rehab—and I didn't even know what that meant.

She came in first and gave me a look that indicated I could relax. He followed behind and looked so much better than he had the last time I saw him. He still didn't look great, or even normal, but on a relative basis, he looked like a new man, and he sounded better too—I was amazed.

"Thanks, Dad. Thanks for getting me out of jail; and thanks for helping me get my car."

I sat there stunned.

"I'm sorry. I had to get some. I was really sick."

"Heroin? Withdrawal?"

"Yes. I was in jail for three days."

"Are you addicted? Can you quit?"

"I can't stop. I've tried. That doctor I go to . . . she wrote me Suboxone prescriptions for two years, and that helped, but she told me she couldn't do it anymore."

"Will you get help? Will you go to rehab?"

"Yes."

"Now? Will you go now?"

"No. I have to do that thing tomorrow with the drug people."

"Ok. After that? Will you go after that?"

"Wednesday. I'll go Wednesday."

"Ok—cool!"

"That's awesome, Jackson," his mother said.

"So, what time tomorrow?" I asked.

"I don't know, about lunchtime. They are going to call me."

"Do you have drugs on you now?"

"No. I used everything before I came home."

"Are you sure?"

"Yes, Dad."

My seventeen year old came in. That ended the conversation we were having. Wendy asked Madeline if she would mind driving me to McDonald's to get Jack's car. She agreed. Madeline and I went to pick up the car. Wendy sat with Jack.

February 25, 2014

Our house starts to get busy about 6:00 AM on school days. Wendy was up and in the shower—she would leave by 6:30. Madeline was a junior and would drive her Jeep to school. The thirteen year old was in the eighth grade, and I would drive her to school about 8:30. Wendy had already taken care of the dog and cat.

I had a standing meeting on Tuesdays at 10:00 AM. It usually went an hour. It was also my mom's birthday—I'd have to call her. And then there was the activity that Jack had planned with the GBI—I would need to figure out what my role might be, as that transpired. I would probably just wait around until he left to meet them at lunchtime.

I took the thirteen year old to school and then came home and checked my emails. It was 9:00 AM. I texted my assistant and told her I was going to work from home this morning. I let her know I would be in about lunchtime. She was cool with it, but let me know via text that my manager was worried about me. I sincerely appreciated that—but I didn't want to tell anyone that my son was a heroin addict; nevertheless, I didn't want to lie either. However, with the rehab and everything coming up tomorrow—I might be missing some work to figure it all out. The phone rang—it was the COO.

"Dude—are you ok? What's going on?"

"It's bad. It is really bad, and I might miss some work."

"What is it?"

"Jack told us he was a heroin addict last night."

"Holy shit, dude. Heroin? Are you serious?"

"I'll tell you all about it sometime, but I have to find a rehab for him."

"Are you taking him now?"

"No. Wednesday."

"Dude—take him now, don't mess around with that shit."

"Listen, he can't go yet; here is what happened . . ."

I went on to tell him about the GBI, the reckless driving, the arrest on Friday night—almost all of it. I did not tell him that I was losing my mind, or that I was having a tough time. He probably knew anyway.

"Dude—that's terrible! Listen. Stay home with him and love on that kid. He's your only son. Figure out what you have to do, and let me know if I can help in any way. I'll be praying for him—for all of y'all."

The call ended shortly after that. I was relieved. Todd always had a way of letting me know that he understood a lot more about what I was saying without making me say it. Sometimes, I wish I had said it. Therapeutically, it would have been better—healthier if I talked more about all this as it happened.

I checked some more mail, responded to a few, deleted a lot. Then I reviewed the agenda for the 10:00 AM meeting. It would take the full hour. I halfheartedly browsed for some rehabs. At first glance, it looked like a lot of sponsored-ad responses were coming back from my search. Nothing stood out to me.

"I'll do it later, at the office," I thought.

February 25, 2014, 10:00 AM

I opened my conference bridge at 10:00 AM. Most of my team was already on and making small talk. I let them all know I was working from home; then we started the meeting.

I pace when I talk on the phone. Well, I walk when I am on the phone. Usually in circles. On this call, I would walk in the front door, through the house to the back door, out onto the deck, then the backyard, up the driveway, and then back in the front door again. It was a nice day, the sun was out, and it was good to be outside. The call was perfectly normal. We were going to run over by a few minutes.

My son had picked up my walking-while-talking-on-the-phone habit. We passed each other once or twice during my conference call. I was going to the front door, and he was coming out. I overheard part of his conversation as he passed by.

"So, I'll meet you there at noon?" I heard him say. "Ok. Ok."

He continued in his direction out. I stopped at the door. His call ended, and he turned to come back inside. I muted my phone so that I could talk to him.

"Who was that?" I asked.

"It was them. I am meeting them at noon, and then we are leaving from there."

I looked at my watch—it was 11:05.

"Ok. I am going to the office—are you good?"

"Fine."

"Ok. Cool."

I walked down the driveway and back up again. My conference call ended when I got to the top. I put my phone in my pocket and removed the earbuds.

I wondered what he was going to have to do. Would he wear a wire? Would he just buy dope? Would he introduce a new junkie to his dealer? The new junkie, of course, being an undercover cop. It seemed dangerous.

Definitely, risk involved, I thought.

I opened the front door and stepped into the entryway. The stairs to the second level of our house were in front of me, and I could see through the open foyer that the upstairs bathroom door was shut.

Probably taking a shower, I thought.

I yelled up the stairs, "Yo, Jack! I am taking off, I'll see you later!"

He didn't hear me. What he was about to do with the cops was scary, and I wanted to tell him goodbye and good luck. I didn't hear the shower water running, so he should hear me. I moved over to the bottom step so that I could yell directly at the bathroom door.

"Hey, JP!!! I am leaving! Jack!"

Just then, and in the subtlest way, I heard what sounded like a full laundry basket hitting the wooden floor—a soft thummmmp. And then another sound, almost exactly like the first thummmmp.

What the hell is he doing? I thought.

I walked halfway up the stairs and had the most unbelievable thought. This is hard to describe, even in conversation, because it didn't come in any words. I wasn't thinking in words—not with this thought.

Like most people, most of my thinking is done consciously and in English—my native language. Much of my thought seems to be a long-running narrative that jumps with ease from topic to topic. The unbelievable thought that I had at that moment did not come in words—no words at all. It was a feeling—a knowing feeling. And the thought was that he had just overdosed on heroin and was dead.

Almost immediately, the narrative returned to take over my mind and control of my actions.

Dude, c'mon. Nothing like this happens to you.

I started back down the stairs. He was fine, and I was making too much of this whole situation. This is not Beverly Hills, 90210—I am just plain old Bob with an uneventful life, in the uninteresting suburbs.

I was two or three steps down when the thoughts that come without a voice or words returned. This time the feeling was complete dread—*he is in trouble.*

I feel that it is important to note that this message was different from any normal thinking. The whole ordeal going all the way back to Friday night—but especially this morning—has been odd—strange. But this stuff, what was happening on the stairs, was bizarre—unique to most of the events in my life. I do not know if it was some sort of subconscious awareness, or higher power, or something mystic. But what I do know is that it was different—way different from the normal mode when I think. And because it was different, I hesitated—I paused—because it was as if I were in a movie or a dream. So much of this WAS happening, but it seemed as if it shouldn't be, or couldn't be. Not to me anyway—and not to anyone I know.

Regardless—the voiceless, wordless message made me turn around and start back up the stairs again. My conscious, normal, thinking voice started again—though with far less confidence—as if it was already not taking responsibility for anything that might be wrong. I was scared.

He's fine; go to work; you do not live in 90210.

My emotions were drowning out my thinking voice. I got to the top of the stairs and walked over to the outer door of the bathroom.

"Jack! Hey, Jack!"

I banged on the six-panel door with the side of my fist.

No response. I felt my lip quiver. I tried to take a deep breath. It kind of shuddered back out before I got it all the way in. I tried the doorknob. It was locked. I banged again and called for him

"Jack."

Nothing. I reached up and felt for the key on the overhead doorjamb. Not there. I was now in a hurry and beginning to panic.

An earring! An earring will work, I thought.

I ran to the other side of the house and found an earring on Wendy's vanity. When I got back to the bathroom door, I plunged the earring shaft into the door lock. It popped, and I turned the handle. When I opened the door, I was disappointed, but not surprised that he was not in the vanity room. I passed the vanity and went to the second door. I repeatedly called his name, as I banged on this door with the same fist I had used outside. The door was locked.

I used the earring to pop the lock and turned the handle. I couldn't push the door open—it would only crack open.

"What the fuck?" I screamed.

The shower was off; he wasn't in it. I pushed the door a little harder—enough to discover that his body was curled up between the toilet and the door that I was trying to open. The best I could tell was that his head was on the floor, face down, with the back of his head against the door I was trying to push open. I might break his neck if I pushed too hard. Fuck!

I didn't feel as if I had many options. I decided I had to push my way into that room. I pushed slowly—trying hard not to hurt him. I am fairly thin and could squeeze through a narrow opening . . . as soon as I thought I could fit—I positioned myself between the door and the jamb. As I was squeezing through the crack, I noticed that he was kind of in a somersault position. The back of his head and neck were up against the door—his back was facing the ceiling, and he was curled in a ball. It is as if he fell off the toilet head first after nodding off and was still in that perfect sitting position—except on the floor.

As my body got through the narrow opening, the door slammed shut. His body was like a spring wedged between the toilet and the door, forcing the door shut.

The small room we were in was large enough for a tub and a toilet, little else. The walls and floor are ceramic tiles—the room might be 5 by 7 feet, with the tub taking up most of that area. The remaining space was now occupied by the toilet, my son's body, and me. Making it more complicated was the fact that the door opened in toward us.

I got down on my knees. His back was facing up, his head was down, and his torso was curled in a ball. I reached across his back and grabbed his far shoulder. Then I rotated him toward me. His head came into the cradle of my left arm.

"Oh! Geezus! Fuck!"

I had never seen so many shades of blue and purple before. I slapped his face and screamed his name—no response. He wasn't breathing.

I checked his wrist for a pulse—I had a hard time gripping his limp arm with one hand without using my thumb. I could feel my heart beating—in my chest, in my neck, in my temples. I couldn't find a pulse in his arm. I must have been doing it wrong. I moved my fingers to his neck. I checked six or seven times up and down the side of his neck. I couldn't find one. His color was enough to tell me he wasn't breathing and hadn't been for a while.

"Holy fuck! Holy fuck! This is not happening to me! Fuck! Jack! Jack! Wake up! Wake the fuck up! God, please don't take him—take me. Take me instead."

I had a few moments of hesitation before dialing 911. Was this normal? What if I call 911 and he wakes up and then the cops arrest him? Fuck, he'd be so pissed. Why don't I know anything about heroin?

"Jack, Jack! Wake up!"

I knew he was dead. I mean no breath and no pulse. That's called dead. I called 911.

"911 operator. What is your location?"

"My son is dead; he's not breathing. I can't find a pulse . . ."

"Sir, where are you? I don't know where you are."

"He overdosed, heroin, he's not breathing."

"Sir, I need to know where to send help, where are you?"

I was sobbing, drooling, nose running, she could have been right next to me, and she wouldn't understand what I was about to say.

"It's 4335 Thrashers Overlook, Acworth." I was upset now. What I just said to her didn't sound anything like it was supposed to.

"Sir, I didn't hear you. Please, slow down and be as clear as you can."

I was pissed. I was on a Bluetooth headset in a 5 by 7 ceramic room crying like a baby and had to pronounce the name of my oddly named street clearly, so the 911 operator could find me.

I screamed at her, "4335 Thrashers Overlook, Acworth!"

"Acworth? Sir, this is Kennesaw, let me get Acworth on the line."

"My son is dying; don't transfer me!"

"Sir, the station heard your call. They are en route. What is the condition of your son?"

"He is blue, no pulse, no breath."

"Sir, you have to do CPR right now—is he flat on the floor?"

"No, he's not flat—we are trapped behind a door."

"Sir, you have to get him out of there—you have to get him flat on the floor right now."

I heard sirens in the background. "I can't . . ."

"Sir, open that door . . . "

I was in a difficult position on the floor. Our lower bodies were tangled and pressed together between the toilet, tub, wall, and the door that opened in toward us. His body was wedged between the toilet and the door.

"Fuck."

I reached across my body with my right hand and grabbed the doorknob. I pulled him closer to my chest in the cradle of my left arm. I pulled on the knob. He was still in the way, and I had no leverage to open the door with my right hand.

"Sir, your son is going to die—open that door."

I pulled him aggressively toward me and smashed myself against the tub—we both rolled away from the inward swing of the door. I yanked on the knob, as I turned it—the door opened just enough for me to get my fingers between the jamb and the door. This was going to hurt him—the edge of the door was going to scrape down his back as the door opened—if it opened. I yanked him once more toward me and pushed the door away from us with my right hand. The door scraped down his back, as I pushed it open as hard as I could from the position I was in.

"Sir, get him out . . . "

I untangled myself from his body and stood up. I stepped out into the vanity room and reached down and grabbed him by the armpits and pulled his body out of the small toilet area into the vanity room.

"Ok, he is out. He is flat on his back."

"Is he breathing, sir?"

"No."

"Ok. You have to do CPR now."

I reached down and felt his chest. His heart was not beating—but it felt like it was fluttering. An extremely high-rate vibration rather than a beat.

"Ok, wait, his heart, I feel his heart."

"Sir, that doesn't matter. You have to breathe into him right now. Do CPR right now!"

I didn't know that CPR had changed since my last certification in the 1980s. Now, in the current era, chest compressions are done regardless of a heartbeat. So, while she was telling me accurately what to do, I had my doubts because when I learned CPR, we didn't do compressions if there were signs of a heartbeat.

"Sir, breathe into him! Sir, breathe into him or he will die."

I couldn't believe this was happening to me; I was crying hard again—heaving type of crying. I could hardly breathe myself.

"God, please, save him. I'll do anything."

I tilted his head back and did the "look—listen—feel"—nothing. But as soon as I turned my head to breathe into him, I heard this short and faint exhale sound. Like a baby-snore exhale.

"Wait! He breathed, he breathed!"

"Is he awake, sir? Is he breathing?"

"No, it was just like a little noise he made."

"Sir, breathe into him."

I waited for another breath. Maybe this was going to be ok after all. The sirens were close now; maybe they were on the street. I did not know that the slight snore sound was the "death rattle."

"Jack! Jack! Wake up!"

My dog was having a fit. The firefighters came flying into the house and up the stairs. They dragged his body out into the hallway at the top of the stairs and started working on him. I stood in the doorjamb, crying so hard it hurt.

This was really happening to me. This was real. There were three, then four, then seven people working on my son in my house. My crying was getting serious; I was only 2 feet from the banister and starting to hyperventilate. I couldn't answer any of the questions they were asking me. Within a few seconds, I had my own pair of emergency responders. They were worried I was going to pass out from shock or hyperventilation and fall over the banister into the foyer below. They moved me into my daughter's room and sat me in her desk chair. I could still see them working on him, while a female emergency medical technician (EMT) tried to calm me down.

I was watching them. After they had dragged him out of the vanity room, they cut off all his clothes. They used CPR and an oxygen mask and gave him a shot with a syringe (I learned later that it was Narcan). There were four people huddled around him. Each was doing some procedure or measuring a vital sign.

"What is his name, sir?"

"Jack."

"Hey, hey, can you hear me? Can you see me? What's your name?"

I didn't hear if he answered or not. The police were here now—five of them. There were five firefighters, four EMTs, and five police officers.

I sat in the dark, cluttered room of my oldest daughter. She was a freshman at New York University. Even though she had been away since last August, her room was alive with her spirit. I sat bewildered as to how two siblings could be so different. One was at NYU pursuing her passion; the other was fighting for his life *because* of his passion. Is that what it is? His passion? Is he so passionate about this, that he is willing to go to jail, damage the family, drive like a maniac, stick needles in his arm, risk his life, and ultimately die—for his passion? Was heroin his passion? The contrast between the two kids was stunning.

The EMT who was tending to me was asking me questions. I wasn't even in the same dimension as she was. She was shaking me by the shoulder and asking if I was ok. Tears were still streaming down my face, my nose was running, and my lips were covered in slime. Before I answered her, I realized that something was different about me now. It was as though the person who I thought I was before today was now but a shadow. Someone who was nearby but no longer a part of me. I shook that thought off and answered her.

"Ye-yeah, I am ok."

"Ok. I have to ask you some questions; is that ok? We need to ask you some questions, so we can make sure your son is going to be ok."

"Ok."

"The police are going to sit here, so they won't have to ask you all these questions again later; is that ok?"

"Yes, of course, that's fine."

"What is your son's full name?

"Jackson Patrick Hobbs, H-O-B-B-S."

"What is his date of birth?"

"January, 12, 1992—he just turned twenty-two."

"Where was he born?"

"Schenectady, New York."

"Does he live here with you?"

"Yes—yes he does."

"Are you still married to his mother? Does she live here?"

"Yes and yes; but she is at school right now."

"Do you know how to reach her?"

"Ye-yeah, I'll figure it out."

She left with her notes and went over to where the others were working on Jack. I heard her asking him the same questions that she had just asked me. If he answered, I could not hear his responses. He was still on the floor with people all around him. He might have still been wearing the oxygen mask as well; I couldn't see his face.

The police, two of them, were still in the room with me.

"Mr. Hobbs, where did you find him?"

I pointed through the wall to the next room.

"In the bathroom—next door."

"Do you mind if we look around?"

"No, please, search the whole place. Bring dogs. I don't want any of that stuff here."

"Thank you, sir."

The two officers walked toward the bathroom and left me alone in the bedroom. I was in a dream. Nothing seemed real—it was foggy. I was so confused; I couldn't think; I couldn't plan; I couldn't do anything but sit there and cry; cry and watch them working to revive my twenty-two-year-old son.

Two EMTs who had left the second floor a few moments earlier were now returning with a gurney. I remembered the last time I saw a gurney in a house that I lived in; it was 1974, my paternal grandmother, "Nanny," had just died in our bathroom. I was seven years old. Gurneys, bodies, bathrooms.

When they got to the top of the stairs, the others cleared out of the way. The captain turned and walked toward me with the EMT who had been tending to me earlier. I caught a glimpse of Jack; he still had the oxygen mask on his face. I wasn't sure what to think about that.

"Mr. Hobbs, I am Captain Nagy with the Cobb County Fire Department," he said, as he reached for my snot-covered hand.

"Hi," I responded, as I shook his hand

"Your son is going to be fine. Right now, we don't see any sign of brain damage. He knows where he is, who he is, and where he is from. He has a faint idea of what has happened. We are taking him to Kennestone for further treatment and testing. After that, he will be observed by the ER staff, and then next steps will be considered. He's lucky. We just started using this heroin antidote called Naloxone (Narcan), it's an amazing drug; it saved his life. Do you want to ride with the ambulance to the hospital?"

The other responders were taking Jack down the stairs on the gurney.

"No, no. I have a few things to do here; I have to reach his mom, I have to talk with the police, and I have to put a few things together for the hospital."

I had no idea what I was saying. I had no plan—I didn't want to get in the ambulance. I needed to be alone and process this as much as I could. I was completely overwhelmed with—well, with everything. My sensory systems were overloaded—I could not take any more input. My body was shaking and in some kind of pain—maybe I was exhausted from crying. Emotionally, I was wasted; that did not stop the emotions from coming; I think I just stopped acknowledging that they were there. And mentally, I don't know; my mind kind of shut down. There was no thinking. It was as if part of my being was on strike.

"Sir, I know you are upset; this is a lot to deal with, but you don't need anything—just go to the hospital in the ambulance."

"No. I have to talk to the police, and I have to take care of a few things. I'll be fine. I'll drive down in my truck."

"Sir, with all due respect, you are not in any condition to drive. Do you believe you can get in that truck and safely drive to Kennestone?"

"Ye-yeah. I'll be ok."

He turned to the EMT who was looking at me as if I were a mental patient. "Go ahead and have them leave—we'll clean-up here and make sure everything is ok," he ordered her.

"Yes, Captain," she said. "Goodbye, Mr. Hobbs, and good luck to you and your son."

"Thanks. Thanks for everything," I muttered.

The police came in, the two who had been in the bathroom. Two others had already gone downstairs with everyone else. The fire captain asked if we could go downstairs and talk.

"Sure, we can go down to the kitchen," I replied.

The captain helped me up and out of the chair. It seemed like hours that I had been in my daughter's bedroom.

"Wh—what time is it?" I asked, as I struggled to gain my balance as I stood.

"Easy, Mr. Hobbs—are you ok?"

"Yeah, I got it."

"It's 11:50."

Wow. It was only forty minutes since I stood on the stairs debating with myself as to whether I should go up or leave for work. I was so tired, so exhausted, so scared.

"Can you walk, Mr. Hobbs?"

"Yeah. I'm ok. Let's go downstairs."

The two cops went ahead of me, and the fire captain nervously followed behind.

"Use the railing, sir," he said.

My dog was waiting at the bottom of the stairs. He was scared too. He looked so much like Murphy—my first Gold Border Collie.

May 2012. Murphy died in my truck—yes, that truck—due to heat exhaustion. Jack had momentarily left the door open in the driveway—and Murph—being excited to go on a ride—jumped right in. Jack walked by a short time later and shut the door. He had no reason to look inside—why would he? Several hours had passed, and I could not find Murph. He didn't run off often. I searched the neighborhood and all the adjoining yards—I couldn't find him.

I was in bed about 11:00 PM and was suddenly overcome with a sense of dread. I had a feeling that Murph was in the truck. I told myself several times no—no he wasn't; but not convincingly enough to prevent me from walking down to the bottom of the drive. I opened the door—there he was.

I cannot describe how much he must have suffered in that heat. He left us plenty of signs that he fought to survive until his last breath. He was a great buddy.

Why is this relevant? When Jack found that Murphy was dead and how he died, he lost it. He blamed himself for Murphy's death and my sadness. It was 11:30 PM, and Jack knelt at the side of my bed and apologized a dozen times. He was sobbing. Then he left—I had no idea where he went.

It was the Friday night before Memorial Day weekend, 2012. Despite texting and calling him at least 150 times during the weekend, I got no response. On Tuesday morning, he called me from the Candler County Jail in middle Georgia—at least a three-hour drive from where we were. He was arrested for possession of methamphetamine, forgery first degree, and forgery second degree—three felonies. I was stunned.

It turned out that he left Friday night with three other junkies and a stolen prescription pad. It sounded like they were writing prescriptions and hitting every pharmacy in Georgia for bottles of pain pills that they would eventually use themselves or sell to other junkies. After almost a year in jail, he pleaded guilty and was sentenced to ten years in prison with credit for time served and the balance on probation with at least two years reporting. The reporting probation was just ending at the time of his overdose.

I petted Berkeley on the head and led the group into the kitchen. We sat down, and the fire captain spoke first, "Like I said upstairs, your son is probably ok. We'll know for sure once the doctors look at him. The Naloxone we just gave him saved his life—but it causes withdrawal symptoms—so we need to monitor him for that, so he doesn't overdose again if he gets sick."

"What happened to him?"

"Jack overdosed on heroin. A heroin overdose is simple really—all that happens is the addict stops breathing. The nonvoluntary, reflex action of breathing is suppressed by the drug. If no one finds him, he suffocates. If someone finds him in time and can restore his breathing or keep oxygen flowing to his brain until help arrives—then he will survive, hopefully without brain damage.

"Was he dead?" I couldn't find a pulse.

"From your perspective, yes. Regardless, there was not much time left. You saved his life."

I started crying uncontrollably. I had gone most of my life with rarely crying. And if a situation developed where I might cry—I avoided it. I even tried to run away to Arizona when I was sixteen to avoid a funeral. Under no circumstances would I cry in front of three grown men—men I didn't even know. I felt like such a sissy. Why could I not remain composed?

The fire captain stood up and told me that I was not alone. "Kids are dying all over Cobb County because of heroin. You are lucky Jack is alive, and he is lucky that you were not at work."

I stared blankly in his general direction without actually looking at him.

"Do you have any questions, Mr. Hobbs?"

"No, not right now. Thank you!"

"Ok—we are right around the corner if you need anything."

"Ok—thanks, Captain."

"And don't forget to call his mom—she needs to know."

"Fuck," I said, and I didn't care about etiquette anymore. Hell, I didn't care about anything.

The captain left, and I turned to the two officers. They asked if I could reach her. I told them she was a teacher, and I would try—but she probably won't answer.

I found her name on my call log and pushed the button next to her name; as expected it went to voicemail. I hung up and was crying again. Not because she didn't answer, but because what if she did?

What the fuck am I going to tell her? I thought to myself. And even if you have something to say, you are gonna scare her because you can't complete a single coherent sentence without bawling.

I tried to text her. I could not accurately hit any buttons. The entire text was garbage. I was frustrated.

One of the officers asked, "Is there someone else you can call? Someone you trust who can reach your wife for you?"

I called her sister, Jenipher, and left a voicemail. I told her that Jack had an emergency and was headed to Kennestone. Then I told the officers I would try my executive assistant at the office. I found Kim's name on my call log and pushed the button.

"Hello—how's Jack?" she asked.

"Kim, I need your help . . ." I couldn't say anything else. The officer took the phone from me. For some reason saying my son overdosed and the thought of telling the story caused me not to be able to speak.

The officer who had the phone put it on speaker.

"Hi, Kim, this is Officer Palmer of the Cobb County Police Department. Everyone is ok. We need you to reach Mrs. Hobbs at school and tell her there is a family emergency and she needs to come home right now."

"What's wrong? Where's Bob?"

"Their son had an accidental overdose of heroin. He is ok and on his way to Kennestone Hospital in an ambulance. Mr. Hobbs is too upset at the moment to speak to you, but he is fine. Can you reach Mrs. Hobbs?"

"Oh, yes! I'll call the school right now. Did you try her cell phone?"

"Yes, we tried the cell phone, and she must be in class."

"Ok, I'll take care of it—I'll get her home right now."

"Thank you, Kim," the officer said, as he hung up.

The cops spent five or ten minutes telling me that they didn't find any drugs other than what was in the bathroom. It was important that I dispose of the syringes and other items left in the bathroom before I leave the house. They were not going to file charges, but they recommended two things.

"Sir, you and your family have a lot of work to do—heroin is nasty. You need to find a detox center and a rehab as soon as possible. And most important, don't bring him back here until he is detoxed; otherwise, he will overdose again once the withdrawal starts."

Again, I looked at him with glazed eyes.

"It is gonna be ok, sir; he is alive; he's got a chance—most of these calls don't end up like this. You are lucky!"

I'm lucky, I thought. "Thanks, officer, thanks for everything."[13]

I followed them out to the front porch. Their patrol car and one other were still in the cul de sac. When the sunlight hit my tear-stained eyes—I couldn't help but think of a Pink Floyd song.

---

[13] I never had an opportunity to show my appreciation for those loving souls who helped Jack and me that day. I cannot thank you all enough! The response time of the Cobb County Fire Department was incredible; I still don't know how they found me! Thanks! The compassion shown by the Cobb County Police Department was remarkable—they knew who my son was and what he did in their neighborhoods. Their priority was saving a life and keeping a family together. Thank you! And to the EMTs—I can't say enough about the loving care you gave both of us! Thank you! And God bless you always.

"That's weird," I thought, as I squinted and shaded my eyes with my hands.

Some neighbors had gathered on the street and were looking at my house as the police cars pulled away. I stood on the porch and stared at them—they looked back at me. I still wonder why they wouldn't walk down and check on me. They probably didn't know any of the details about my morning—anything could have happened. But you would think that with two fire trucks, an ambulance, and two cop cars in front of my house for close to an hour, you might need to check on your neighbor. I think the right thing to do would be to walk down and check on this person left alone in his house after all this traumatic activity—but they just stood there talking to each other looking at me. Why? I'll never know.

I went inside. The house was so different than it was just an hour ago. It was scary in here alone; it didn't feel safe; it didn't feel like home anymore. It is hard to explain what was happening because I didn't *know* anything was happening. It would take almost three years to even get close to the answers. But one thing was certain—I was sincerely beginning to lose my mind.

I had to go to the hospital, probably for a while. I started looking for my iPad and various device chargers—my phone, the tablet, my computer. I put all these items in a shopping bag.

I got a text from Kim: "Wendy is on her way home."

Wait a minute, I thought—she should go to Kennestone.

"Please send her to Kennestone—he is probably there already," I replied.

"Ok."

I didn't type that text; I used voice recognition. I got a text right back that said Wendy was headed to Kennestone. In the meantime, Jen called and was alarmed. I was able to tell her that Jack had an overdose, Wendy was on her way there, and she should meet her at Kennestone. She agreed and hung up.

When I got in the truck, I started to realize how bright it was outside. It became apparent that I couldn't drive before I got out of the driveway. I was shaky, couldn't focus, and could not see well.

Why can't I drive, I wondered. I drove around in circles on the cul de sac—hoping my condition would clear. It didn't. My vision was blurry, and my depth perception was terrible. It was the strangest thing. I parked and sat for a minute.

Wendy was going to beat me to the hospital. I didn't want her to be alone—but Jen was on her way there too hopefully.

"Why didn't I get in that ambulance?"

Kim called me. "Hey. Are you ok? Let me help you."

"I can't drive," I told her; the tears were falling again.

"I'll come get you," she said.

"No, Kim. I'll figure it out."

"I'll be there in twenty minutes—bye." She hung up. She knew how stubborn and prideful I was.

I was relieved actually. I couldn't drive, and she would be a big comfort. I was glad she was coming, despite the humiliation and shame I was sure to feel. The problem was—I was going to be alone in the house for twenty minutes.

I went inside and mindlessly went upstairs. I went into the bathroom where I had found him. The police had put the syringe and spoon on the toilet tank. I wrapped them up in toilet paper and walked all the way down the stairs and down the driveway to throw them in the garbage bin.

I went back upstairs and as I approached the bathroom door—I glanced at the crucifix that was just outside the doorjamb. It was an old-fashioned crucifix that had candles and holy water inside—just in case "last rites" needed to be administered in a rush. Wow.

I decided that Wendy and the girls did not need to see his cutup jeans and shirt. As I gathered them up, I saw the silver cross that Jack wore around his neck. Again, wow. That's twice. It felt like déjà vu. Didn't I just find this cross after another tragedy of his?

There was also some medical debris left behind by the EMTs. A pair of rolled-up surgical gloves, some adhesive tape, and a sticky tab. I gathered it all up and made the long walk back to the bin and tossed it all, except the cross.

I went back upstairs for the third time and walked straight into the bathroom where it all took place. I sat on the side of the tub and noticed Wendy's earring on the floor. I was struck by how much my life had changed since I last held that earring in my hand. Then without any warning or prompting, images of his blue face and crumpled body raced through the screen in my mind. The shock of pulling him into the cradle of my arm and seeing that blue face—the same cradle that held him on the day he took his first breaths some twenty-two years ago. Why was I so sentimental? This was crazy. First tears, then heaving, then all-out sobbing.

"Fuck. Fuck. Fuck. What is happening to me?"

The doorbell rang—I wasn't ready. I grabbed a towel and started wiping my eyes and then unrolled some toilet paper and jammed it into my pocket.

"Hello . . ." Kim was inside. I walked out and looked down at her from the spot where I had almost fallen over the banister.

"Oh—sweetie, I am so sorry," she said, as she started to cry.

I went down to her, and she gave me a much-needed hug. I clung to her; I didn't care if it was "inappropriate." I had lost all appreciation for time—I didn't know if this had all started three hours or three days ago. But I had been isolated and alone until just now. I cried on her shoulder, as she held me with love and support.

I calmed down, and she was ready to help do whatever needed to be done. She had a mental list of things to worry about; she always had a list.

"What do you need?" she asked.

"That shopping bag with all the chargers and my backpack out of the truck."

"Do you have Jack's phone, charger, and some clothes?" she asked.

"No. I don't have any of that stuff," I muttered, wondering why I hadn't thought of that. "Oh, and remind me to call the judge in Paulding County too. I don't want him to get arrested for blowing off the GBI today."

Until just now, I had forgotten all about the appointment he had with the GBI. He is probably in *big trouble* for blowing off a superior court judge AND the GBI—probably seven years in prison.

Kim went through the house, as if she lived there, making sure we had whatever might be needed.

My coworker is at my house putting together personal items for my heroin-addicted son, because I can't drive to the hospital following his overdose—common executive problem, I thought.

I didn't care, though, as in the big scheme of things, her going through the house was nothing. I went out to the truck and got my backpack. We met at her car at the top of the driveway, got in, and left.

I called the judge and spoke with him for about ten minutes. He could tell that I was upset and handled me with charity and grace. He told me that he and his wife would be praying for us and that he hoped my son would get help. It could not have gone better.

As we drove to the hospital, I explained everything to Kim. She was a great listener, and her main concern was whether I was ok. Of course, I told her I was fine.

Maybe she forgets, I am Bob Hobbs, nothing fazes me for long, I thought.

We parked in ER parking, and Kim walked me in. She wanted to offer Wendy her love and support. We saw Wendy and Jenipher waiting on the far side of the ER waiting room. They stood as we approached them; Jen gave me a really warm and comforting hug and asked me if I was ok. Wendy and I hugged for just a brief moment.

We sat together for a few minutes, while Kim made sure we knew that she would do anything we needed—including taking care of the girls. Jen had already volunteered for girl duty, so we let Kim know how much we loved her and appreciated her help. She was going to call in a few hours to see if we were ok. We stood, said our goodbyes, and, with tears in her eyes, Kim left.

Wendy and Jen updated me on what was going on at the hospital. No one had seen him yet, but he was ok and under observation. They would get us when we could see him.

Jen was a nurse. I asked her what was going on back there and she honestly didn't know. She assumed that there would be a wide array of testing, drug screens, sexually transmitted diseases (STD) screens, psychiatric evaluations, and suicide questionnaires. But she didn't know what the policy was here.

"I don't want to see him; not yet; you guys go make sure everything is ok, and I'll go back after I know everything is ok."

"What happened, hon?" Jen asked.

"Well . . ." I started crying—openly—in public. What the hell was wrong with me?

I told the story as best I could. It was littered with starts and stops, due to my crying or needing to blow my nose. I told them what the officers told me about rehab, detox, and the suggestion that we do not allow the hospital to discharge him under any circumstances.

A short time later, a nurse came out and called for Hobbs. Wendy and Jen got up and went back to see him. I stayed in the waiting room—alone again. I did not want to look at him. I was afraid—of what? I don't know—but my mind was firm. Stay away from him for now.

It was thirty or forty-five minutes before Jen came out. She reported to me both as my sister-in-law and a medical professional.

"He is fine, no brain damage. He is really sick and is on suicide watch, which is normal procedure here at Kennestone after an overdose. He knows that he passed out, and then woke up with EMTs working on him."

"Ok," I said.

"You should go back; Wendy will need you. I have to go to your house and take care of the girls, do you need anything else?"

"Nah."

"Ok, Bobo. Call me if you need me. I love you!"

"Thanks, Niffy, I love you too."

It took me a while to work up the courage to go back. I didn't know what I would do, or what I would say. I didn't want to cry in front of him. I didn't know if I was angry, sad, forgiving, relieved, or scared. I was numb—I was full of so many emotions that my total net emotion was numb. I was at a tipping point. I couldn't take any more.

When I did go back and saw him for the first time, I was surprised at how he looked. This was the fourth extremely unique appearance he had had in two days. He was sick and dirty and greasy at the jail. He looked like a new man after he shot up that evening. He was dead and blue this morning. Now he looks wrung out. He looks like a junkie—skinny, dark sunken eyes, hollow cheeks. Wrung out—like a used dishcloth—he looked wrung out.

The Impact of an Overdose

In the moments immediately following my belief that my son was dead, I had two conflicting emotions. This is not something I enjoy reflecting on, as it brings up overwhelming feelings of guilt when I do.

But, this book is for those trying to make sense of what is going on in the life-and-death situations faced by addicts and their families. Others might feel the way I felt, and, for that reason, I must speak of my experience.

I was mourning as any father would mourn the death of his child. I felt a tremendous loss, tremendous despair, tremendous guilt, and a strong sense of failure. There was also shame, embarrassment, and humiliation. My first-born child, my only son, was gone. Part of the mourning process is the consideration of how to tell his mom, his sisters, and his grandparents. How raw would that be?

I don't want to lead you to believe that I was not in the moment during all this chaos and desperation—because I was. But the mind does what it does. Mine was everywhere and nowhere all day. You might wonder how all this could be happening in such a small timeframe, and I don't know how to answer that question other than this explanation.

If you walk into a cathedral with your eyes closed, and then open your eyes to witness its beauty for just one instant, you can walk out into the street and describe what you saw in that instant in great detail. It was only an instant, but your mind somehow captured it in a snapshot. That's how it was that day for me; it was a series of instants, many of them I captured in great detail.

I was relieved. I had a tremendous sense of relief in the instant where I was mourning his death. I felt that he was safe; that his suffering was over. However, selfishly, I was relieved for myself. This is where the guilt comes in. I was relieved that I would not need to deal with this bullshit anymore. What I just described in these opening chapters captures only three or four days of more than eight years of incredibly bad and terrifying behavior. For me, I was in constant fear, constant worry, and constant despair.

Of course, there were glimmers of brilliance during these eight years. More often than not, my feelings would turn quickly from anxiety and regret to hope and pride.

"Maybe it *was* just a phase—he's gonna be fine—thank God!"

I'd let people know at work and in the extended family that I thought the worst was behind us—that he turned the corner—that it was finally over . . .

But whether it was a week, or a month, or six months, those periods were always dashed with even bigger problems. My hopes and feelings of pride would be flattened, steamrolled, by yet another unexplainable, self-destructive fuckup. In time, like many of us, I learned not to get my hopes up—to not believe in good outcomes.

I hate to write that I had enough—that it was killing me—and that though I was mourning his loss—I was relieved it was over.

As I look back on it now, I think that had he died, I eventually would have recovered, as family members do following such a loss. But in my case, I mourned his death—and was relieved that our suffering was at an end—however, he came back from the death that I had witnessed. The relief was gone; the mourning remains to this day.

Many of the things that followed in my life, and the lives of my loved ones, might not have happened had he not been revived. Please, do not think that I wish he had died—because that is not true—I am simply trying to work through the psychological impact of what happened. I want to share it as honestly and truthfully as I can, so that if something this horrible happens to others—they know that what is happening inside their heads has happened before—and they should relieve themselves of any guilt they might carry.

The feelings of mourning did not leave me. I have become so convinced this will happen again, that I have set myself up to be in a constant state of mourning. Maybe my brain has decided to just stay in this state and minimize the trauma when death comes. I don't know. But three years later, I live in fear and sadness.

The relief I felt because this whole painful phase of my life was at an end was smashed by the reality that it wasn't over. And I would continue to fight with him and his addiction well into the future. There was no known endpoint to this madness. Soon I would learn that even after rehab—there was likely a relapse, likely an overdose, likely more rehabs. I was being educated that I needed to accept this as my reality—and, at the same time, let it go—let it go. I still can't believe that is the therapy we get—it's gonna happen again—nothing you can do about it—let it go.

Any relief that I had felt at the thought of his death was fully replaced with anxiety after his revival. I was more convinced than ever, that I was going to be shot at the front door by a pissed-off dealer or customer and probably only after I found Jack dead again.

I think these last few paragraphs portray the root of my emotional disorders, which include posttraumatic stress disorder (PTSD), anxiety, and major depressive disorder.

Chapter 3 Concepts

1. You might get caught between helping an addict and protecting yourself or others.
2. You and your spouse/partner must remain aligned.
3. Know in advance what heroin does and how it kills.
4. You can't predict how others will respond to your dilemma.
5. You can't control anything.
6. God, the Tao, the Universe, a higher power is with you.
7. Overdoses are scary and not a time to panic; you must be able to save a life.
8. Have Narcan available when with an addict.
9. Heroin overdoses require a hospital visit.
10. Heroin addicts have little comprehension of what it is like saving their lives.

Chapter 4

What I Didn't Know When I Needed To

There's no darkness except ignorance.
~William Shakespeare

Discover: Know What You Are Up Against

There were many signs available to me that I either ignored or missed. The track Jack was on was of his own doing, and there is likely nothing I could have done to prevent his overdose in 2014. However, I could have been better prepared for the eventual overdose and the aftermath that followed.

I could have done better in understanding the degree of his drug usage and the effects of the drugs he was using. The biggest problem was I didn't even know he was using heroin, and I should have. Not that it was my responsibility to know, but I was one of those parents who didn't want to know. I didn't want to know the depths that my child had sunk to. It was as if the longer it took to admit the truth, the longer it wouldn't be true. It wouldn't be true that his life was in jeopardy. I made many mistakes in this journey—the biggest, though, was avoiding the truth. I must have believed that the longer I denied the obvious, the longer he would live. It is a terrible place for a parent denying the obvious, as it unfolds before your eyes, revealing how foolish you truly are.

The evidence that he was a heroin addict came over a long period of time. Until the overdose, there was never a crime scene where everything was available all at once. There were sporadic odd occurrences that didn't fit with my view of normal. Had I simply done a few hours of Web searching on some of the weird things he did, I likely would have concluded he was a heroin addict. I could have searched on these topics:

- My son pawned everything.
- My son forged my checks.
- Why are my spoons missing?
- What is Suboxone?
- What are painkillers?
- Why does a spoon have burn marks on the bottom?

Had I genuinely wanted to know, I could have discovered the source of his eventual killer. But I was in denial, due to fear or shame or both. I did not want to discover the truth. Looking back, it is easy to see what was happening, but as it unfolded in real time, it was not so easy, not for me, the parent. I urge anyone reading this, to be honest with yourself. Discover the truth as soon as you can, and then take aggressive action. The consequences of doing little, or waiting for more evidence, are too tragic to allow.

The piece of evidence I regret ignoring the most was Suboxone. He was on a Suboxone prescription, written by a licensed medical doctor, for close to two years. He went to this doctor every two weeks, as if his life depended on it. I never bothered to check into it. I figured it was between him and his doctor. Had I looked it up and asked enough questions, I might have discovered the depths of his problems. It might not have changed anything, had I known, but we could have been better prepared for what was coming. I did not know what Suboxone was, and I never tried to figure it out.

So, the first suggestion of this chapter is to know what you are up against. This will require that you overcome the denial that is so strong in your heart. You will have to gather the courage to snoop around your loved one's personal items, ask probing questions, and get to the bottom of what they are dealing with. It is not fun, and it might not feel ethical or moral, and it might not be. But this could be a matter of life and death. If your loved one's behavior is cause for concern, and if you think narcotics are involved, you must act quickly. Do not delay! The sooner you know what you are dealing with, the better you can prepare for what lies ahead.

If you do begin to discover some ugly truths, some disturbing evidence, you must force yourself to accept it and to evaluate it fairly. The parental voice of denial is strong, and it will do everything in its power to convince you that your child is not involved in something so dirty and dangerous. I often think that the voice that compels the addict to use, the seductive heroin voice, is the same voice that whispers to parents that the evidence we are seeing is not real, that there are explanations for it, that our child is not capable of such nonsense. I urge you to ignore that voice of denial, for it is also the voice of death.

Educate: Learn Everything You Can

If your loved one is using heroin, there is at least a one in four likelihood that he or she is addicted. If addicted, there is a one in fifteen (6 percent) chance that they will die from an overdose. The most urgent thing that you, your family, and others who are frequently with your loved one need to know is how to save the life of an overdosed heroin addict. Everything else can wait until this vital step is mastered.

In Chapter 2, we described how heroin and other opioids cause euphoria, pain relief, and a sense of relaxation by working on the brain and the nervous system's neurotransmitters via opiate receptors. In an overdose, the number of morphine molecules and the potency or strength of the drug can overwhelm the opiate receptors and the victim, causing the nonvoluntary reflex action of breathing to stop. This is the life-threatening reaction to an overdose—no breathing.

Saving a Life

To save an overdose victim's life, a responder must restore breathing or provide the victim with oxygen until breathing can be restored. If breathing is not restored or oxygen provided via emergency breathing, the victim will suffocate and die. Alternatively, if the victim is found too late or oxygen is delayed, the victim can suffer brain damage or become comatose.

Here are the recommended steps to follow in the event of an overdose due to heroin or another opioid:

Step	Instruction	Note
1	Call 911—understand limits of mobile phones. Or know the emergency number of the country where you are.	Have another person call, if available.
2	Determine if victim is breathing.	
3	If not breathing, perform CPR—do not stop CPR until victim recovers.	
4	Administer Narcan—per instructions.	If available.
5	Continue CPR (step 3).	
6	Administer second dose of Narcan—per instructions.	If available.
7	Continue CPR (step 3).	
8	Get victim to the emergency room, as soon as possible.	Understand risks of second overdose and withdrawal due to Narcan.

Figure 6: Recommended Steps to Follow after an Overdose.

I cannot overemphasize that time is of the essence. Do not delay in starting these steps and carrying them out. You will likely be afraid, maybe even in shock. This is why preparation is so important. You and those who spend time with your addicted loved one must be prepared to save his or her life under extreme duress in an emergency. If the person has been "down" for just a minute or so, they might begin to turn blue— starting with their nails and lips. If it has been longer, their entire face might be shaded blue. It is not an easy thing to look at, but you must overcome your emotions and get your mind straight, so that you can save a life.

You might have a thought similar to this: "What if he gets in trouble when I call 911?" He might. He might die too. Better safe than sorry. If you come across a nonresponsive heroin addict, you must put everything aside, except your desire to save his life.

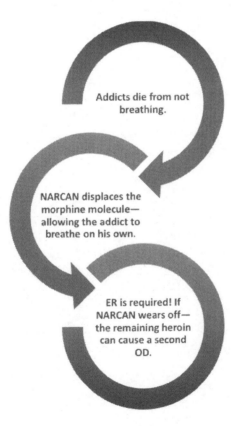

Figure 7: Saving a Life.

Detailed Steps

Step 1, Call for Help

It is preferred that you have another person call 911. If someone else is not available, I suggest that you dial 911 and put your phone on "speaker" or use some hands-free device, if possible. This will allow you to work on the victim while talking to the 911 agent.

You should know that if you are calling from a mobile phone, there is a high probability that the agent will not know where you are located. There is a major flaw in the US mobile phone 911 service concerning your location. Do not be surprised if the agent wants to know where you are before wanting to know why you are calling. It is crucial that you speak clearly and calmly in helping the agent understand your location.

Once they know where you are, be clear in describing your belief that you are trying to save the victim of a heroin overdose. If you have Narcan—let them know. Otherwise, prepare yourself for CPR.

Steps 2 and 3, Check Breathing and CPR

It would be great if you and everyone around your addicted loved one could be trained and certified in CPR. However, that wish is not practical. You could and should read up on CPR techniques and watch a few instructional videos on YouTube. Kneeling over a blue, dead heroin addict is not the time to remember what you learned about CPR in the eighth grade—you will panic and fail. Learn it now while you are calm.

Some basic tips are as follows: Try to get the victim flat on his back on a firm surface. Verify the airway is clear of obstruction before breathing into the mouth. Obviously, if there are indications that moving the victim might cause serious injury or death, use your best judgment on the scene. Do your best to get air into them.

Important note: When checking breathing, do not confuse the "death rattle" with breathing. The slight indication of an exhale that sounds like a baby snore is NOT breathing. It is a sign that death is near.

Follow CPR procedures until the victim is revived, help arrives, or you are too exhausted to continue.

Step 4, Administer Narcan

If you have Narcan, follow the instructions and any previous training you might have received and administer it. CPR might still be required following the first dose, if the victim's breathing is not restored. The 911 operator might be able to guide you, but remember time is of the essence.

Steps 5, 6, and 7, Continue CPR

Continue CPR. If available, administer a second dose of Narcan per the instructions or your previous training. CPR might still be required.

Step 8, Obtain Emergency Services

It is vital that the victim be taken to an emergency room as soon as possible, once breathing is restored or emergency responders arrive. The risk of a second overdose is especially high at this time for two reasons. First, the Narcan will wear off, and if sufficient heroin remains in the addict's body, he can overdose again, once the Narcan is gone. Second, Narcan rapidly removes morphine molecules from opiate receptors, thereby forcing an "artificial" withdrawal. The addict will feel all the symptoms of heroin withdrawal and will physically crave heroin and risk a second overdose.

Another reason to get to the ER is so the addict is in the "virtual custody" of medical services. This might be the best opportunity to get him or her into a treatment program, beginning with detox. If the ER was avoided for whatever reason, there is virtually no chance to get an addict into treatment, and the next stop is probably the morgue. But the drama and trauma associated with the 911 call and the ER visit, coupled with your insistence can trigger the addict's willingness to begin treatment. I strongly urge you to treat this tragedy as an opportunity to get your addict (and your family) the help they need. You might not get another chance.

You should avoid taking your addict anywhere other than directly to detox from the ER. If the addict goes home after ER, they will likely have access to heroin and will have a reduced motivation to go to treatment. The best advice I can give is the same as the police gave me— do not allow your addict to be discharged from the ER following an overdose. Your best chance to save them is while they are in the ER. Do not take no for an answer.

Hopefully, after you finish this book, but before a tragedy, you will have created an emergency plan based on the information provided. If so, you should be prepared for this situation.

A Note on Narcan

Narcan (Naloxone) is an amazing antidote to heroin and other opioids. It consists of molecules that have a higher propensity than the morphine molecule to attach to the opiate receptors in the brain and nervous system. Quickly after administration, the Narcan molecules attach to the opiate receptors prohibiting the morphine molecules from attaching. This allows the victim's nervous system to recover and begin breathing again. Sometimes the dose of heroin taken is so high and potent that the second dose of Narcan is needed to displace enough morphine molecules for the victim to begin breathing again. Always follow the instructions provided with the Narcan you are using.

Chapter 4 Concepts

1. Know how to save an overdose victim's life.
2. Have Narcan on hand.
3. Know CPR.
4. Know that a heroin overdose is simply the loss of respiration; the victim needs oxygen.
5. Learn everything you can about heroin addiction.

Chapter 5

And Just Like That—Putting a Recently Dead Addict Back on the Street

The difference between stupidity and genius is that genius has its limits.
~Albert Einstein

They Tell Me the Emergency Is Over

I looked down at him as he lay in his hospital bed. It wasn't that long ago that we were here in the ER with him.

Why was that? I thought

It was then that the silver cross, déjà vu moment slammed into my awareness. I did find the cross on the ground at the scene of another one of his drug-related incidents.

It was almost a year ago—just before Karen's high school graduation in May 2013.

Jack had just gotten out of the Candler County Jail after serving almost a full year for perjury convictions. He was shopping with his mom at a local department store when he bumped into one of his "customers." This guy was pissed off with Jack, allegedly (and likely), Jack had stolen more than $1,000 from him.

Somehow, Jack ended up outside, behind the store with this guy and his buddy. They beat the shit out of Jack—which he probably deserved— but they took it even further. For good measure, they got in their truck and ran over Jack's leg, and then they backed up the truck and ran over it a second time. It seemed like a lifetime ago, but it was less than one year. Time is a funny phenomenon when living with an addict.

The police had to interview him after the assault, of course. He didn't want to press charges initially, for obvious reasons—that part is not important here. But what is important is that while he was in the hospital following the assault—he told me that he had lost his silver cross during the fight and asked me if I would go try to find it. So, I went to the scene of the crime, and because the setting sun was shining just right, I saw the glare coming from his silver cross lying in the parking lot behind the department store.

Wow. That's weird, I thought to myself, now looking at him following his overdose.

Narcotic overdoses follow special protocols in emergency rooms, at least in our jurisdiction. The hospitals have certain protocols and procedures that are self-imposed, and then those that are imposed by the government. These all required that a variety of specialists and administrators, in addition to the ER staff, visit with him while he was under observation.

Jack was twenty-two years old; so, Wendy and I have no legal rights, or standing, concerning any of the procedures or information being shared. For some of his interviews, we were asked to excuse ourselves, and for others, we were allowed to stay. I don't know what the differences were, but I know that one of his interviews was about sexually transmitted diseases—and I am sure we were excused for that one. Who would want to discuss that stuff in front of their parents?

He was on suicide watch. The healthcare professionals assume that every overdose is likely a suicide attempt until they have evidence that it was accidental. The evidence could be the patient's description of what happened and those conversations confirmed by witnesses; or, in our case, a series of psych evaluations could be passed to give the hospital a sense of ease regarding the self-destructive nature of the patient. In this case, I didn't know. I thought he could have been so frightened by becoming a narc that he would rather kill himself than go through with it.

He was in the ER for six or seven hours, as I remember. During that time, there were several people discussing his release, and at some point, the attending ER physician came in and informed us that Jack would be released within an hour, and we could go home. Immediately, the Cobb County police officer's warning flashed into my head—and then flew out of my mouth.

"We are not leaving here until he is detoxed," I didn't know what that meant. "We are not leaving this hospital until we have a place to go. We are not going home under any circumstances."

"Sir, we do not detox here."

"I don't care—we are not leaving this hospital until we have a place to go—and we are most definitely not going home. He was dead eight hours ago—we are not going anywhere until I know he is safe."

I didn't know if I was more concerned about his safety or mine. I certainly could not go through another overdose. I was firm with my posture and my tone of voice. The doctor walked out, saying he would be back.

Fifteen minutes later, he returned and told me the hospital had no medical reason to keep him. He was stable, was not experiencing any withdrawal symptoms, was not suicidal, and besides—he was twenty-two years old. He reminded me that I had no legal standing here.

As I started to protest yet again, Wendy interrupted, "Jack, what do *youuuuuu* want to do?" she asked. Apparently, she had been talking with him and knew what he would say.

"I am going to do whatever you and Dad tell me to do," he said.

Holy crap, did he just say that? I thought to myself—pleased and stunned at the same time. I looked at the doctor, "Please, Doc, there has to be something you can do. You know as well as I do that if we go home, the risk is high that this is going to happen again," I stated with authority. In truth, I didn't know. I didn't know shit, other than what the officer told me, and that was all I had to go by right now.

"I'll go make some calls," the doctor said.

I guess he did know as well as I did.

"Thank you!"

A psychiatrist came into his room a short time later. Jack recognized her. I guessed that she worked with him through the suicide observation. She introduced herself to Wendy and me and asked Jack how he was doing. Then she started telling us "the rules" and the way "things are done here."

"Mr. Hobbs, we cannot keep your son. There is no medical reason to keep him. He is not in any danger of harming himself, and his physical condition is stable. I understand your position, but we simply do not have a reason to keep him. Insurance is not going to cover his stay with us, if we don't have a reason to admit him. Asking us to admit him because he might overdose again is like asking us to admit you because you might get sick again—there is no reason at this time."

"You do have a reason!" I exclaimed. "He is a heroin addict; he just overdosed and almost died. If we go home, he is going to get sick, and then he is going to use again, and he is going to die again. You should have seen what he did on Monday after spending three days in jail. We are lucky that he didn't kill a dozen people trying to get to his dealer's house."

"Sir, he has no symptoms of withdrawal; have you found a rehab center? Maybe they will detox him."

This person didn't know what she was talking about. I could tell. She would be willing to help me, if she knew what to do. But since she did not know what to do, she was hiding her ignorance behind policy and procedures.

"Ma'am, this is Wellstar," I stated. "It is a huge company. Somebody in this company knows what to do, and we are not leaving until we talk to that person!"

She left. I was not sure we would see her again. Wendy was starting to get that look on her face that I usually only saw at the car dealership when she thought that I had negotiated long enough. That look usually came about what turned out to be the halfway point. If she had that look now—I had a few doctors and a few rejections left before I would have to accept their refusal to help me.

I needed to talk with somebody and get advice. I was betting all of this on what the cop had told me—I didn't know whether he knew what he was saying or not—but he was all I had so far. I had no one to call— and what would I say if I did?

"Hey, man, when your son overdosed on heroin, what did you do?" I mean really—there was nowhere to go, no one to turn to. I was lost.

Now what? Now what am I supposed to do, I thought.

This was nuts. There absolutely had to be a solution—no way were we the first family in this situation.

The psychiatrist came back and asked me to sit down. Maybe she felt I was threatening. I looked behind her to see if security was following.

"Sir, I spoke with my department head. We don't offer detox services here at Kennestone. South Cobb Hospital has a program called New Vision, which is a detox program, but only for alcohol, not heroin. The reason is that alcohol withdrawal can kill an alcoholic. Heroin withdrawal is horrible; but not life-threatening."

"Ma'am, that is ridiculous. The Cobb County police told me specifically not to allow you to discharge my son. He told me that Cobb County was expecting more than 300 heroin overdose deaths this year— 2014. I refuse to believe that Wellstar does not have a program to treat this problem, and I refuse to allow my son to be one of the 300. Did you call New Vision? Did you call them, Doctor, and ask them about heroin?"

"No. They do not offer detox for narcotics, sir."

"Ma'am, go call them. Please. We cannot leave here. I am begging you to please call New Vision and get us in."

"I'll call them Mr. Hobbs, but they only do alcohol."

"Thank you."

The attending nurse came in and took the required vitals and asked the required questions. She asked if Jack was ready to go home and if he had gotten his discharge papers yet. I about blew a chip.

"We ARE NOT leaving here without a place to go—so we DO NOT have discharge papers yet!" I scolded.

Minutes seem like hours in the emergency room; hell, anywhere in the hospital for that matter. It seemed like forever, but it was only ten or twenty minutes before the psychiatrist returned.

"Mr. Hobbs, I apologize. I was wrong about New Vision; they do detox heroin patients."

"Thank God," Wendy said. Probably because she was tiring of my stubbornness—but definitely because she saw a step to take to make this all better.

"The problem is your son doesn't have any symptoms yet, so we cannot transfer him. It is probably going to be two or three days before he has any symptoms—so we can't keep him here. But, I have an idea. You guys listen to what I say and then decide if you want to follow-through with what I suggest. It might work."

"I'm listening," I said

"We will discharge you from here. Go immediately to the ER at South Cobb and complain about being sick and worried about withdrawals. That will get you in. If you are lucky, withdrawals will start soon—or you will have an empathetic physician. This is the best I can do for you at this time. I am sorry."

She then looked at Jack. "This is entirely up to you. You are twenty-two years old. You are only going to get well if you decide it is time to get well. Good luck to you. Good luck, Mr. and Mrs. Hobbs."

"Thank you, Doctor," Wendy said.

"Thanks, Doc," I said.

The discharge didn't take long, as they were ready for us to leave. Jack got dressed and gathered his things. He had his phone—which was probably a risk, but he was trying to get a message to the GBI. I am not sure if he ever reached them, but I had reached the judge, and I hoped that would be enough.

We went through the Steak 'n Shake drive-through to get him something to eat. It had been a long day, and this would be his first food. Wendy and I decided we would get something after he was settled at South Cobb. I wanted a beer—several actually.

Checking into the ER was a bit awkward. Here was a twenty-two-year-old checking into the hospital with his parents doing all the talking. Certainly, we were over-parenting from a certain point of view, but I considered this a life-and-death situation, and I felt that the slightest misstep might result in the bad outcome of death. We presented the insurance card and answered the intake questions as best we could. We reminded the intake administrator that all his important information was just collected at their sister hospital and they could get all of it from there.

We had a seat in the waiting room, and it wasn't long before we were called back. It seemed that the drug and alcohol program ran its own independent emergency service through the ER. Once he was taken back to the ER examining area, we were told that he would be moving upstairs to a standard room, once a bed became available. Wendy and I waited long enough to make sure that he had a place to stay at the hospital, and that he wasn't going to check himself out, and then we left to get a bite to eat.

It is hard to describe how I felt once I was settled to the idea that he would be staying at the hospital. You might think I was relieved or grateful or pleased, and maybe I should have been. But the reality at the time was overwhelming negative emotions. My body had been flooded with so much emotion for seemingly so long that it had reached a new normal. The new normal was a general feeling of dread and sadness. For me, feeling "good" consisted of a lower-than-average level of those two emotions.

Today, though, I was full. All circuits were busy. New emotions were still generated and were in the pipeline to be processed, but all circuits were busy—there was nowhere for the new feelings to go anymore. I don't know if they were stored up somewhere and would come out eventually, or if they dissipated in place, never to be dealt with. But my feelings that day did not vary much after a certain point. They were overwhelmingly terrible, and they stayed that way for a long time.

Mentally, there was not a lot of brain activity. I wasn't thinking; I was dwelling. Dwelling on what I saw; dwelling on what I did and what I didn't do. There wasn't much room for me to think or to tap into any form of intelligence. It would be a few days before my mental state switched from dwelling on the morning of February 25 to dreading any day in the future. It was tough being so sad—it became impossible being terrified every day.

I was wrapped tight. All this had to be released at some point—holding on to it was a mighty task. My whole body was in pain, perhaps due to carrying both the burden of regret with the fear of parental failure. The pain was deep—in my bones—in the essence of my being. I cried almost all day, and crying has its own way of wearing out a body. I did not feel good, but I was soon to discover a simple remedy that would help me deal with these new-to-me problems.

Wendy and I went to Red Lobster for a late snack/dinner. We sat at a booth in the bar, and I think it was then that she got her first really good look at me. I don't know what she saw, but she became sympathetic—as if she were looking at a broken old man. I appreciated the look of support and compassion I noticed from her. It didn't stop me from breaking down, though; and I didn't care that we were in the middle of a restaurant bar. My pride was destroyed today—ripped from me—developed over 45 years, the pride I had in myself, my abilities, my family, my accomplishments, and my upbringing—all of it was completely smashed in a few short hours. There was nothing I was proud of anymore.

Wendy assured me that he was going to be fine and that everything was going to be ok. I told her that the overdose was not the only thing that I was upset about—there was more.

This was going to be worse than confession, I thought.

We ordered soup and appetizers, and I ordered a tall draft beer. As soon as the glass hit the table, I picked it up and gulped a third of the glass. Almost immediately, I felt a deep sense of easing. The overwhelming tension in my body started to fade ever so little—and even though I still felt terrible—it was a better terrible. I quickly finished that first beer and eagerly ordered a second one.

I hesitated in telling Wendy what was bothering me. I mean, I am the only person in the universe who knows what happened in that room today. I did not want her to think less of me—but, hell—I didn't recognize who "me" was at the moment. I was reaching into space for some marker, some reminder, or some restoration program that could help me with my identity. I have never found it. Did I want to tell her that I was a fraud? A phony? A failure? I had to admit it to someone—and she was the person available—so I took the risk and let it fly.

"Wendy, I wasn't able to save him," I said. The tears started to come, as that admission of shame and guilt left my mouth.

"What do you mean? He is alive."

"Not because of me. They screamed at me to do CPR, begged me to do it. I didn't do it. I never did it, and I don't know why."

"Bob, he is fine, you saved his life."

"No, the fire department did. I always believed that given an opportunity to be a hero that I would rise to the occasion. Today, when he was dead on the floor, and the 911 people were begging me to breathe into him, I froze. I failed to do what was needed. I couldn't even be a hero with a family member in my own home; imagine how bad I would be on a battlefield or in a car crash. I am so ashamed of myself." I said, continuing to cry.

She was holding my hand from across the table. Normally in this situation, she would be holding both; but one was busy lifting the magic elixir of beer to my lips. The tension was leaving my body, as I drank those beers.

We sat quietly while we ate our snacks and I drank beer. When we were finished, we returned to the ER to wait for his room assignment in the New Vision detox program.

He ended up staying in the ER, unadmitted to the hospital, for three nights. They cared for him as if he were in a room, but he was not yet admitted to the hospital, and he was still considered an Emergency Room patient. I am not sure what was behind all of it. Certainly, my apparent insanity played a role; regardless, whatever it was that motivated them to provide special treatment for us, I am grateful for all they did.

They reminded us regularly that the detox program could not take him until he was ready for detox and showing symptoms of withdrawal. Every once in a while, my doubt would creep in, and I would become convinced they were going to discharge him—thankfully, they never did.

Jack knew all about withdrawal and the symptoms he could expect. He spoke to the medical staff with ease about what he had experienced in the past and what he was expecting now. By noon on the fourth day—

Thursday—he was fairly sure he was starting to feel the last of the morphine molecules leave his body. To my surprise, it wasn't an "all of a sudden" acute pain with vomiting and rolling around. All of that came—but subtly and slowly. It was as if the heroin was letting its host know that there was still time—"All this eventual, inevitable pain can still be avoided—just get a fix. Only you can prevent the pain—get some before this gets any worse."

On Thursday, they admitted him and moved him "upstairs" to the New Vision program. Finally, after three days of walking in the dark, we got to talk to experts on the subject of heroin abuse, opioid addiction, and the crisis gripping our county and the entire country. I was shocked at what I didn't know. Hell, actor Philip Seymour Hoffman died of a heroin overdose in Greenwich Village, where my daughter lives, just three weeks earlier. I never had a clue. I never started to connect the dots . . . until now.

I had been researching rehab centers online. There was still no one to ask—no family or friends or neighbors had ever been through anything like this before; if they had, they were quiet about it—like we were being. The shame and humiliation are so strong that they protect the epidemic; they are part of the epidemic. Even if I did find someone to ask, what was I going to say? "Hey, man, when your son overdosed on heroin, what rehab did you choose and why?" It sounded ridiculous.

And even if I did buck up the courage to overcome my shame—how would someone answer that question? Even if they were experts dealing with the exact same issue, they might remain silent. No one wants to be associated with this stuff—especially those with several children still in school. Again, part of the reason heroin is so successfully growing in unabated popularity, despite the carnage it delivers on its users and their families, is because no one wants to discuss it. It is a secret. And secrecy is one of heroin's biggest allies.

I found a couple of local treatment centers that seemed to have experience with heroin. But their websites and brochures were crappy—they looked like they were going broke. There were also many national rehabs with wonderful websites, glitzy brochures, and wonderful call center agents. Some of these wanted $80,000 or more for sixty to ninety days. There was no way I was going to figure that kind of money out in three or four days—not with a kid at NYU. These places looked legit though—Malibu, South Florida, great destination rehabs.

Insurance was an issue too. Not many rehab programs took our insurance—or any insurance for that matter. It took me some thinking to determine my decision criteria. I had visited a bunch of websites, read dozens of brochures, and talked to five or six intake managers. Everyone was a salesperson—they all had a pitch, and they were all well trained in capitalizing on fear—uncertainty—and doubt. In almost all cases, I felt like I was talking to a business—not a mental health facility.

Some centers pitched their recovery rate or their client reviews; others pitched their venue or the quality of their cafeteria or dining room. Some bragged on their first visit success rate and the number of heroin users they had treated, were currently treating, or had on their staff. Others had crappy websites, black-and-white brochures, and an answering machine.

I didn't know what I wanted, but on my own intuition, I decided that I would prefer a place that would cure him the first time. I couldn't afford for this to not work. I was so naïve—so ignorant. I also wanted him to go away, because staying near here would be too distracting, too tempting. I also considered extensive heroin experience to be a must—I didn't know anything about it and needed to know—or feel comfortable that the staff dealing with him were experienced heroin addicts. Hopefully, they would teach me a thing or two in the process. I started focusing on these criteria, as I spoke to different treatment centers.

Meanwhile, Jack's withdrawal symptoms were progressing. By Thursday evening, he was getting sick and looking like death warmed over. His skin color was pale and chalky. His face was more like a skeleton, than a fully alive person. He would have periods of profuse sweating followed by periods of extreme clamminess. He didn't eat, and he didn't get out of bed. The attending nurse wanted to discuss medication options with him. I was about to learn a little bit about drugs.

She started off with Suboxone—and asked Jack if he wanted to taper off the heroin using the Suboxone. I did not know what she was talking about—he declined the Suboxone. He said he wanted to stay clean. She asked if he was sure, and then offered that he could always change his mind later. Then she asked him about benzodiazepines—benzos. He knew what they were—I didn't. What I learned was that benzos are tranquilizers and they include commonly prescribed psych drugs, such as Xanax and Klonopin. Again, he declined. My thoughts drifted to Xanax.

Fall 2006

A month or so after he sat in the front seat of my truck, as a freshman in high school, and told me fervently to stay out of his life, things seemed to be better than they were through the summer. He was competing for the number 1 spot on the varsity cross-country team, and he was playing well on two hockey teams. On one Monday in September, he had his name on the school announcements for winning a cross-country meet and for scoring two goals in a varsity hockey game. You would think this would be enough exposure for a freshman. But no.

The cross-country team was heading from Atlanta to Orlando for a large cross-country meet and some team bonding at Disney World. They chartered a bus and reserved hotel rooms and were expecting a wonderful experience for the kids and the staff.

When the team arrived in Orlando, Jack had difficulty getting off the bus. When the coaches asked him if he was ok, he couldn't speak. A little later at the team dinner, he made some sexual advances on a married female coach. Later that night, we received a call from the head coach who told us that our freshman ate two Xanax with a senior buddy while on the bus. He would be suspended for the next meet or so.

I never looked up Xanax back then. The Xanax incident was the first time he had tried something I had never tried—and he was only a freshman. It seemed as if we were always facing something like this, from 2006 until this day. The thing about being a parent of a person who does this, regardless of whether they are a minor, is that there is no eject handle. There is no escape, no way out. Eventually, this becomes extremely frustrating and emotionally destructive for any caring parent.

Today he declined Xanax. *How ironical*, I thought. He told her he wanted to take Advil or Tylenol, but no prescription drugs. She talked to him about restless leg syndrome and other discomforts she was sure he would experience in the coming hours. He still declined the pills. Finally, she asked about sleeping meds, and he said he would wait and see how it went. Right now, no, but check back at bedtime. He had been "clean" of everything since Monday morning, so maybe he was committed to staying that way. Maybe he was committed to this.

Everyone on the staff (at least who we spoke to) was an addiction specialist in their given role. The doctors, the nurses, the counselors, even the nurse's aides. In fact, I got the best advice and direction from a nurse's aide. I wish I could remember his name. He helped me get my head on straight about how to choose a rehab and what was coming at me during the next several weeks—whether I was ready for it or not.

When I first started talking with the nurse's aide, our conversation was mostly about sports. It is usually easy to start a conversation, and often a friendship, with some sport's current event. We were both walking toward the elevator when he asked me what we were going to do next with Jack. I told him that I was looking for a remote ninety-day rehab location, where Jack could start recovering with little distraction from his loser friends who lived near here. I also voiced my desire to find a center where there was heroin expertise, and a high, first-visit success rate.

He chuckled at me, not mockingly, but warmly, and he invited me to walk with him a while longer instead of heading to my truck. I didn't hesitate; if he knew something in this area, I wanted to hear it. Sarcastically, he asked me if I was leaning toward one of those treatment centers with a slick website, great reviews, and high success rates.

"Of course! Isn't that just common sense?" I said.

"C'mon man," he said. "You are a smart guy! Don't fall for one of those marketing companies that does rehab; find a rehab that is so focused on treatment that marketing is an afterthought, and then only if there is a budget for it. Find one like that, and you might have a chance, and you won't waste your money chasing fantasies like "first-time heroin recovery.""

I thought about what he just said; here was a nurse's aide schooling me in common business sense.

"What else you got for me, man?" I asked.

He continued breaking down what he considered to be my flawed thinking.

"Well, the way I see it, your son lives in Cobb County. You are gonna send him away to some remote city for rehab—and he'll probably be a rehab all-star, an honor grad. He'll come out with a fancy referral letter and a shiny certificate. But when he's done, guess what happens next? He comes home to Cobb County. This is where he lives; this is where his life happens. Once he is back here, he has no support group, no sponsor, no doctors; all he has are his loser buddies. It won't take long until that fancy rehab is a distant memory, and your son will go back out, and ultimately, he will end up right back in here again. I see it all the time, dude."

"Holy shit," I said. "How do you know all this?"

"Work here, man. See 'em come, see 'em go. See 'em come back again. It's sad, it really is. And that's the other thing." He paused and made sure he had my attention. "This is heroin, man. There is no such thing as a one-and-done rehab—not that I've seen. Don't go mortgaging the house chasing recovery rates and online reviews. I don't know any addicts, no heroin addicts, who don't relapse—and more than once too."

"But, dude, some of these places are pitching recovery rates like 75–80 percent!"

"Not heroin, man. No way. Maybe if they blend everything together—all alcohol and all drugs. And they probably include all people who check-in—hell, parents check kids in who drank once or smoked weed once. It's all just statistics. How many people do you think answer their treatment center's survey call one year out or two years out? I guarantee you all the clean ones answer, and few, if any, of the relapsers do. They aren't boldfaced lies, man—but it ain't straight either. It's all marketing and sales—people know you are scared and they wanna capitalize."

"Man! You're awesome! I never thought about it like that. I am pissed about the one-and-done thing; but you gave me a lot to think about."

"You're scared shitless, dude. Of course, you ain't thinking. I got two places I recommend. Tangu is local. Call them. They save lives. If it ain't right for you, call me, and I'll give you my remote recommendation."

"Tangu? I called them this morning—got voicemail. And their website isn't that good."

"Websites don't heal addicts. Neither do sales guys. Doctors and other addicts help addicts."

"Ok. I'll check them out, but I don't think they take my insurance."

"They are good people. They will work with you."

"Ok, thanks for the tip."

"You are welcome, dude. Good luck!"

I found my way back to the car and got my notebook and then headed back to Jack's room. I felt like I had just gone to grad school on addiction recovery.

Watching an Addict Suffer

On Friday morning, Jack was in full withdrawal. He hadn't slept the night before. He was now exhausted; even so, he could not lay still.

His legs were moving almost constantly, and when they weren't, he was tossing and turning. I could see why they were offering him sleeping pills and tranquilizers—even that Suboxone. I often thought in those hours that he probably wished he was dead—he was suffering, and there was little he could do to stop it. Torture. That's what it was—torture. I could not understand. Clearly, it was not his first time going through this. I wondered then and still do—"If an addict knows this outcome in advance—why would they ever use? Getting through all this pain was an accomplishment—why go back? It was insanity."

I learned some years later that often an addict experiences euphoria so strong, that the urge to replicate it is stronger than the urge for sex. That's powerful. But I also learned that many long-time addicts begin to experience a feeling of nothing—absolute nothing. I have tried to imagine what that might feel like, and in my condition with PTSD, anxiety, and depression, it is hard to fathom.

I don't want to ever know how bad a person must be suffering to obtain an obsession with feeling nothing—a feeling of nothingness. Their suffering must be horrible. Think about it, these humans are willing to risk everything to feel nothing. The feeling they are willing to die for is no feeling at all. Interesting, isn't it? Paradoxical even?

I tried to hang in there with him and support him, as long as I could, through the pain. I really wanted him to finish this detox, but was beginning to worry that he might just get up and leave. He was free to leave the hospital at any time as he was of age, and was under no court order or other authority to go through this. I probably should have given him more credit for this.

We tried to go for a walk once or twice, but we didn't fare well. He would make an effort to get out of bed and start off, but he quickly would lose interest and go back to bed. This was a kid who could run 3.1 miles in seventeen minutes; a kid who could fly around the ice for hours frontward and backward with a rubber disk at the end of a stick, while avoiding two thugs who wanted to break his bones. I was proud that he didn't want to take any drugs, but at the same time, this was terrible to watch, and I wished the nurses would do something to help him.

I would fall to tears anytime I spoke with someone about where I was or what was going on. Sometimes, the simple act of leaving his room and looking out a window would bring tears. I was scared and sad, and at any given time, I didn't know which was going to dominate.

I had called Tangu; the local rehab center that the nurse's aide had told me about. One of the associates was going to come by and meet us at the hospital. I also had an appointment for a conference call later Friday afternoon with a rehab in North Carolina. I was down to two.

When the Tangu rep arrived in Jack's room, she didn't want to talk much with Wendy and me. At least not yet. She wanted to get to know Jack and gain an understanding of where he was with all that was happening. The two of them talked like old friends; she seemed to know firsthand what he was going through. I figured it was because she meets so many addicts as a part of her job. I learned later that she was a heroin addict with almost three years clean. Unfortunately, as with most heroin addicts, she eventually relapsed some months later.

Before she left us, she invited Wendy and me to the treatment center, on Saturday, so that we could meet a few members of the team. I had never been to a rehab before, and Wendy wanted to see the residential facilities. We both imagined that he would be sleeping on a cot, in a hut with a dirt floor, with rodents running around. That's an exaggeration, of course, but we didn't have any frame of reference. We were going to find out tomorrow.

I spoke with the North Carolina people later that day. They seemed legit, but were pushing hard for my commitment. It was if they had a quota to fill or something. Jack had already told me that he was afraid to stay here, but he needed to learn how to live here, and therefore wanted to try Tangu.

We went to Tangu the next morning and met the managing director, Gerald Rhett.[14] Gerald was a smart, experienced therapist from New York City—definitely uptown—way uptown. I knew he was from New York because of his accent and because of his Yankee hat. He had just come to the office from the gym so that he could meet us.

I was immediately impressed with his compassion; he knew we were suffering. And even though Jack was going to be his patient, Gerald was already providing therapy to Wendy and me. We were both fairly beat up

---

[14] Gerald Rhett is currently managing his own clinic, Recovery Unlimited, in Douglasville, Georgia.

by this point. We were emotionally exhausted, but the emotions kept coming at us anyway. As I said before, all circuits were busy; the overwhelm was so . . . I don't have a word for it. Numbing comes to mind—but I was certainly not numb.

Gerald focused on three things during our meeting.

First, Jack needed life skills so that he could live on his own. A twenty-two-year-old man should not be living with his parents.

Second, Jack needed to learn how to cope with his addiction in his natural habitat. There would be little success if he didn't build a support network where he lives.

Third, the entire family needed to participate in the process. Tangu has a family night every Wednesday evening, and all friends and family are welcome.

Gerald then spent some time describing the curriculum, how the clients would be spending their days and weeks, the makeup of the current roster of clients, and a profile of the professional and clinical staff. He also covered rules and protocol, phone policy, driving privileges, and other policies. It was an informative session. Gerald had the manager of Residential Life meet us in the lobby.

He introduced himself as Davis and was a young-looking fellow with a ton of enthusiasm. The mismatch in emotional energy between the two of us was enormous—but he made me feel better. Just being near such a positive person made me feel better.

Davis drove us to the residential complex. We checked out the facilities and the amenities before entering one of the units. It was a typical, three-bedroom apartment. I thought it was really nice, way too nice for heroin addicts. We looked at all the rooms, and Wendy asked a bunch of questions. I really didn't care too much about this part of it, other than security—meaning security of the addicts. I wanted to know when they were allowed to leave, who checked on them, how often, and related type of information.

At one point, Davis started a conversation by asking me what my son's drug of choice was. I had not heard that terminology before.

"I don't know, but he is in detox for heroin."

Davis smiled. "Is he an IV user?" he asked.

"Huh?" I had never heard that term.

"IV or intravenous, does he use needles?"

"Uh, yeah. Is there another way?" I really felt "uncool." A nerdy dad with no clue what his son was up to all these years, and that was the irony; I had done everything I could to know what he was up to all these years. No way could I explain all that to Davis. I know absolutely nothing about the drug that almost killed my son and was about to spend tens of thousands of dollars to try to save him from it.

"I am recovering from heroin," Davis said.

No way. There was no way that this bright, cheerful, intelligent, young man was ever hooked on heroin. I wanted to believe him. I really did. That would give me hope that Jack had a chance.

"It was really hard. I went away for a long time to get clean. I didn't use needles, though, I smoked and snorted mostly. I am lucky," Davis explained

At the time, I think Davis told me he had six years clean; if correct, that means he is approaching nine years—which is by far the most clean-time I am aware of for heroin addicts. However, the addicts who relapse would be quick to point out that Davis was not an IV user—he was not one of them. Davis is a therapist now at a local clinic, and he is working hard to build his practice. He is a healer. If I ever go through anything like this again, Davis will be one of the first people I call for help.

When we finished the tour, Wendy and I left Tangu. We needed to talk through what we wanted to do. Jack's detox at New Vision was coming to an end, and we needed to have a place for him to go. We had lunch and considered all the criteria and decision points. A local center had become important to both of us—Gerald did a good job emphasizing that point. Jack's preference was to stay nearby. We had no faith or confidence that he could go away for three months and then come back and stay clean on his own. We decided on Tangu.[15]

I called and let them know we wanted to enroll at Tangu. They were pleased and offered to open the office the following day—Sunday—in the event Jack was discharged.

Meanwhile, Jack was continuing to suffer with hot flashes, cold flashes, and general misery. He would just lay there and moan softly in pain. I could easily see why some people would never even try to quit, and why they would go to almost any length to not feel what he was

---

[15] Tangu is owned and operated by Dr. Walter Brooks. There is not enough space to express the gratitude we have for our experiences at Tangu. Dr. Brooks and his staff became our extended family during a difficult time in our lives.

feeling. Assault, battery, robbery, forgery, theft, lying, cheating, pawning everything owned, reckless driving, incarcerations—there was no obstacle too high for many addicts when it came between them and a fix.

Chapter 5 Concepts

1. Never let a recently overdosed heroin addict go back home.
2. Review and write a plan. Then use it!
3. You will never have a better opportunity than now (in the hospital), to get your addict into treatment.
4. Don't take no for an answer. Get the best results you possibly can from every healthcare service professional involved.
5. In transitions, be careful of the addict's use of phones. Heroin dealers deliver, like pizza.
6. Work with your insurance provider. Learn every available option. Do not be afraid to "play dumb."
7. Do not choose rehabs based on websites and salespeople.

Chapter 6

Withdrawal and Detox—Dying Might Be Better

Much of your pain is self-chosen.
It is the bitter potion by which the physician within you heals your sick self.
Therefore trust the physician, and drink his remedy in silence and tranquility:
For his hand, though heavy and hard, is guided by the tender hand of the Unseen,
And the cup he brings, though it burn your lips, has been fashioned of the clay
which the Potter has moistened with His own sacred tears.
~Kahlil Gibran, "On Pain"

Regardless of addiction (*definition*: biochemical changes in the brain that result in irrational behavior associated with the addictive substance), over time, opiate users develop a physical dependency (*definition*: physical changes in the body that build tolerance to a given compound as evidenced by the ensuing illness or other physical reactions that develop when the compound is removed) on the morphine molecule.

As described earlier, the body builds a tolerance to the morphine molecule as a defensive mechanism to its presence. As tolerance develops, the effects of using heroin are diminished. The user will then repeatedly increase dosage as tolerance increases to experience the same level of euphoria. When the morphine molecule is abruptly withdrawn, the presence of the body's defenses is now an overcompensation and results in withdrawal symptoms. These symptoms will remain until the morphine molecule is reintroduced, or the body's defenses are lowered, as it returns to a normal state.

It is important to note here that many deadly overdoses occur following a sustained period of withdrawal or detoxification. This is due to the body reducing its defenses in the absence of the morphine molecule and thus its tolerance. The user, having become accustomed to taking a certain amount of heroin, relapses without reducing the normal dose. The amount of heroin introduced to a body with lower tolerance often overwhelms the nervous system, especially the part controlling the respiratory system, and results in death.

As the body adjusts to the absence of the morphine molecule, the following symptoms are common in heroin addicts:

Extreme pain	Flu-like symptoms
Restlessness	Runny nose
Restless legs	Watery eyes; hay-fever symptoms
Insomnia	Body aches
Drowsiness	Extreme cravings to use
Anxiety	Depression, sadness

The degree of suffering during withdrawal and the duration of symptoms are dependent on the usage habits of the addict. From a timing perspective, symptoms can begin within one to three days, and then persist for another three to four days. In all, the physical withdrawal from opiates can last as long as ten days following the last dose of heroin. Even after those ten days, many addicts continue to live in a haze or fog. In my experience, I have witnessed recovering heroin addicts noticeably improve in physical health after thirty to ninety days.

Detoxification is simply the body's natural process of ridding itself of impurities and toxins, while restoring its normal and natural chemistry. As long as an addict doesn't use during the ten or so days of the detox process, they will become "detoxed."

It is possible, though uncomfortable, to withdraw/detox from heroin without the support of a physician and prescription medications. Although, the addict might believe they are on death's door during the withdrawal, it is not likely heroin withdrawal will result in death. Most addicts find it necessary to use some assortment of medications while detoxing. Medical professionals are concerned with helping the addict complete the detox and are willing to prescribe meds to that end. No one wants a withdrawing heroin addict to quit in the middle of detox due to pain and discomfort.

There are a variety of medications that an addict can choose from, with consent of their doctor, to ease the pain of withdrawal. These medications range from specialized drugs designed specifically for opiate withdrawal, to standard sleeping medications, tranquilizers, and over-the-counter (OTC) pain relievers.

These specialized opiate medications are designed to help taper or titrate the addict down from a high level of morphine to a lower level of morphine, and then to no morphine. Sometimes the drug contains a benign compound that attaches to the opioid receptors in the brain and nervous system to reduce the symptoms of withdrawal. Suboxone, Subutex, and Methadone are some of the drugs that might be used.

Benzodiazepines, also known as benzos, are tranquilizers that act to help relax and calm a patient physically and mentally. They have a particularly good reputation in reducing anxiety. They are also highly addictive and highly abused. Common brands that you might have heard of are Xanax and Klonopin. Consult with your addict's doctor when considering the use of these medications. When push comes to shove— it's better to get off the heroin and then worry about benzos. But don't underestimate the danger of benzos.

Sleep can be an issue during detox. Doctors are willing to help here as well with both OTC sleep aids and prescription meds. Sleep is likely going to be hard to come by during the first ten days of detox, and I would suggest that the more time the addict sleeps, the better off they will be during withdrawal.

I would not advise a detox from heroin be conducted at home. It is critically important that the whole process be supervised by medical professionals who are specifically trained and educated in addiction. A family doctor or general practitioner is more dangerous than helpful—the more well meaning they are, the more dangerous they are. Do not overlook this statement. Your addict knows that all the pain and suffering they are experiencing can be made to disappear with a simple call to a pizza delivery, black tar heroin dealer. Cravings are high; tolerance is low—risk of death is considerable. Don't fudge here. Be with experts who know what they are doing.

The balance you are looking for here is elusive. But stated simply— you want to provide as much comfort to your addict during withdrawal as you can, so that he or she can complete the detox, while minimizing any potential dependency or interest in new substances, such as benzos or methadone. In other words, use as few support meds as you can while keeping them in detox.[16]

---

[16] Some severe, long-time addicts might require an extended titration period of forty-five to sixty days. In these extreme cases, follow the doctor's recommendations. My personal feeling is that these individuals should be in 24/7 care under the supervision of addiction specialists. Otherwise, Suboxone just serves as a temporary substitute to heroin—or worse—something to sell in order to get heroin.

Chapter 6 Concepts

1. Be thoughtful about detoxification medications. Normally, medication should only be used for ten days or so. In extreme cases, it might take thirty to forty-five days. Ask questions.
2. Know the difference between physical dependence and addiction.
3. Be there to support and comfort an addict in withdrawal.
4. Benzos are highly addictive and deadly; be careful.

Chapter 7

Detox to Rehab

The only way to make sense out of change is to plunge into it,
move with it, and join the dance.
~Alan Watts

Things were better for him on Sunday morning. He had finally gotten some sleep and didn't seem so restless. He was in a fog, though, trance like. It was as if he had just gotten over a bad illness, such as pneumonia or strep throat. I could tell his body was exhausted from the torment of withdrawal. His mind was probably tired too, from resisting the urge to end the pain by using or by taking the offered prescription meds. It was ten days since his arrest, seven days since he drove like a maniac, six days since his overdose. All three of us were zombies. How we kept going and why we kept going is hard to answer, especially because none of us knew where we were going or when we would get there. I can only say that somewhere deep within each of us individually, and somehow joined collectively, was a small glimmer of hope—hope that had no rational reason to exist.

We were all eager to check out of the hospital. It was seven full days of nurses and doctors. We threw together the few items he had in his room. We thanked the staff as they wished us well—and we left.[17]

Wendy had packed a small bag of clothes and toiletries that he would need to get started at rehab. A small team of Tangu's staff was meeting us at noon. The intake process would take a couple of hours, and then he would move into the residence.

For at least the first ten days, he would be under twenty-four-hour supervision. One of his roommates would be a member of the Tangu staff and the other would be a client with some clean time behind him.

A man named Gary met us in the parking lot. He was fifteen years clean of some narcotic, not heroin. He was the security manager for Tangu and was going to search Jack and all his belongings before admitting him to the residence. He was meticulous, as he helped us unpack the car and take Jack's stuff into the office. I could tell it had

---

[17] To this day, we have never heard from the GBI.

been several years since an addict successfully pulled something over on Gary—and he was proud of that fact.

Once everyone and everything was inside, Gary let us know that he lived on campus and that he was the security manager, and that he provided transportation for those clients who did not yet have driving privileges. He would drive the clients to at least one Alcoholics Anonymous (AA) meeting every day and would take them shopping, to treatment, and to any medical care they might need.

He explained that Wendy and I were to meet with Gerald again while he strip-searched Jack and went through all his stuff. I thought this was a serious way to get started—but then I considered all the things that Jack pulled on us through the years. I am sure a percentage of new clients try to sneak some contraband into the facility.

Jack took his shirt off as I was leaving. As I walked out of the room, I caught a glimpse of him standing there in just his faded jeans. Gary closed the door, while I drifted off to a time Jack was standing shirtless in jeans.

Sometime in 2008

Jack was sixteen years old and was shooting hoops at the bottom of the driveway—it was quite warm and he had taken his shirt off. His plaid boxers were well above the waistband of his faded and fashionably torn blue jeans. Wendy and I had just pulled in from running a few nearby errands. I walked down the driveway to see what was up with him and he turned to me and started acting crazy. He looked at me with his deep dark eyes and took a fighting stance. He raised his fists and started bouncing around like Muhammad Ali.

"C'mon, old man, I'm gonna kick your ass," he screamed at me without the slightest regard for many of our neighbors who were enjoying the fresh air of spring.

"I'm gonna kick your fuckin' ass, let's go," he screamed again.

I didn't know what this was about—but he was serious. I wondered if he had a knife or some other kind of weapon, because surely he didn't think he could beat me. I outweighed him by 40 pounds. Having grown up the oldest of seven boys—I knew how to win altercations like this. He knew it too—I told him all the time that none of my brothers could ever whup me because I was willing to cheat, to do whatever it took not to lose. Maybe he took a lesson or something?

"I'm going to kick the shit out of you—but I ain't goin' to jail, so you got to hit me first. C'mon, old man, hit me. Right here, one time," he commanded, as he stuck his chin out at me and lowered his left hand.

"Knock it off, Jack," I scolded. *"I am not going to punch you."*

Even after everything he pulled on us through the years, I never punched him. Not in the face, anyway. I might have tried to neutralize him once my knocking the wind out of him with a brisk blow to the belly—but I even doubted that. Hell, he was rarely spanked unless he lied—and even then—not always. If I slapped him every time he lied, he'd get beat every day. He wasn't backing off.

Now what. Now, what do I do? *I thought.*

I took a fighting stance and let him back me into the house so that the neighbors would not have to endure the insanity. We danced around each other, as he continued to taunt me into hitting him first, presumably, so he could claim self-defense after beating my ass and avoid jail. It was comical really. He was only 140 pounds—I was 180. I was a runner; he was a smoker. His fighting posture was not overly coordinated, as he bounced around like a pro fighter in the ring. It was totally ridiculous. As much as he deserved to have his ass beat—I wasn't going to give him what he wanted. I figured at some point I'd just fall on top of him and he'd tire, struggling to get out from under me.

Our little dance, which is literally what it was, continued into the hallway and then just outside the bathroom door. I had a brilliant idea just then. I would lure him into the bathroom, as we continued the dance, and I would turn so that his back was to the tub. Then, I would simply push him in and lay on top of him until he surrendered. He would have absolutely no leverage in the tub—none—as his legs would be up over the edge with his feet off the ground while his upper body was pinned by me in the basin.

So, that's what I did. And man, did it work! There was absolutely nothing he could do other than scream obscenities at me for being a chicken to fight him. He was threatening to get me again later. It was then that I decided I was going to really scare the shit out of him. I pushed his face to the side and held his head in the bottom of the basin. He was looking right at the drain when I turned the water on.

"You better knock this shit off, or I will close that fucking drain," I said, as I stared down at him.

"Fuck you, asshole, fuck you!"

So I closed the drain with his head pinned right there. Water was splashing on his face. I could not believe I was doing this. This was indeed crazy. Why couldn't we just play catch or go to a ballgame? The whole scenario was insane, and the guilt that was filling my mind was overwhelming. I considered stopping but easily convinced myself that if he didn't surrender, one of us was going to get hurt. If my option was this or a fistfight—I chose this. I was totally in control of him and though he hadn't admitted it yet, he was completely at my mercy.

It would take a while for the water level in the tub to be high enough to cover his mouth and nose. There was enough water now, so the side of his head that was pinned to the bottom was soaked. I imagined that he was having a little hearing difficulty in that ear. He started screaming for his mom. I had asked her earlier, in the driveway, to please stay away until this was over. He screamed like a schoolgirl, and I don't say that to belittle him; he was truly terrified now.

"Mom!! Mommmmmm! He is gonna kill me. He's drowning me," he wailed.

I looked down at him. His eyes were huge. "She's not coming, man! Knock this shit off!"

"Fuck you! Mom! Save me . . . He has the wa-water on . . . Ma . . ."

If I pushed his head slightly, I could get the side of his mouth in the water. He was tasting it now. It was getting to the point where I would have to decide how much further I was going to carry this out. I sure as hell wasn't going to drown him. Besides, I was really feeling bad about what I was doing—I mean who does this to their kid? Somehow, a fistfight was prevented, at least so far, but the cost of prevention was getting high; at least in my psyche. He choked a little bit—more on the bitter taste of fear and defeat than the water in the tub.

"Ok, Stop. Stop. Stop. Stahhp! Dad!"

"What?" I said.

"Ok, I'm sorry, Dad, I'm sorry; please, let me up, I quit."

I couldn't believe it. In an instant, he went from raving lunatic to humble child.

"Dad, please stop. I love you. I am sorry, Dad!"

"I am going to let you up," I said. "But you are going right back in if you start your shit again."

I let him up, but stood right against his body while the tub was still behind him—just in case he tried something again. I still don't believe what happened next.

"I love you, Dad; I am sorry," he said, as he hugged me.

Geezus, what just happened? *I thought.*

To this day, nine years later, I have no idea what happened. In hindsight, I consider the possibility that he was on some narcotic. Other than that, there is no explanation.

"And then Davis will accompany you to the residence and get you settled over there," Gerald said.

I had missed this entire conversation, as I reflected on the tub incident. Here we are, six years later, checking into rehab. How did we get so fucked up?

Wendy had been filling out papers and signing forms. While Gerald talked, I daydreamed, and we all waited for Gary to bring Jack down.

Gary knocked and immediately opened the door. Jack stepped in, and Gary introduced him to Gerald.

"Hi. I am Gerald Rhett!" Gerald said firmly, as he stood to greet Jack.

Jack extended his hand, palm up, and looked eye-to-eye with Gerald.

"Jack Hobbs," he said, as he firmly shook Gerald's hand.

There's one thing I taught him that he remembers, I thought, as I watched him properly greet Gerald.

Gerald went over everything with Jack in great detail. He talked about the residence, contraband, females, visitors, female staff members, drug testing, life skills development, relapse prevention, probation, and privilege levels—there was a lot to know.

Once he finished with his introduction to Tangu and the rules, Gerald had Jack sign a few papers. Gary had already taken his phone, debit card, credit card, and cash. Those were all in an envelope, and Gary handed it to Gerald. Gerald checked off the inventory sheet, signed it, and put all of it in his office safe. Jack signed the inventory sheet indicating his agreement with what was now in Gerald's custody.

Gerald then spoke with Jack about the physician he was going to see in the morning. They talked about how Jack felt and if he needed or wanted any meds: Suboxone, benzos, sleep aids, etc. Technically, he was still in detox. Jack said that he was tired and feeling hazy—but that he would wait on getting any meds until he saw the doctor.

Then Gerald explained something that was important, at least in my mind. Within a week, if Jack had no sign of opiates in his blood (including from Suboxone), they were going to start an oral Vivitrol treatment program. If he stayed clean for thirty days, he would transition from an oral to an injection program, where he would receive a Vivitrol shot monthly. The monthly treatment would last as long as he was clean and for at least twelve months.

"What the hell is Vivitrol?" I asked.

"Vivitrol is a specialized treatment that reduces the risk of relapse in heroin addicts," Gerald stated.

"Really? Why didn't we just do that to begin with?" I asked.

"Well, if you take Vivitrol while you are actively using, you'll get deathly ill," Gerald answered. "And, Vivitrol does nothing to stop cravings—all it really does is eliminate heroin from having any effect on the user. What I mean is, when using this medicine, if an addict shoots up, the heroin will not work at all, and the addict will get sick. It is a great deterrent, because it renders heroin as a useless waste of money."

"The problem is that some addicts become so obsessed with the cravings that they try to overcome the Vivitrol by using more and more heroin, and eventually they overdose and die. Roughly 3 percent of Vivitrol patients try to overcome it."

"Man, that sounds dangerous," I said

"It is," Gerald said. "That is why it should only be administered by treatment professionals who have direct supervision and observation of the patient.

"I can see that," I said.

The discussion continued for another ten minutes. Gerald made sure all the required forms were filled out and signed. Once everyone's questions were answered, Gerald excused himself—it was Sunday. Davis came in and the five of us—Gary, Davis, Jack, Wendy, and me—left for the residences. Jack rode with Gary.

Once at the residences, there wasn't much for Wendy and me to do. Gary, Davis, and Jack handled all the moving. Gary suggested that Wendy and I go shopping and get a week's worth of groceries for Jack and any other noncontraband items that he might need. He also suggested that we bring back $20 cash that he would hold for Jack in the event they stopped off for coffee or ice cream when headed to and from AA meetings.

"There is a Walmart right across the street from the office," Gary said. "We'll be getting oriented here—call us when you get back, the gate code is 1980#."

"Ok," I said.

We said some quick goodbyes and Wendy and I left for Walmart.

We returned with more than a week's worth of groceries. We overdid everything. Gary went through the bags to make sure there was no contraband. We had bought cigarettes, and he gave them to Jack and then quickly bummed one. *That was funny,* I thought.

The time came to say goodbye. It was inconsequential, as we were going to see him Wednesday at family night. However, once again, I could not prevent myself from becoming emotional. We had been through so much. I thought we had made a ton of progress in a week. After all, he was dead on Monday. We had come a long way—saved his life, kept him safe, got him detoxed, found a rehab, and got him checked into an apartment. I had hope. But despite how far we had come—there was still the scratching in the back of my head, *You just put your kid in heroin rehab and you consider that successful? Seriously?"* Insanity, man, all I can say.

When we drove away, I cried once again. A week ending in rehab is a great week. Wow. That's how the addiction thing works. It has a ton of patience in its long-term strategy to destroy you—we were in year eight. Slowly during all this time, values, beliefs, and identities, were all eroded to the fundamental bedrock of the ego's nature. Not just for the addicts, for everyone around them.

It was a successful week, I thought, shaking my head. *I just left him in a ninety-day heroin rehab, and it is a successful week.*

Life wasn't done with us. There was more to come.

Family Night, Our First Wednesday

Monday morning came, and I had to go back to work. I had not been to the office since Friday, February 21. It was only a week since I bailed him out of the Paulding County Jail; and just six days since I found him on the bathroom floor. The last time I saw Kim was in the waiting room at Kennestone. Somehow it seemed as though I had lived an entire lifetime since the last time I was in the office. She was happy to see me, and we managed to have a good talk, without getting too deep into the messy business of rehab.

I sat in my office and it was as if it belonged to somebody else. It had a different feel. I was restless as I sat there; my body hurt, I had butterflies, and my hips were tight.

I had kept up via email and phone with the many projects that were underway; I generally knew what was going on in my departments; I just wasn't directly overseeing anything at the moment. There was always stress at work. It was a 24/7 operation and if anything went wrong, it was something I had to get involved in. There wasn't any room in me for more stress; maybe that is hard to understand—but I was emotionally maxed out. More and more could happen to me, but the impact wasn't always that great. I was already fully impacted. Maybe that took a little of the edge off at the office. Everything was still important, but it didn't feel important. Not to me. How could it? My kid just overdosed on heroin and was in rehab. How bad could a broken computer be?

I was unusually sensitive around my friends and colleagues. No one was trying to upset me—I was just generally upset. I had known some of them for almost eleven years—and even their kindest concerns were met with resistance. Not because I didn't want to share with them or show them appreciation for the concern they had for me—but because I didn't want to cry at work. In those days that followed the overdose, I was continuously on edge between safe and sorry when it came to tears. And even though everyone knew what had happened—I didn't want to admit it to anyone. I did not want to validate any of the shame or humiliation that I was feeling by admitting what was wrong with my son, and thus my family and ultimately me.

There were two people in the office who really knew most of what had been going on at my house during the past eight years. Both had been around for a long time and were finally both promoted to the vice president (VP) level. I confided in both—we had been through hell through the years at work—if I couldn't trust them—who could I trust? I often would try to be self-deprecating and humorous when I told stories of Jack's antics. Many of the things he did were hard to believe anyway—so adding a little humor made the whole ordeal more appetizing.

Through the years, both of them, one a new father, the other a young mother, warned me that I was going to crack-up eventually; and they were always surprised that it hadn't happened already. By crack, they meant the big crack—the nervous breakdown kind of crack-up. I was always able to brush that part of the conversation aside—but would wonder if I would know if I had a nervous breakdown. *Seriously, I thought, do the victims of a nervous breakdown know they had one?*

I would tell them that I was unaffected by feelings and emotions. I was, of course, and they knew it—but it helped me avoid facing my truth.

I wasn't so sure about myself today; in fact, I had no confidence that I wouldn't lose it at any moment. I did take a few minutes to fill them both in on what had been transpiring and where we were in the process. Normally, they made light of the situation with a hint of sarcasm or a petty joke. Not this time. They were both careful not to push me—maybe I looked as fragile as I felt.

The senior executives were a separate matter. Even though I am sure Kim was keeping them updated, out of concern for my well-being, I did not wish to tell them many details. The whole thing could be looked at as a failure; my lack of CPR performance was just icing on the shit-cake of failure. But it wasn't that one of their executives was failing, that I wanted to keep from them; that was probably impossible. What I was hoping to hide was my inability to handle the situation on an emotional level. There was a lot of perceived pressure and stress on me, and the guys on my team most of the time. I did not want to show any signs of weakness. I just felt that if they sensed a lack of confidence on my part that they might lose confidence in me too. I kept reminding myself that I was so good at hiding my grief, that they would never need to deal with it because they would never know—at least for a little while longer.

It was hard being there. It really was. I had just spent the past seven days in constant contact with Jack and now he was in rehab and I was at work. I desperately wanted to know what was happening with him, what was he doing, and was he safe. There was definite separation anxiety on my side. That anxiety, coupled with my emotional overwhelm, the physical pain that was forefront in both my body, and my consciousness, made it difficult to focus on anything or anyone. I tried. I really tried. But I would drift off to the past sadness or the future fear—never was I present.

It must have been obvious—to whom exactly, I don't know. Maybe Wendy called Kim—or someone talked to Human Resources about me. Anyway, Kim came to my office and suggested we start looking for a therapist or a counselor. I laughed it off at first—but she didn't budge.

She stood her ground and asked me who she could call, because she was making me an appointment this week. I wasn't really taken aback by her strong desire to make this happen; so much as it made me reflect on how I must be presenting myself. I know how I felt, but I thought that I was doing a great job covering it up. I guess not.

I had never gone to a psychologist or psychiatrist. I didn't know who to call or even where to look. So, Kim decided she was going to use the Employee Assistance Program (EAP) and our company's insurance carrier's mental health hotline to get some referrals. She was also going to schedule an appointment for me to see my family doctor just to make sure that there was no waiting to start medications if he felt they were necessary.

The EAP and insurance carrier turned up nothing useful. We did schedule two visits via EAP with two separate healthcare providers. They were both terrible. No way was I going to keep visiting them. Later that week, I saw the family doctor and he was quite concerned; he immediately started me on anti-anxiety meds and told me to contact the Wellstar psychiatry office as soon as I returned to the office.

I had Kim call Wellstar. I don't think I had a choice in the matter—she had taken responsibility for getting me help. Help that I still didn't think I needed. When she called Wellstar, they were not taking any new patients and we were placed on a waiting list. It turned out that most mental health providers in the metro Atlanta area were oversubscribed. Finding someone to verify I wasn't going to lose my marbles was proving tricky.

Eventually, Kim became frustrated and called my family doctor and complained about not being able to find any help. We still don't know what he did—but he got me an appointment for the first of the following week. Although many months would pass where Kim and others would worry about my well-being—they were relieved that I had a scheduled appointment with a reputable practice in the near term.

Wednesday, March 5, 2014

Jack was technically only on his third day in rehab when our first family night arrived. We didn't know what to expect.

Maybe it was a reception or a meet and greet, I wondered. We just didn't know anything other than it was family night, and we were supposed to attend.

We were early—a concept that seems to escape most members of my family. We had the opportunity to take Jack to dinner before the event. The pizza came quickly; so we were able to head to the treatment center ahead of schedule. Being early in a strange place with strange people made me antsy. I didn't know what to do with myself. I was restless and agitated. I ended up just wandering around, pretending to read brochures and trade journals. I was nervous and afraid. I had never met the families of any heroin addicts before and certainly didn't know any addicts.

What kind of people am I going to get mixed up with? I wondered.

It is embarrassing, and I am ashamed to admit it, but I was expecting to be surrounded by people—parents and addicts alike—who just couldn't figure out how life worked. Certainly, my situation was an anomaly; because the way I was raised and the way I raised my kids would never produce an addict, heroin or otherwise. No. My family was a statistical outlier—it had to be because I did everything right. I did everything "by the book." All these people—who had yet even to arrive—were all certainly problem children. The parents weren't raised right and then they raised rotten kids who married rotten spouses.

I bet they all get along with each other here, I thought. *No way am I going to fit in with any of these people.*

I was such an idiot. So naïve. So terribly wrong about so many things.

It wasn't long before other families started coming in. I nervously greeted those who looked like they would reciprocate. I vividly remember the first person I met. She was probably ten years older than I was. Clearly—she was a hippie.

Figures, I thought.

My prejudice was soon blown away though when she first spoke to me, because she was incredibly articulate and brilliant. She took charge of the waiting room crowd and moved us into the meeting room area. I was soon overcome by a sense of dread, because as I entered the room, I noticed that the chairs—thirty of them—were arranged in a large circle.

Oh, dear, I thought. *This is family therapy. We were going to share our family issues with other families. No way are these people going to hear my story.*

At the time, being humble usually meant being humiliated, and I was not going to humiliate myself with these drug-addicted families. After all, I was better than this.[18]

I met the "hippie's" husband. From all I could tell, he was a successful and well-educated professional. I supposed he was likely a lawyer of some kind—likely in Buckhead.

How did this guy end up with a hippie wife and a heroin-addicted kid? I wondered.

I could write a hundred pages describing what my expectations were going into this meeting and how terribly wrong they turned out to be. This realization alone forced a ton of guilt into my spirit. There are probably four or five psychoanalysis lessons that could be developed from my experiences that evening. I was so judgmental, so egotistical, and so arrogant. I was blinded not only by my lack of exposure to such things, but by my flawed values and beliefs about myself, my family, and society in general. I am truly ashamed of the person I was then.

The families gathered and were seated. Each family sat together usually in groups of three—sometimes more, sometimes less. As I looked around at each addict and their loved ones, I was overcome with regret.

What am I doing here? Geezus! I don't belong here; I don't deserve this! I thought.

Right away, I started judging every single person in the room. Every father was labeled and categorized into some likely flaw of character defect that resulted in his family's arrival here. Each mother was evaluated as too passive, too controlling, too masculine, or too feminine, and, in one case, too hippie. The addicts varied widely in category—much more than I would have anticipated. Don't get me wrong—there was a large population with varying degrees of tattoos and body

---

[18] Looking back on this now, I realize how foolish I was. Not just that night, but for many years prior. I was ignorant to all that was happening around me. It was as if I would surround myself only with people and things that fit into my nice, controlled world. Anything that didn't fit was excluded. Controlling my environment in this way resulted in becoming an adult man with a narrow and limited view on the real world. It has taken a long time to overcome this notion of my reality being true and correct. As the real world has humbled me, I have grown in understanding and compassion. I was completely and totally forced out of my world, so that I could see things as they are—at first bitterly and then willingly. The world—the way it exists—is not the way I created it in my mind, and it does not comply with my rules of operation.

piercings. There was too much makeup, too little clothing, too hipster, too gangster, etc. There were a few conservative-looking addicts—they looked almost "normal," as if they could be my neighbors. I figured they had to be here because their mom or dad were defective.

No one had even spoken yet! Already, I had ranked every person from first to last in intelligence, income level, education level, parenting skills, family values, and criminal record. All we needed was the experiment to unfold during the meeting so that I could compare my expected results to the real-life data. The meeting was set to begin. For about five minutes, I had forgotten that I was *actually one of them*. The mind is a peculiar phenomenon.

Every Wednesday, the family group meeting started the same way. The facilitator—a therapist—asked a person to introduce himself and to describe briefly how the week has gone. The general assumption was that the person was here the previous week. Then, family by family, each individual describes who they are, why they are there, and how their week has gone. The addicts will add their clean and sober time—usually in a number of days.

Wow. I could talk all night about my week, I thought.

The therapist started with his own introduction. His name was Tommy, and he was an IV heroin addict with three years clean.[19] I liked him. Immediately, I felt that he could serve as a role model for Jack. A person who could offer him hope and direction—a roadmap to recovery and future success. Tommy looked successful—he played the part extremely well. He was well dressed, well funded, carried two phones, and an e-cigarette. He drove an extremely ugly, yet expensive Mercedes SUV. The only thing I didn't care for were the argyle socks—I never liked them.

The way the room was arranged, I was going to introduce myself after Wendy and Jack and just before the last family in the circle.

In trying to express how I felt and what was going through my mind after joining the addiction community, I hope the reader didn't lose track of my demeanor at the time. Nothing had changed yet emotionally. I was still overwhelmed with emotions with many new feelings queuing for their turn to rattle me, if and when the circuitry of my central nervous system ever cleared. I was extremely depressed and extremely afraid. I

---

[19] Tommy eventually relapsed and overdosed. I still pray for him.

did not look good; I had aged considerably. I was not sleeping. I still had no answers as to what was happening to me.

I listened intently, as each family took its turn sharing. At first, my interest was to identify where they fucked up. What was the cause of all this? But it wasn't long before I was listening with more empathy. These were real and painful stories of true suffering—just like mine. All the families in attendance had been here before, and everyone knew one another. My family was new.

What struck me as most revealing in the early stages of the introductions was how articulate, intelligent, and well read the addicts were. In fact, through the years since, rarely have I met a heroin addict who I would classify as a gangster. By gangster—I mean the type of people who dress down on purpose and talk in a dialect that only gangsters understand; for example, the word "that" is pronounced "dat" in their world, and the waistband of their underpants (plaid boxers or thongs) is well above that of their trousers. Every addict at tonight's meeting was surprisingly smart. I could not believe it. How do these smart people—obviously well raised—end up sticking needles in their arms? How do they end up in rehab? It was amazing and confusing.

For the most part, my premeeting analysis and categorization of the parents was also wrong. None of the parents seemed to be too far to an edge of any spectrum. They were all normal people. I was shocked. How did normal people get here? It hadn't soaked in completely yet—but I had much more in common with these people than I had differences. Eventually, my acceptance of them would help with their acceptance of me—and, in a strange way, help with my acceptance of myself.

Some families were well into the ninety-day program. Many weeks had passed since they sat broken and torn in their first family meeting. They seemed to have some level of happiness or hope or relief that I certainly did not have and did not think I ever could have. It was weird.

Maybe these happy people's kids aren't as fucked up as mine is, I thought.

It did not take long to blow that thought out of the water. Some of the addict's stories were so horribly tragic that I felt bad about how weak I must be to be so screwed-up about what my kid did. There are some amazing stories of what lengths an addict would go to get high, to stay high. Stories that at times I wished would just end—because I could not imagine the pain, the sadness, the depths to which a human could descend. But for most of them—the comeback—even though just beginning—was just as amazing. People would describe levels so low that a turnaround would seem impossible—let alone rise. But these people found a way—they found a way to start the comeback. My story almost seemed insignificant. And I felt bad that I was so messed up because of it. When it came to heroin addiction—I didn't know anything. And when it came to pain—mine was a pinprick.

Jack went first when it was our family's turn. He was not nearly as clear and concise as the other addicts had been. He was only eight days clean and was still in a hazy, foggy place between withdrawal and sobriety. He had gotten to know the other addicts during the past few days, and they were all supportive of him. I found some solace in the thought that they were looking after him; but then I reminded myself that they were heroin addicts—not necessarily a positive thing. I trusted no one.

Wendy was brief. She wanted to be a supportive mom, but she too was ashamed to be there and was still raw emotionally. She teared up and grabbed my hand as she spoke about why we were there. The other moms looked at her with complete empathy and compassion as she ended. The hippie offered to speak with her after the meeting and to help in any way she could. I wasn't sure if I liked the hippie yet. She might be smarter than me.

It was my turn. So many new emotions started flooding in on top of the already overdrawn circuits. The old emotions had yet to drain away. I think that somehow the adrenaline rush that was common before I spoke publicly was opening up room for new, raw feelings. I was extremely vulnerable, and I did not like it. I was resisting. Some of the addicts had mentioned that this was their fourth or fifth time in rehab. One had been at Tangu for nine months.

"I am Bob, Wendy's husband, Jack's father," I stated softly.

A tear fell down my cheek. I thought about having to do this again and again and again. For some reason, I thought about my mom and dad, my football coaches, all the people who had helped me growing up. They helped me with great hope that I would do something special; how did I let everyone down? How did this happen?

I drifted away from the room. I couldn't form a word. I couldn't speak.

Tommy repositioned his chair. He moved to the middle of the circle and faced me directly. He let me cry. He let me struggle. I wasn't heaving, crying. But I was overcome with debilitating sadness. I wanted to share—I just couldn't.

Tommy was gentle when he said, "I see a broken man; you look so utterly defeated. Obviously, you love your son very much. You did everything you could to keep him safe. You ended up saving his life. You haven't lost yet."

He paused and said, "It's ok to mourn."

I managed to speak, "I'm scared. I'm sad. I listened to all these stories. Some people were going through this for the fourth or fifth time. Hayes has been here for nine months. I can't imagine this happening again. I still am having a hard time getting through it once."

"Your son is a heroin addict," he said, as a matter of fact.

"Yes. But this is rehab, and it has to work; I can't go through life thinking that I am going to find his dead, blue body on the bathroom floor again," I mumbled.

"If he stays here long enough, and listens and learns, he will have a chance. If he uses again, it will because he makes a choice to do so. He will know the consequences, and he will have many options before sticking that needle in his arm. That is the best outcome we can offer— that anyone can offer. It is up to him after that," Tommy said.

I was crying. *That's not good enough.*

Tommy looked around the room. What he was about to say, I am certain they had heard many times. "From experience, heroin is tough to beat. The relapse rate for IV heroin users following thirty days on inpatient treatment is 87 percent within the first year. The probability of your son never using heroin again is low. But like I said, if he does use again, it will be because he chooses to with full knowledge of the consequences and with a full set of tools he can use to prevent it."

I was slouching lower in my chair—without realizing it. Tommy continued, as tears fell from my chin to my shirt. "There will probably be 47,000 overdose deaths this year [2014]—25,000 to 30,000 due to opiates. These are the numbers you and your family are faced with."

He wasn't making me feel any better.

"I know you probably feel worse. But we are not going to mislead you. The last thing you need is to have smoke blown up your ass. I'm not going to do that. You guys need to be prepared for this, because it is not easy. It is not one and done. It is forever. But, I will promise you that you will start to feel better; eventually, you will feel better."

"I am so afraid," I said.

"I understand, but look at your son; he is here, and he is safe."

Tommy looked around the room—family to family. "Some of you have heard me tell this story before. The front of the human brain, the prefrontal cortex, is relatively new from an evolutionary perspective. The base of the brain, ancient in evolutionary terms, is well formed and present in all animals. It is where the survival responses of fight, flight, and freeze are generated in response to threats. Responses are generally fear or anger and can produce strong mental and physical sensations.

"When a rabbit sees a fox, it becomes terrified and runs into the brush. Once safe in the brush, it is happy again, almost instantly, with no memory or concern for the fox. When a cub is threatened, the mama bear becomes enraged and fights off the threat. But once the threat is removed, the mama bear quickly forgets and becomes playful with her cubs. Rabbits and bears have no prefrontal cortex.

"Humans on the other hand, because of the prefrontal cortex, have the ability to recreate scenarios from their pasts and imagine potential threats in their futures. There is no threat to their survival during these memories and dreams. But the front of the brain creates the same chemistry and signaling as if the scenarios were real; the base of the brain doesn't know the difference—to it, neurons are neurons. So, it triggers the fight, flight, or freeze responses, just as it would if a real threat to survival existed. But there is no fox; there is no threat.

"Part of what you are going to have to learn how to do is to remind yourself of what is real and not real. It is going to take a lot of work, and you will need a lot of help. Right now, Jack is here, he is safe, and so are you."

Tommy had taken all the remaining time to work with me on my broken heart. I was happy that he cared. But yet, I was devastated. I had just learned that my son was likely going to relapse. I also learned that I kept reproducing the horror that I felt that day by reliving the scenario in my mind and forecasting it into the future. If I was ever going to feel better, I was going to have to get out of the past and out of the future. At the time, I didn't know that such a thing as the present was a possibility.

After the meeting, all the families took a few moments to get to know one another. Everyone introduced themselves to us and welcomed us to Tangu. I was reassured that it would get better and my tension about the night was starting to ease. There was so much love and hope in their eyes, as they greeted others with warm hugs and enormous compassion. Never had I read so many people so wrong in my entire life. Or, maybe only now was I right about people for the first time in my life. I was confused about my perception. I would remain so for quite some time.

The hippie implored us to join Families Anonymous or Al-Anon, as soon as we could. We should have listened. You should listen! We felt we were so wrapped up in saving Jack that we believed the investment in the current effort was more than sufficient. We were wrong. No matter what we did, we could not save him. All we could do was save ourselves. Despite strong advice to the contrary, we didn't listen. All our eggs were in his basket—if he failed—we were all going to fail. Please don't make this mistake! You can save yourself, while supporting your addict. Don't make the mistake of investing everything you have in the addiction—get busy also investing in yourself.

As we said our goodbyes, I felt that something about me was melting away. Perhaps it was my pride, or maybe it was my strong urge to control everything and everyone. I am not sure. There were a lot of glaciers in my world. If I were ever to regain a sense of normalcy, I would require a lot of melting.[20]

The Zoloft antidepressant medication I was taking was beginning to work; at least to the extent that such drugs do. I can't say that the enormous overwhelm of emotion subsided, because it didn't. Not yet anyway. I was crying less often and less intensely. I was getting some sleep—not much. I spent a lot of time researching heroin statistics[21]—I was looking for some glitch in the data, some loophole that would tell me my son could escape. I also felt way behind the curve—everybody knew more than I did. For quite some time, heroin was the only topic I could focus on.

---

[20] Some weeks later, as a veteran member of the family group, I would happily embrace new families and reassure them that it was going to get better. But on this first night, no one could convince me of such an outcome.

[21] It is still frustrating that the available statistics run a year or more behind. Although overdose deaths are growing exponentially as of 2016, the available statistics are one year behind and somewhat hide the true magnitude of the epidemic.

The Psychiatrist

Academically, I knew the difference between a psychiatrist and a psychologist. I didn't know the difference in practice. My appointment with the psychiatry office started with a thirty-minute session with a social worker or maybe a nurse practitioner. She was quite thorough and efficient in getting to the nature of my problems and why I was there. She also had the benefit of my family doctor's evaluation. I had a difficult time describing the whole overdose scene again—and particularly struggled to describe my inability to do CPR.

After almost two weeks, it seemed silly that I couldn't do it. The CPR situation was going to be an issue for me for a long time. Occasionally, during our talk, she would show some compassionate understanding or provide me with some advice. Ultimately, though, her purpose was to collect information so that the doctor could quickly decide what meds to prescribe.

At the end of our session, she excused herself and went to talk with the doctor. I sat quietly in her office—alone. I was once again questioning what was happening to me.

Is this normal? Am I normal?

They were recurring questions. Everyone I asked responded supportively. But how else would they respond? No one is going to tell a dad that his reaction to his child's overdose is abnormal—besides—who would know?

I wonder if anyone can answer those questions, I thought.

There is a certain amount of fear that should be expected when someone is in the uncharted waters of life's circumstances. As far as I know, none of my friends or family has ever gone through something like this. Therefore, I had no reference on which to judge whether or not my reaction and my current emotional state were normal responses to what I had experienced. I just didn't know where I was, and worse maybe, I didn't know if it was ok for me to be there—that was the scary part.

I walked into the office of Dr. Chris Riddell with fresh images of my son's blue face and a vivid memory of the terror I felt in the moments I believed him to be dead. Chris had photos of his wife and kids on display; ski vacations and holiday parties.

How did we get so fucked up? I thought, as I looked around.

Chris was well briefed on what was happening with me; so fortunately, I didn't need to go through the story again. I could tell that he had sat with guys like me many, many times in his career. He probably already knew what to do and how to do it. He went through the motions anyway.

He asked me to describe what I was feeling and how I was feeling it. I tried to express to him that I didn't know enough words to adequately describe the sensations I was feeling. There was nothing that I could come up with that was a reference that another person would have experienced that would have been similar to what I felt. I didn't use the words anxiety or depression—because at the time I didn't know exactly what those words meant.

So, I told him that I felt pain in my body—all the time. The pain was usually strongest in my hips, and it made me uncomfortable—restless even. I tried to compare it to the nervousness or the butterflies that I felt before a high school football game—except it never goes away—there is no game. Another explanation I tried to use was that it was like being in trouble—like sitting outside the principal's office, or in front of a police car, and not knowing yet what I had done or how much trouble I was in. It was a sense of fear that something bad was coming but not knowing how bad. And finally, I told him that this pain was always in the forefront of my mind. I was conscious of it—constantly. All by itself, this pain was enough to wear me out.

He asked some clarifying questions and then went on to tell me what he thought. His diagnosis was that I had gone through some severe trauma. My initial response to that trauma was some level of shock, followed by a traumatic stress disorder. He said that I was suffering from what I would know as PTSD—but that I was still in the active trauma stage. The post stage had not yet happened. I essentially had TSD, and, at some point, the post would come. He went on to tell me that I would need a lot of therapy and that if I hadn't found anyone yet that he would recommend someone. Meanwhile, he was going to start me on a drug called Klonopin, and he would double the dosage of Zoloft that my family doctor had prescribed.

It was hard to believe that I was going to be taking a tranquilizer and an anti-anxiety medication daily. Neither of us knew that this was only the beginning. The doctor walked me out to the reception area and handed me a card and a brochure for The Anxiety & Stress Management

Institute. He told me to give them a call when I arrived back at work. I had Kim set me up for the following week.

Wednesday came relatively quickly, and before we knew it, we were eating pizza with Jack again. The three of us were apprehensive, because some families were not afraid to hash out personal family business in front of the others. They aired a lot of dirty laundry about one another. Certainly, we had our secrets too, and we hoped that they would be kept private by our loved ones. Our anxieties were markedly different from the ones we experienced the previous week where the fear of the unknown was front and center. Even though this was only our second family night, we were feeling like veterans.

Jack was now looking and feeling a lot better. He was fifteen days clean and today was his tenth day at Tangu. He would be visiting with his clinical advisor the following morning to determine if he would be changing rooms and what privileges he would be entitled to. At dinner, he told us that fifteen days was the longest period of clean time he had outside of jail in years. He was nearly human again. The overall change in him was remarkable.

When we arrived at the treatment center, we greeted the families we had met the previous week, as if they were old lifelong friends. Funny how addiction can draw people together. Not in a neighborhood or subdivision, mind you—but only in the addiction community itself. One day, I hope to see communities treat addiction as compassionately as they treat cancer or other life-threatening diseases.

Gerald Rhett was the facilitating therapist this night, and I was glad to see him. Though I thoroughly enjoyed Tommy, I wanted Gerald to validate some of Tommy's claims and statistics from the previous meeting.

Gerald introduced himself as a "recovering person"—I found that hard to believe. How could a man as vibrant and alive as Gerald ever have been as hopeless and helpless as Jack was? Eventually, I learned that Gerald was not a heroin addict, so my quest to discover one with more than three years clean continued.

As Gerald went around the room, family to family, he landed on the topic of relapse. I wanted to learn more about Tommy's numbers—so when I saw the opportunity, I threw my question out at Gerald.

"Gerald, Tommy said that the relapse rate within one year after thirty days in treatment was about 87 percent—that can't be right, can it?"

"I am surprised it is that low," Gerald said. "I would put it in the 90s for heroin. What's out there now is stronger, more potent, more addictive," he said.

That was depressing. Instead of getting good or neutral news, I got worse news.

"Gerald, my son used heroin for four years and we didn't know. How the hell do we know if he relapses once he leaves here?" I asked.

Gerald told us the same thing that Tommy did the week before.

"He might relapse—but if he does it will because he consciously makes the decision to use again. With a clear mind and full knowledge of the consequences, if he uses again, he will ignore everything he is learning and will intently refuse to use any of the tools he is developing," Gerald said.

"As far as how will you know?" Gerald leaned up in his chair and looked me straight in the eyes. "First thing you must never forget is that addicts are liars. They will always lie to you—never tell the truth. Ignore this fact at your own peril. The second thing is if you get that gut feeling that he is out there using, that he relapsed, there is no need to ask any questions, no need for evidence to prove your point, when you get that gut feel—it's too late—he relapsed."

Progressing through Rehab

Jack was a stellar client at Tangu. Soon after his ten days were over, he earned the use of his phone. He was learning life skills, such as managing money, maintaining an apartment, doing laundry, grocery shopping, and managing a schedule.

By the thirtieth day in Tangu, he had thirty-five days clean. The Vivitrol treatment was now via monthly injection and that alone gave me a certain degree of relief. He was doing well, and for a while there, we all thought that he would eventually end up as an addiction counselor. He had gotten his driving privileges restored and had his car at the residential complex. This was a big deal for him, as he was allowed to drive himself and his friends back and forth to treatment and AA meetings.

As always, the individual with the car assumes a certain level of leadership in the social circle. I could tell that his confidence was growing, and he was assuming more and more of a leadership role among the residents. Often, on family nights, other clients would highlight something that he did or said during the week that had inspired them. He was asserting himself—in a positive way. It was pleasant to watch. I was able to relax a little. He was clean. He was at Tangu. He was safe.

Eventually, Jack got a job landscaping. He lived at the Tangu residences but was working most days from early to late. He had difficulty getting to family night on time—I don't think he made it to one before the meeting started. There were several meetings he had to attend each week as a part of his deal with Gerald. Most important, he was to attend relapse prevention. He was also under close supervision and monitoring due to the monthly Vivitrol treatment, so he was expected to show up on request.

Personally, I thought he was working too much and too soon. He had the rest of his life to work. He was always impatient and felt like he was "so far behind" in his life. I could understand that, to a certain extent, but being behind in life was better than being dead. It wasn't in his best interest to be working as much as he was, especially at the expense of his treatment time. I would imagine everyone at Tangu would agree—but Jack was persuasive. When it came to making a convincing argument about why he should have his way—Jack was a master. He got his way and—as with most addicted persons—we'd find out eventually that his way doesn't work.

My situation was unfolding. The Klonopin and Zoloft were doing what they were supposed to do. The Klonopin helped me sleep and helped reduce the nervous tension that was always so prevalent in my body. It was never eliminated, and I always thought about it, but it did become more tolerable with time. I wish—in looking back—that I would have worked with the doctor to eliminate the pain entirely, because its constant presence was driving me crazy—literally. At the same time, though, I have to be cognizant that it might not have been possible to eliminate it entirely with meds—at least not while remaining somewhat functional.

My therapy at The Anxiety & Stress Management Institute was wonderful. It introduced me to a whole new way of life and one that I continue to explore and benefit from. My teacher/coach/counselor was a man named Adam Funderburk, a licensed mental health counselor with a specialization in mindfulness. Mindfulness was something that I had never heard of, and had someone introduced it to me before my son's overdose (before I needed it), I would have laughed at them.

When I first started my mindfulness practice—which quickly became a meditation practice—I could not sit for five minutes without becoming frustrated. I learned through research that mindfulness and meditation were paths to nirvana and if anyone needed to land there, it was me. Naturally, my Western mind wanted all the benefits immediately—they didn't come that fast. For some reason, though, I continued practicing mindfulness, began studying meditation, and expanded into yoga. Eventually, I could sit for five minutes. I wasn't calm for many of those 300 seconds, but there were brief moments of pure awareness—maybe even concentration from time to time. Those moments were enough to keep me coming back and trying to get deeper.

My company was sold in the spring of 2014. I had eleven years with what was just a start-up in 2003. The buyer was going to change our name, our colors, and eventually our focus. I wanted to make the transition work for me—but I could never latch on with the new company. Not because of them—but because of me. The timing wasn't good, obviously; I was in a shitty place mentally, emotionally, and spiritually. That, coupled with the feelings of loss generated as they stripped our logos and color scheme from our offices and website and "my company," made it tough. I designed that logo—I picked those colors.

Despite my mindfulness practice, the Zoloft, the Klonopin, and my weekly meetings with Adam, I was still suffering excessively from time to time. The suffering—or the pain if you will—was easily mitigated with just a drink or two. Usually no big deal. Occasionally, though, if I were feeling alone in my pain or during a particularly disturbing event, I would find myself dwelling on the recent past while staring deeply into the depths of a dark lager or deep cabernet. By staring into the surface of what I was drinking, I could watch my sad past repeat itself, or my scary future unfold, as if on a movie screen.

I drank alone, and I am sure for others at the bar, they looked at me with pity—for they knew that whatever I was processing it was deep, dark, powerful, and might destroy me. I hope I didn't frighten anyone. On these occasions where more than my pain was at stake—I would overindulge and become quite drunk—even incapacitated. At no time did

I ever have the intent of drinking more than one or two—but sometimes back then—it happened.

Jack's treatment progressed to the point where Tangu was just a halfway house, at best. He wanted to leave, and Tangu wanted more money. Certainly, the Vivitrol, the monitoring, the screening, and supervision associated with that treatment were worth something. We were always welcome at family night, and we continued to go for quite some time even after he was discharged.

In the end, I think we paid a small amount of money so that he could stay at the residence for another thirty days. The money would also cover the cost of the Vivitrol and associated treatment through the end of the year. At the end of the thirty days, he was moving back home—and eventually he did.

Of the many addicts who I met in those days, there are sadly some who are no longer with us. Many, many others have relapsed and have either started the process again or are still out there—out there in the hell of active heroin addiction. I can never know the suffering that these poor souls endure—but I am sympathetic to their plight. My love and compassion are sent to them daily, and my prayer is that they find their way back. Other addicts from those days have stayed clean. This population is small. At least one has done so well that he is becoming an addiction therapist. When he does—he will be awesome. He is perfectly suited to save lives! (Go, Hayes!)[22, 23]

---

[22] This chapter is being drafted at 5:35 PM EST, January 26, 2017. I just received a text from a high school friend and classmate that her son overdosed and is on a breathing machine in ICU. This addiction stuff is so much more common than we think. God bless him! God bless all of them.

[23] It is April 2, 2017. I am proofreading this edited version just prior to release. My friend in the previous footnote had her daughter put in jail. This is just after she was left dead in a ditch by her "friends." Fortunately, after TEN doses of Narcan, she was revived. She is only 29. I cannot believe the pain my friend is living in.

Chapter 7 Concepts

1. Intake to a treatment center is a rather formal process. Be prepared.
2. Know in advance, what you need or can have at rehab.
3. You are going to continuously question your motives, your past, and your feelings. Guilt, blame, and regret are going to grasp at your heart. The time to get help from Al-Anon and a therapist is now. Do not wait!
4. Do not think others in your family are not affected by what is happening. Everyone needs help now. If you want to keep the family together, get everyone to counseling immediately.
5. Other families in heroin addiction are more like yours than different. Don't judge; love!
6. Heroin relapse rates are high; the number of years in clean recovery is low.
7. Do not be afraid to use antidepressants or anti-anxiety medications to help get through this difficult time.
8. Involve the whole family in the addict's treatment, to the extent possible.
9. Be open to prayer and meditation.
10. Celebrate successes of those who are winning.

Chapter 8

Don't Mortgage the House

Money can buy you a bed but not sleep.
Money can buy you a clock but not time.
Money can buy you a book but not knowledge.
Money can buy you a position but not respect.
Money can buy you medicine but not health.
Money can buy you blood but not life.
Money can buy you sex but not love.
~Unknown

Money can buy you treatment but not recovery.
~Me

When Fear, Panic, Guilt, Love, and Ignorance Intersect

Choosing a rehabilitation treatment provider was far and away the most difficult mental and emotional exercise we had to complete during this whole process. Because we didn't know what was happening in advance, we were caught completely unprepared emotionally, mentally, financially, and spiritually for what transpired. In a situation of great emotional stress, tremendous levels of guilt, and extreme fear, we were faced with making a relatively large financial decision that would play directly into the life-and-death situation of our son. We were ignorant.

- How much money would you spend to save your child's life?
- Do you feel guilty if the answer is less than everything you have?
- What about your other children?
- What if you are blaming yourself for his addiction and overdose?
- What if your spouse/partner is blaming you?
- How do the numbers change?
- Are you afraid you might make yet another mistake that might cost him his life?

How do you rationally make a decision?

Before I continue—I must suggest Al-Anon and Families Anonymous. These groups can help you figure out the answers to these otherwise impossible moral dilemmas.

Continuing—these are questions that you are going to need to answer—either in advance of a tragedy or the throes of chaos created by one. I strongly suggest that you think about it now and use whatever resources are available to you to make a rational decision. Talk to other people about the moral dilemma you face—money versus life. Ask your spiritual leader, your doctor, your therapist, your siblings, your parents, ask! Ask and listen.

Open a discussion, ask the question, and then listen and appreciate what people say to you. I promise you the decision you make in advance after getting input from other people will be far better than one you will make under duress. At some point, after the tragedy, this subject will be approached with these people—not because you are looking for advice, but because you are looking for support. Don't put yourself in another guilt-ridden "I wish I woulda" situation. Be proactive.

Asking for Advice

As hard as it might be for you to try Al-Anon or Families Anonymous, I urge you to do so. There are people in these groups who have suffered your burden and survived. They can provide you with suggestions that you will not find anywhere else. And, as mentioned several times already, finding this information in advance of needing it will lead to better decision making on your part later. I will venture to suggest that any work you do before you need it will result in a stronger recovery for your loved one and an improved financial situation for you. As we will discover in the relapse chapter—the financial savings is important—because you will likely need to do this again and again with your heroin addict. So, don't go spending all your savings just yet—you are going to need to support him again in three years or less. Sorry!

When you talk with people about this subject, you don't need to disclose any personal information. Your questions should be light, something like, "Hey, I have a loved one who might be in need of some inpatient treatment for heroin addiction. Do you have any suggestions in this area?"

Then let the person answer you. If they offer you information, write it down or ask them to email or text it to you. Don't rely on your memory—

it will likely fail you. If they have no advice, follow up with this, "I see. Well, do you know of anyone you trust who might have experience with something like this?"

Again, let them answer and document what they tell you. When you are finished, simply end with, "Thank you for your help. I will let you know how it turns out."

That's it. Leave it at that. If you end up learning something that might be helpful to the people you spoke with—share your results with them.

Internet

When you start searching the Internet for information about rehab, you are going to be inundated with ads and sponsored results. (You will notice the word "AD" boxed-in, next to the results.) The first five to ten search results will almost certainly be "sponsored" and the following five to ten results might not be ads but will be linked to one of the sponsor's websites.

This is a money business, and these businesses know you are desperate. Many times, their sales technique is based on your fear, uncertainty, and doubt (FUD). They are betting that you do not know anything, you are afraid, and you are in a hurry to find help for your loved one. They are going to take advantage of your situation. I do not have a problem with what they do—they are American businesses—but you need to be able to recognize how the game is played, so that you get the best possible treatment for the least amount of money.

As you scroll through all the results, you will eventually find blogs, bulletin boards, and other sites that discuss topics that interest you. These can be great sources of information, especially when kept current and run by a parent or loved one of an addict. However, much time can be wasted looking for a site that is current and legit.

One more place to look is nonprofit foundations that focus on heroin and other drug addictions in your area. You might be surprised to find a parent who has started a nonprofit with the expressed purpose of helping someone like you. These types of organizations might turn out to be your best sources of information.

Another idea to keep in mind, as you begin to accept that this addiction thing is a big money business, is that the recovery community is incestuous. In a regional area, everyone in the business gets to know everyone else. In time, they begin to help one another with referrals. Generally, in business, that is healthy—but if kickbacks or commissions are paid to your advisors by the people they refer you to, then that should raise a red flag. It is not a disqualifier—you just need to understand your advisor's motivation might be monetary rather than your best interests.

You should also be aware that some treatment facilities in various geographies might be under some investigation related to fraud, conspiracy, or false advertising. My best advice is to go into this with your eyes wide open. Recognize it for what it is, and choose based on personal buying experience and preference. In the end, it should feel right to you, and you must be able to live with your choice.

There are a wide variety of treatment centers to choose from. They range in "perceived quality" from low end to high end. Think about the food service industry—there are soup kitchens, fast-food drive-throughs, family buffets, family sit-downs, and exclusive five-star locations. So it is with rehabs—there are publicly funded, charity funded, semi-private, private, nonprofit, for-profit, and exclusive luxury "destination" treatment centers. You need to keep in mind that they all do the same thing—provide addiction treatment to addicts. Just like everyone in the food service industry serves food.

When you begin considering your options, it is likely your first impression will be from a website. DON'T JUDGE! There are good rehabs with awesome websites. There are also bad rehabs with awesome websites. Likewise, there are awesome rehabs with crappy websites. The same is true with online brochures and the method by which the facility answers your call—IF they answer your call. What you need to know is that choosing a place that is going to take your loved one's life into its hands and $25,000 or more of your money is not easy and cannot be done online alone. Especially if your addict has overdosed and you are under emotional stress while trying to decide.

When you contact many of these facilities, you will likely be speaking with someone who is compensated in some way if you say yes to them. Their apparent sales approach will be one of compassion and sympathy, but, as stated earlier, their closing technique might try to leverage FUD. The fact that they are trying to leverage fear, uncertainty, and doubt does not mean that they cannot treat your addict—it just means that their closing technique is a shortcut to you saying yes to them.

Instead of deciding on what to do based on salespeople or commissioned agents, perhaps there are better people you can speak with at the treatment center. If I were to go through this again, I would want to speak with the manager, supervisor, or clinician who is responsible for all the employees who would have contact with my loved one. All locations differ in size and scope, but there are some people I would want to talk with while making my decision.

Executive Director

This is the person who, on behalf of the founder or the board of trustees, manages the day-to-day operation of the facility. This person will have direct knowledge of the types of therapies in use, the residential life program, security, progression, visitation, discipline, medication, and, of course, staffing profiles, client profiles, relapse ratios, and cost of attendance. This person will be the key influencer in your decision making.

Chief Therapist/Counselor

There is often a doctoral-level therapist or psychologist on staff who has designed and will administer the treatment curriculum, including the strategies and philosophies used in treatment. You will want to hear the person describe what is done at the center and why, therapeutically. The depth of knowledge and the level of enthusiasm this person displays toward the program is a good indicator of how well the staff implements it.

Residential Manager/Director

You will want to speak with the person responsible for your loved one's well-being while they are away from treatment. Learning the overall philosophy about residential life, life skills development, client interaction, recreational programs, and off-site events, such as AA meetings, is important. Your loved one will be in treatment for thirty to ninety days. Keeping them from feeling imprisoned, while freeing them from addiction, is an important consideration. The best treatment in the world is worthless if the addict leaves early because the living conditions become unbearable. This does not mean the addict should be pampered—it means that addiction recovery can be mentally and emotionally taxing, and there must be some reasonable "down" time.

The Medical Doctor

There almost always is a person on staff who writes prescriptions for the clients. It might be a doctor or a nurse practitioner (NP) or a physician's assistant (PA). Usually, these prescriptions are all encompassing—meaning the facility will only dispense medications to clients that were written by this physician or under his supervision. This means that blood pressure meds, cholesterol meds, birth control, cold and flu, allergy, all of it is usually prescribed and administered via the staff under the supervision of the prescribing onsite physician.

You will want to speak with this person, if possible, about his or her philosophy on the various medications available in treatment. Specifically, you will want to hear the doctor discuss sleeping meds, benzos, Subutex, Suboxone, methadone, Vivitrol, etc. You will want to know when such meds would be used, under what circumstances, and for how long—both during and after treatment of your loved one. Pay special attention to the Vivitrol discussion.

Intake Coordinator

You will want to speak with the intake coordinator to get a feel for what to expect on the first day your loved one arrives for treatment. There is usually a fair amount of paperwork to complete and certain required items to bring and contraband items to leave behind. The easier and less stressful the first day is for your loved one, the better transition he or she will make into the treatment community.

Decision Criteria

There are so many dimensions to choosing a treatment facility that it is easy to get lost in what you are trying to accomplish. Just like buying a new car—a car's only purpose is to get you from Point A to Point B. They ALL do that. Everything else—automatic transmission, air conditioning, AM-FM stereo, sunroof, leather seats, side airbags—is just accessories. They are nice to have, but they are not fulfilling the car's purpose.

Treatment facilities all have the same purpose—to provide their clients with the proper level of care during their first thirty to ninety days of recovery, so they have the best opportunity to remain clean and sober for life.

Given this basic purpose, your main criteria should be something similar to this: "Select the best **available** treatment for my addict that I can reasonably afford, knowing that it might be necessary to do this again and again (at my discretion)."

Outside this basic statement, it is unlikely that you know what you want or need. And if you have followed my advice so far, it is likely that you have become confused by all the information you have collected.

In the next few sections, I am going to discuss some criteria that I think are important for you to consider in your evaluation. As you read these, remember, you are looking for the **best** location that you can reasonably afford. There is no perfect choice, and, with few exceptions, I do not believe there are big life-ending mistakes that you can make if you do your own due diligence. Your addict needs treatment—and you are going to provide it.

Heroin Experience

This one is obvious. You would not want your fancy German sports car worked on by a mechanic who has only worked on Chevys. In my opinion, heroin addicts have such a unique experience with the drug that when two or more of them get together, a unique relationship is formed. It's like a fraternity or sorority. There are those who have experienced the euphoria and deadly grip of heroin and those who haven't. There are those who "know" and then everyone else. I do not think that even the best healers in the world have a reasonable chance of saving a heroin addict from relapse, if the healer doesn't "know." The best healer of a heroin addict, in my mind, is another heroin addict.

With that stated, you should focus your search on treatment facilities that have vast experience with heroin addicts. I would suggest that many of their clinical staff and more than 50 percent of their current clientele should be heroin addicts or recovering heroin addicts. Remember, this is a community your addict is going to join and live in 24/7 for thirty to ninety days. There should be ample opportunity for him to connect with a person who understands firsthand what he is experiencing. If your addict has a hard time making such a connection, he might have a difficult time completing the program. This does not mean that the doctors on staff, the lead psychologists, and counselors must be recovered heroin addicts—I think that would be a huge ask. You'd be fortunate to find such a place.

Local Versus Remote

This is one of the most widely used, key, selling points that you will hear when speaking to prospective treatment centers. The remote facilities are going to tell you that your addict needs to "get away" from the people, places, and things that have kept them using all this time. They will tell you that your addict has so much to work on to get healthy—certainly, they don't need the distractions of home to impede their progress.

Meanwhile, the local providers will tell you horror stories of huge sums of money spent to send addicts away to locations where they became "all-star" clients only to return home to no support, no network, no known meeting schedule, no sponsor, and a rapid decline to relapse. They will tell you that your addict needs to learn how to live, work, and play clean and sober in the community they call home. It is important that your loved one builds a strong local network so that he can continue the difficult trials of recovery after treatment.

In my opinion, if the family and other loved ones can participate in the recovery process locally, then that would tip the scales toward a local provider. However, this is a personal decision based on the traits and behaviors of your loved one.

Cost

Obviously, if you cannot afford treatment from a given facility, then that particular location should be scratched. My belief (and experience) is that recovery from heroin addiction is going to take more than one visit to rehab. As you consider what you spend the first time, you ought to think about a second and third trip to treatment. I don't wish to destroy your hope—I only wish to help you make a practical decision based on the reality of this situation. You might only be able to afford one trip, and if that is so, then you do your best with what you have and move forward.

I suggest that you and your family (and maybe even your addict) consider how many times you would be willing or able to fund treatment. From there, you can decide how much to spend the first time. The main point is this—please do not mortgage the house to pay for treatment with the expectation that it will be a one and done—this is a path to disappointment and financial ruin. In fact, don't mortgage the house at all. There might be "free" options.

I cannot predict which rehab visit will be the costliest, nor can I guess at how many visits there will be. My intuition tells me that the first visit is the most educational and intensive and therefore presumably the costliest. Follow-on visits to rehab should be of shorter duration and therefore less money. With that said, there are many examples of addicts who went to traditional treatment several times without success only to go to a work-camp rehab for a year or more before getting clean. Many professionals will tell you that treatment will work when the addict is ready—and, unfortunately, many are not ready the first time. I think it is important to keep in mind as you go through this that after thirty to ninety days of treatment, it is not likely that any addict is healed NOR is it likely that any addict is doomed.

In thinking through your options, insurance is important. You should use every means at your disposal to get your health insurance company to help fund treatment. Sometimes it will and sometimes it won't. If you have difficulty, there might still be possibilities to get the company to help defray the costs. Perhaps you can work with your family doctor or therapist in looking for a way that they can help you get funded through referrals.

While in treatment, though insurance might not cover the inpatient care for addiction, it might cover some medications, some hours of individual therapy, and maybe some well-visit care. Repeatedly, we faced unsatisfactory answers to our inquiries. Always, some rule or procedure was quoted in dealing with people on the phone. I cannot guarantee positive results—but I do encourage you to not take no for an answer—be persistent, and keep looking for a better answer and a better outcome. Often, but not always, you will be rewarded for your persistence.

If You Cannot Afford Anything

If your addict needs treatment, and you have no source of funding, you should look at publicly funded facilities. In 2013, more than 300,000 heroin addicts were admitted to public inpatient treatment centers.[24] In Atlanta, Georgia, there is access to facilities that are focused on homeless addicts and alcoholics. These are sometimes the best locations for

---

[24] DEA. (2016). National Heroin Threat Assessment Summary—Updated (DEA-DCT-DIR-031-16). Retrieved February 2017 from
https://www.dea.gov/divisions/hq/2016/hq062716_attach.pdf

recovery, due to the dedication of the staff who invest their entire lives to these facilities. There are also locations that offer addicts low-wage employment and a place to stay for a low weekly fee. The jobs they get, pay just enough for room and board, leaving no money for drugs. I encourage you to continue looking for help until you find it. You have little to lose.

Research tips: Call state and local government agencies. Contact addiction hotlines. Search online for terms that include public treatment, nonprofit treatment, nonprofit addiction foundations, and free heroin help.

Residential Programs

As discussed in the introduction to this chapter, your loved one will be spending thirty to ninety days in the treatment center that you select. The first ten to fifteen days are going to be extraordinarily difficult for them, as they begin to deal directly with the life situation they are in. The sixteen- to ninety-day period is less intense and might become boring or uninteresting—and a bored, disinterested addict is a danger to himself. Don't get me wrong, addicts absolutely must learn how to deal with boredom—but I believe that certain levels, if left unattenuated, will bring bad results.

The residential program must provide safety and security for the residents throughout their stay. The first week should be spent under 24/7 supervision, where additional care is provided for the addict as they adjust from detoxification to residential life. The client's ability to leave and return to and from the facility should be closely monitored and scrutinized. Visitors must be preapproved by the administration of the facility.

Following the first phase, the residence staff should have social and recreational programs available that promote the development of healthy, sober-living relationships, while fending off excessive boredom. Visitation privileges and procedures should be clearly communicated, so that the addict and his family know what to expect and when. The family should be highly encouraged to attend all available events. Likewise, rules and regulations regarding the use of house phones should be clearly defined and understood.

The residential program is also responsible for the nutrition of the residents. You should take care to understand the dining schedule, menus, and snacks available during the addict's stay, and any responsibility the clients have in self-preparing meals while in residence.

Medical Programming

The short- and long-term prescription of drugs related to recovery is an important element to consider. There are pros and cons of using any drug, and it is important that you understand the underlying philosophy of the facility you choose.

I am not a medical professional, but I realize that addicts have complex needs. I have developed a few basic beliefs that I would consider important in choosing a location for the typical addict. First, the use of Subutex, Suboxone, or methadone should be temporary, only during the detox process. The dose administered should be tapering toward zero, and the goal should be no such meds after a certain date, which should be in early recovery. Any additional use should be on a case-by-case basis—not standard practice.

Likewise, any use of benzos, except where warranted psychologically, should be temporary, and only in the treatment of the withdrawal process and associated anxieties. Long-term reliance on benzos in treating heroin addiction is not a good solution. Again, I am just a dad; addiction doctors know better than I do and should treat these issues on an individual basis. However, if a treatment center has a reputation or a habit of prescribing benzos and other treatments—as a general rule, rather than the exception—I would take issue with that, short of a really good explanation by the medical and clinical staff.

I do believe that a Vivitrol treatment program of at least twelve months is a critical element in the recovery process, and that the cost should be included as a part of the initial treatment. This might be a big ask; however, the odds of successfully recovering from addiction increase after one year. The first year is critical, and Vivitrol makes a huge difference. You should have a good understanding of how and when Vivitrol will be administered in the treatment program you are choosing.

Note on Meds

Vivitrol: Long-acting form of naltrexone that is injected once per month, eliminating the need for daily dosing as is required with the oral form of naltrexone, known as Revia.

Naltrexone: An opioid antagonist (resists effects of opioids) medication that can only be used after a patient has completed detoxification. Naltrexone is not addictive or sedating and does not result in physical dependence.

Subutex: Buprenorphine, a partial opioid agonist (substitute) for the treatment of opioid addiction that relieves drug cravings without producing the "high" or dangerous side effects of other opioids.

Suboxone: Buprenorphine and Naloxone, a partial opioid agonist blended with an opioid receptor antagonist, which is designed to reduce cravings for opioids while minimizing the effect any opiate abuse might have on the patient.

It goes without saying that any medications, OTC or otherwise, should be administered directly to the patient in the presence of a staff member. There should be no medications of any kind in the residence.

Health and Wellness Monitoring

The basic health and wellness of all clients should be monitored and tended to during their stay. Basic indicators, such as body weight, blood pressure, temperature, temperament, and appearance, should be tracked and any deviations investigated. In the event of an emergency, the center should have arrangements with nearby health providers and hospitals.

Random drug screening should also be routinely conducted, in addition to drug screens required in accordance with the administration of Vivitrol.

Life Skills and Clinical Treatment

For many heroin addicts, the development of age-appropriate life skills is lacking. This is due to addicts' primary purpose of acquiring and using heroin, rather than building a healthy life for themselves. Some might not know how to write a check, let alone balance a checkbook. Even the most basic survival skills, such as grocery shopping, cleaning, laundry, budgeting, paying bills, and addressing an envelope are underdeveloped. Often when released to the "real world," the lack of these skills frustrates the addict and the likelihood of relapse increases. Some treatment centers might focus on life skills development as a priority—and I think it is beneficial when balanced with clinical treatment. There is probably some merit in theories that codependence arises from dependence, and an independent addict has a better long-term recovery opportunity than a dependent addict.

First-time clients have little knowledge of addiction or recovery. Typically, they possess expert knowledge on drugs and withdrawal; but know little about how heroin works, why withdrawal hurts, and how to stop using. It is important that the program you choose invests significant time educating addicts on the specifics of their drug of choice, dependence, addiction, and recovery. The more addicts understand, the better suited they will be when they have to deal with the drug in the real world.

There should be a balance between clinical treatment and life skills training; both are necessary for the medium- and long-term success of recovery.

Relapse Prevention

You need to get the details regarding relapse prevention training. There should be regularly scheduled sessions that are specifically targeted at understanding relapse from soup to nuts. At the end of the day, the addict's only defense against relapse is recognizing certain triggers and taking preventive steps instead of relapse steps. If the concept of trigger and prevention step is not drilled repeatedly—the relapse defense will not be available when it's needed. One-on-one therapy, group therapy, and immersion into a twelve-step recovery program should help the addict develop self-awareness and recognition of increasing risk or appearance of a relapse trigger, and then provide him with certain actions he can take to avoid relapse. By sharing experiences with other addicts, especially those who have some clean time, the addict can learn how-to tips and tricks to avoid relapse.

The Vivitrol program is an important component of the relapse prevention design. As discussed, it should extend beyond the thirty to ninety day treatment period and into and beyond an intensive outpatient program (IOP), which is the next phase of recovery. IOP transition should be a topic of discussion that you have with your treatment center.

IOP Transition

The next step after rehab is IOP, which helps addicts transition successfully from a 24/7 residential program to something less structured. There are a variety of IOP formats, and often they are custom designed by the inpatient clinical staff before the addict graduates. Hopefully, your rehab provider will have a plan in place based on your loved one's specific needs.

Sometimes the inpatient providers will also provide IOP. If not, they will often have recommended providers that you can choose from. You should know that IOP is not included in the cost of inpatient treatment and will result in additional charges to you and your insurance provider, if applicable. These costs should be considered when developing your overall budget. We will look at IOP in greater detail in Chapter 10.

Chapter 8 Concepts

1. Deciding on a treatment provider is not easy.
2. Discover all funding options in advance.
3. Use the Selection Criteria Score Sheet (provided at the end of this chapter) and the questions in this chapter to help guide your decision making.
4. Talk to people. Ask questions.
5. Don't be "sold." Know what you want and buy it.
6. Plan this treatment in advance of needing it.
7. Use the experience and wisdom of Al-Anon.
8. Have a plan for post-treatment—IOP.
9. Have a residential plan for post-treatment.
10. Have a transportation plan for your addict, especially, if driving privileges are suspended.
11. Know and understand the medicines involved in treatment.

Some Questions to Start

1. What is a typical day? A typical weekend?
2. What therapy is available for the family to participate in?
3. How much individual therapy is provided?
4. How much group therapy is provided?
5. How is my loved one kept safe?

6. Can my addict work while in rehab?
7. Will the facility help my addict find a job after rehab?
8. Will the staff help my addict with legal issues?
9. Does the facility monitor the money flow of my loved one?
10. How many "alumni" return for additional treatment? How many relapses? How long after treatment?
11. Do successful "alumni" return to share with struggling newcomers?
12. If transportation is an issue, how will my loved one get to outside meeting, appointments, or court appearances?

Selection Criteria Score Sheet[25]

Decision Criteria	Score 1 to 10	Provider 1	Provider 2	Provider 3	Provider 4	Provider 5
Cost (lowest)	1-10					
Insurance						
Out-of-Pocket						
Heroin Experience	1-10					
Staff						
Current Clients						
Alumni						
Location	1-10					
Local						
Remote						
Residential Housing	1-10					
On Campus						
Remote						
Security						
Quality						
Residential - Social Progrms	1-10					
Client Interaction						
Boredome Management						
Personnel	1-10					
Fit with Addict						
Personality/Energy						
Medical Philosophy	1-10					
Detox Meds						
Vivitrol Program						
Screening/Monitoring						
Treatment Strategy/Curriculuum	1-10					
Relapse Prevention Program	1-10					
Life Skills Development	1-10					
IOP Transition	1-10					
Other1	1-10					
Other2	1-10					
Other3	1-10					
Other4	1-10					
Other5	1-10					
Total	Sum					

---

[25] Full-color files from this book are available free at www.heroinlivinganddying.com.

Chapter 9

After Tangu: There and Back Again

*You can never make the same mistake twice because the second time
you make it, it's not a mistake, it's a choice.*
~Steven Denn

Jack didn't do an intensive outpatient program (IOP) following his treatment at Tangu. In fact, he didn't do much, and he devolved into no program fairly quickly.[26] As was his typical pattern following any incarceration—jail or now rehab—he became totally wrapped up in work. Work and money became his primary focus as he chased this illusion of catching up with other people his age. He left behind all the drug and heroin carnage he instigated and moved on, as if it didn't even happen. I was extremely frustrated and upset with him. Although he might set all that happened aside, and move on with his life, I couldn't. I couldn't put this behind me, by any stretch of the imagination. My anxiety rose sharply—I should have gone back for more meds, because I was soon to begin a track of my own self-destruction. The more he drifted away from his recovery program, the more I drifted toward needing one. I continued my mindfulness based stress reduction (MBSR) program and psychiatric treatments—but the sense of dread was clouding everything in my life.

By fall 2014, Jack was missing his scheduled Vivitrol shot. At first by a few days, then by a week, then by two weeks, and then he never went back. Every month, I would fight with him about whether he had gotten his shot and when he would get it. It was a pain in the ass and causing a ton of discontent at home. He always had an excuse—usually work related.

I was becoming more convinced that he didn't want the drug screen. I didn't see any other evidence—but I rarely saw him. I suppose that the lack of evidence of a recovery program is evidence of a relapse. I was still so deeply in the typical codependent mode of hoping so badly that I was wrong about him, that I missed the clues that indicated his probable demise.

---

[26] This is a guaranteed relapse predictor.

And he wasn't just missing Vivitrol shots. He never went to any AA meetings, he frequently missed relapse prevention, and ultimately attendance at family night also dissipated.

I don't recall the exact dates, but at some point between leaving Tangu and the end of 2014, Jack totaled his second car—another Cadillac. Fortunately, for him, his Aunt Jenipher was kind enough to give him her older Nissan Maxima—it was a nice car for him.

As had become typical before his overdose—Wendy and I would argue about him and what he was supposed to be doing. I had always felt that she sided with him and gave him the benefit of the doubt on all things. I was used to the two-on-one nature of our disagreements. I think Wendy was a great mom, and I believe that I was a good dad. However, I think as a couple—we were not great parents. I always felt that at some point one of our kids would drive a wedge between us that would break us up, and my money was on Jack. He was a master manipulator, and he had an easier time getting what he wanted when his mom and I were divided. Once we were divided, he usually had all the room he needed.

Sometimes it felt as though I was an outsider looking in. The plot was unfolding right in front of me—and I felt like I was a part of it—but all I could do was observe. I was like a ghost—I had no physical interactions with the real world.

As for Wendy, unlike her previous behavior toward him, where she would side with him about my concerns, this post-rehab behavior was different, or maybe indifferent. She was likely behaving the way she was taught at Tangu, which was to allow Jack to make his own choices. So, it wasn't that she was siding with him so much, as she wasn't siding with me, and my desire to get out in front of his eventual relapse. For example—when I would complain about him missing AA meetings, she would remind me that it was his decision.

"He knows what he is supposed to do, and it is his decision not to do it," she would say.

Meanwhile, I was terrified that I would see him dead again. So, although I felt slighted for her refusal to stand by me on items like the missed AA meetings, the missed shots, and the missed relapse prevention classes, she probably did play those right. I can't complain about her behavior. But the fact remains that Wendy and I were fighting and having general friction in our marriage, because of our twenty-two-year-old heroin addict son who was living with us. There were plenty of other things the two of us could have been doing to make our marriage better. We just never seemed to get the chance, because some issue like this was right in front of us. As for me, the fact is I didn't want to see another overdose; I didn't want to get shot at the front door; and I was becoming more convinced and frightened that he was going to relapse. It was consuming me. I was just a bundle of fear waiting for something terrible to happen.

For me, this was a signature of my parenting style. In a way, I think I felt that if I would remind him enough, nag him enough, push hard enough, he would do what he was supposed to do. It was the same in hockey, football, cross country, homework, and probation. In the end, the truth was the truth—he was going to do it his way—regardless of how hard I pushed.

The terror of his eventual relapse haunted me. I just needed him to do what the professionals had told him to do—but he refused. Somehow, it seemed, he believed he was this special type of heroin addict, one with a unique superhero power, a chosen one—he could stay clean with no program, despite the reality that 87 percent of addicts who are in recovery programs relapse. He believed that he didn't need to follow any guidelines and he would recover anyway.

Gerald's words rang true. "Trust your gut and remember addicts always lie."

My eventual nervous breakdown was in full prep mode.

By October 2014, I was certain of a relapse. He was at least two weeks late for his Vivitrol shot, and I was then convinced that he was missing on purpose. He would delay his Vivitrol shot, so that he could be sure the prior month's shot wouldn't make him sick; he could get high, wait to clear up so he would pass his piss test, and then get the shot and wait thirty days before getting high again. Addicts always lie, trust your gut.

He was working regularly at the landscaping company with a fellow Tangu client named Jimmy. I loved Jimmy. One day Jack came home and was pissed that Jimmy had stolen $300 or $400 from the glove compartment of Jack's car. Jack went so far as to file a complaint with Tangu, and he might have even filed a police report. I don't recall exactly, but as far as I was concerned, wrecked cars, shady behavior, and missing money almost always indicate the presence of drugs.

In October, I made it clear to Wendy that I thought he had relapsed; if he hadn't, he soon would. I can't blame her for not wanting to believe me.

I didn't want to believe me. As far as I was concerned, this whole thing became about life and death. I had seen death, and I didn't like it. I didn't want to see it again, and I didn't want my daughters to find him dead on the bathroom floor. This time we fought about it. I hadn't confronted him yet—but she took his side in advance.

"He hasn't done anything wrong; he is working hard and trying to get his life together! Why do you have to try to bring him down?" she asked.

It was almost comical. After everything we had been through, this was going to end up about me wanting to bring him down. Conversations like this were always the most frustrating. I had saved his life! I wanted to now prevent his DEATH! But somehow, she thought I had some ulterior motive? What on Earth could that possibly be?

In retrospect, I'd like to think that she believed deeply, in her heart of hearts, that if she could win this fight with me, that it would somehow mean he wasn't relapsing. I know that sounds insane—but that's what we parents were at this point, insane. We become so desperate to make something false out of absolutely observable truth. In her mind, if I couldn't prove he was using, then he wasn't; she could rest easier now.

In November 2014, there was no doubt, absolutely none, that he had relapsed. I did confront him this time, and—as was his usual initial reaction—he was ignorant and rude toward me. It was if he was saying, "Who the hell do you think you are asking me such a stupid question?"

I didn't care what he said or what anyone said. He was using, and I knew it. She and I fought some more about it. This was our life together it seemed. We never really ever fought about money or things that "normal" couples fought over. Our fights were always about our kids—and most of the time our son. I was pissed, and I shut off from everyone.

You scrape his dead carcass off the bathroom floor, I thought when I looked at her.

To the rest of our family, our kids, our parents, our siblings, so little of this madness was visible to them—or to anyone. The continuous and never-ending struggle against this evil and invisible force was destroying us. As individuals, as a family, as a couple—destruction. We were all dying while we were living. I wish we had gotten everyone into Al-Anon then. Maybe it would have helped us better understand one another. But the shame, humiliation, and embarrassment were too much for us.

My anxiety was at an all-time high. I was a nervous wreck, believing death or jail were imminent for him. I didn't want to see him dead again—

not on the bathroom floor and not at the morgue. Thoughts of him driving like he did the day he got out of jail and then killing some three-year-old girl visited my dreams, as often as the front door shooter. In late 2014, no matter where I went, fear accompanied me. My mind was in continuous survival mode—by keeping me afraid, it was keeping me safe. Outside my fearful thoughts, little was happening. I was going through the motions of life—or life as I saw it. Nothing was real; nothing was genuine. Even my job had become artificial—or so it seemed. Somewhere along the way, in all the turmoil and chaos, real and imagined, I lost track of what was real and what was not real, what was important and what wasn't. I was drifting—but at least at this point, I was still aware that I was drifting. Later, a time would come when I was adrift and didn't know.

The Thanksgiving and Christmas holidays were flat. We all got together and lived up to our long-standing traditions. Thank goodness for traditions, they were able to guide us through some rather difficult times and allowed us to at least provide some semblance of holiday cheer for those less affected by our addiction issues. I was in pain, and I assume that at some level Jack was in pain too—though to this day I do not know.

I knew he relapsed; he knew that I knew he relapsed. But, of course, that didn't stop him from lying and defending himself with ever more ridiculous alibis. He had his mom fooled; though I think she was more in denial than believing his bullshit. Sometimes parents believe that until they admit something to be true about their children, that it's not. The longer she could put off admitting it—the longer he was safe in her mind. This is all she had left, if you think about it. The only place he could be safe was in her mind.

In January 2015, there was no question that he was using with regularity. He couldn't hide it, but he couldn't admit it either. He maintained the illusion that I was an insane father putting him down. He wasn't sleeping and was always lethargic. Often his speech was slurred and whatever he said was untrue. He had lost weight, and his cheeks were hollowed. To say that he was easily agitated would be an understatement.

You might think, as he did, that I had become obsessed with the whole relapse thing. Maybe you would be right; I don't know. This was a life-and-death situation for me; I had seen it. I did not believe there were second chances if I fucked this up—he would be dead, and I would live the rest of my life wondering what else I should have done to save him. I did not want to live that way—I would do whatever I had to—to prevent that from happening. I was terrified that he would die and, despite everything I should have learned about my inability to control his behavior, I still was trying to intervene; to exert my will over his. He was lying to me, and that pissed me off more than anything. Further, he was putting my daughters in jeopardy.

As for the girls, my trying to protect them probably didn't matter. They were living with a father suffering from PTSD, anxiety, and major depressive disorder—and obsession with his son's eventual relapse. Their environment was probably quite caustic. Couple that with Wendy's public denial but private acceptance of his relapse, and I am sure the girls were confused and unhappy too.

One day while he was out, I searched his room. I went through some old shoeboxes at the bottom of his closet, and, sure enough, I found a few syringes—just like the one I threw away when I was cleaning up after his overdose. Instantly, the events of that day crashed into my consciousness. That had been the last time I saw a syringe—when I was cleaning up the bathroom, so his sisters wouldn't see the tools of his addiction.

I crumpled to the floor, immobilized by deep levels of despair, regret, and fear. It's one thing to know in your heart; visual proof has an impact.

How we transitioned from this moment of debilitation in his bedroom to him re-enrolled at Tangu I can't remember. He did re-enroll at Tangu, with my blessing and my financial support.[27] There wasn't much activity at his second trip to rehab. He might have made it three weeks before I heard from Gerald Rhett.

No Way!

Gerald Rhett was calling my phone.

"Odd, I thought I paid them," I muttered to myself, as I picked up the phone with an enthusiastic greeting for Gerald.

By the way he responded to my happy greeting, I could tell something was wrong. He was solemn—I thought I was in trouble by the way he spoke.

"Mr. Hobbs, I am sitting here with your son, and we have some unfortunate news to share," he said, with the authority of a school principal.

"Ok, what's up?" I was at work when they called.

---

[27] I had vowed to not pay after the first time.

"You are on speaker here in my office, Mr. Hobbs. Jack, do you want to tell your dad what's happening?"

"Mummmmnndt mmmm." I couldn't understand what he said.

"What's that? I can't hear him," I said.

"I relapsed!" Jack said, as if he were pissed at me or as if to say "now, are you happy?"

"No shit!" I said, "You relapsed in rehab? Awesome!"

"What do you want to do now, sir?" Gerald asked.

"What do I want to do? Nothing. I don't want to do one damn thing," I said.

Gerald explained to me that he had given Jack two options. Actually, it was only one option, and Jack didn't like it.

Tangu has a more intensive inpatient treatment center in downtown Atlanta. Gerald wanted Jack to go there for some additional relapse prevention training. Jack refused. He maintained that he wasn't going to learn anything he didn't already know and was not going downtown.

Gerald told him to pack his stuff and go to the Atlanta facility or pack his stuff and leave Tangu. Jack elected to leave treatment and leave Tangu—I had paid for four weeks—he didn't make three.

Gerald apologized to me. I was pissed. Disappointed. Scared. This kid was killed by heroin less than one year ago, and since his ninety-day rehab, he had relapsed twice—and one of those times was *in rehab,* for Chrissake!

Early 2015—Not Recognizing My Collapse

In early 2015, I was dealing with a flurry of issues. Jack had relapsed in October, though we didn't prove it until January. He entered rehab and then relapsed in rehab. Not a good start for him and not a good start for me. I was still seeing Adam and the psychiatrist. As a result of my obsession with Jack's relapse and the resulting proof of it, my Klonopin dose was doubled, and my Zoloft dose was increased to the maximum allowed. I was also given a "break-the-glass" prescription for Xanax. If I got into any trouble or panic—pop a Xani.

I was often panicked during these days and weeks, because his death had become a certainty in my mind. Scenarios played through on how it was going to happen, who was going to be affected, and how much damage it was going to cause for the rest of us. My dreams were consistently showing the death of a three-year-old girl who he took with him on his way out. Predictably, it was another incredible car crash that would kill them both.

In addition to his relapses, his departure from Tangu, and my expectation of his tragic death, much more was occurring. I learned that my nephew had stolen $8,000 from a business account he had access to. I can only assume that most of it was used on drugs—mostly heroin. In February, my dad was really sick. In March, I lost a major account in my small photography business, due to major errors at a processing lab. Many local families were angry at my company and me because of screwed-up pictures. I broke a couple of ribs and was drinking excessively. I was trying to drown out the inevitable, the visions, the images, not only of his death but of the funeral, the tombstone, the irreparable harm in my relationships that he would leave behind. And regret—the deep regret that I didn't figure it out on time. I was terribly sad and extremely frightened. Alcohol and Klonopin made things easier. I didn't use my Xanax prescription—at least not yet. Maybe I should have.

The feeling of absolute helplessness had become a rather common feeling in my life. My son was going to die—and I couldn't help it. In addition to the extreme sadness and fear of impending tragedy, I felt as though I was in a hopeless situation from which I could never escape. I was always going to be his father, and, as long as he was alive, I was going to have to deal with his addiction and the damage he caused while he saw it through to the end. If he died—I would have to live with that and my failure to prevent it. There was no way out—I was trapped by him, by his addiction, and by my inability to let go. I wanted out so bad—but there is no escape from the life of a heroin addict. He can't escape the addiction, and I couldn't escape him. It was a lifelong sentence of hell. No matter what I tried, I could not find a way to not worry, to not fear what was going to happen to him and the people around him.

I thought that I had done everything I could and that he was now in God's hands. It is easy to say—difficult to accept. I couldn't let go. I still can't.[28] This was my dilemma.

The anger that I had about my stolen $8,000 was nothing in comparison to everything else that I was dealing with emotionally, especially after Jack totaled his car—the Nissan Maxima that Aunt Jen had

---

[28] Thank God for mindfulness and meditation. They have saved my sanity and my life. I still struggle when I think about him—but I can find the present much easier to deal with than in those days.

given him. At least this time he was the only car in the accident—he hit a wall on the Interstate, I think. This was the third car that he totaled; fourth, if you count the pick-up truck he took with him in the first accident. By the time April 2015 rolled around, I was so numb to his behavior that nothing would shock me. I tried to equate, with some hope, that nothing would shock me to nothing would affect me—I was wrong.

On April 26, 2015, my forty-ninth birthday, Jack called to let me know that he had wrecked my truck. Yes, that truck; the truck we drove to hockey tournaments, the truck he sat in when told me to get the fuck out of his life, the truck that Murphy died in, the truck he chewed my ass for bailing him out of jail, and the truck he evaded me while driving 85 mph in a drug-induced frenzy. That truck was now totaled and gone from my life—how fitting that it would be him who would destroy it.

When I saw the truck at the junkyard, I was amazed at how the passenger side of the cab had been crushed from the top down. By some miracle, the female passenger who was with him was not killed (Figure 8). I couldn't see how she wasn't.

Figure 8: Damaged truck.

My now eighteen-year-old daughter was preparing for her graduation from high school in May 2015. Everyone was excited for her, because she had an excellent chance to be valedictorian. It was a lifelong dream of hers, because she wanted to give the graduation address to her class, just like her childhood idol—Elle Woods of *Legally Blonde.* We were fortunate that she did fulfill her dream—despite everything that was going on around her.

Through April and May, there were many preparations getting the house ready for her graduation celebration. We did a major remodeling, had the house painted and recarpeted, had the deck stained, and had landscaping done. My parents were both feeling better and were down for the ceremony—it was always great to have them around.

They were only here for a few days, when they came down to the basement where I was working. They stood in the doorway, crying. Both my parents crying at the same time could only mean bad news. My mom told me what happened. "Bobby, your brother, David, died," my mom said.

"What did you just say?" I asked, almost pissed off.

"David's dead," she sobbed.

I went back into shock, I think. Not because my brother died—but because of this whole crazy and insane sequence of life events that was occurring. I stood up and walked over to where they were. I hugged them both at the same time—a three-way hug of tears—crying for the loss of my brother. There was not much more I could take; I was in serious jeopardy.

My daughter's graduation was close at hand, so we decided that we would have services for David in early to mid-June. This would give my parents time to celebrate the graduation and then get home and arrange everything for the funeral.

It was sad. Especially for my mom and dad. They had been caring for David, while he suffered major losses to diabetes. He had lost his legs, neither kidney functioned, and his heart was failing. It was unlikely that he would survive a heart transplant and a kidney transplant, so he couldn't get on the recipient list for either. I had a good idea of how my parents felt. Watching your own child die is an unnatural experience.

Jack was staying with Wendy's dad. He needed a car and eventually settled on a Korean sedan. He liked the car, even though it was a far cry from his taste in Caddies. Meanwhile, my older daughter had invited him to live with her in Athens for the summer, about an hour from Atlanta. She was attending the University of Georgia (UGA) and had her own place. She helped him get a job at the local country club where she worked. Once he had transportation, there was no reason not to go. She cleared it with us, and then he moved into her place in Athens.

It was only two or three weeks later that I got a call from my nephew—the one who stole the $8,000. He was crying when I picked up the phone.

"Uncle Bob, it's AJ. Jack just got arrested by the Cobb County police," he sobbed.

"AJ, Jack moved to Athens. It is Wednesday night, a work night. He is not in Cobb County," I said.

"Yeah, I know, but I invited him to this party I was at with my buddies, so he drove here. Just before he got here, the party was busted, and while the cops were inside searching everyone, Jack walked in. They searched him and found heroin in his sock. He's gone, Uncle Bob. I couldn't warn him in time, and now he is gone."

"They found heroin on Jack, and he was arrested?" I asked.

"Yep," he said.

I hung up on him. This couldn't be real. He just moved to Athens; who in their right mind would drive all the way back here for a party on a work night? No one. But he is not in his right mind, the answer came silently.

This was going to make things interesting; he was on felony probation in Candler County for six or seven more years. He had an outstanding set of felony charges in Paulding County for possession and intent to distribute, and now he had new felony charges in Cobb County.

"How the hell does he not go to prison now?" I wondered out loud.

As soon as I completed the thought, I went back to believing this wasn't real. The 90120 guy—this can't be happening to me, to my son, to my family. For Chrissake! There was so much mother-fucking drama happening, I couldn't figure out which tragedy to try to keep track of. Something had to give, and maybe it already had.[29] It would be some time before I figured it out.

My whole body stiffened. There were not enough tranquilizers or psych drugs available to make this go away. We had just buried my brother. I went alone to Ohio; I was playing tough guy. We buried him, and then I got home, and this was the call I get. Geezus!

"Now what? Now, what am I supposed to do?"

I didn't wait for an answer; I didn't want one. I was officially checking out on life. I had had enough. I didn't realize it yet, of course, but it was probably on this call where my physiology said to itself, "You know what,

---

[29] Sinking into a "breakdown" doesn't happen instantly, not for me anyway. It happened gradually, throughout many traumas, none of which were adequately dealt with before another came. Once the breakdown occurred, there was no road sign that said: "Danger, you have now lost your mind." It took time for certain behaviors to emerge and for other people to take notice and take action. Think of it like this. When you are in a pitch-black room, it's hard to find the walls—in fact—maybe you don't trust that there are walls—maybe you think they are cliffs. I didn't know where I was—for a long time.

there is way too much going on in this guy's world. We can't process all of it—hell, none of it, so we are shutting down for a while."

It did.

There was a major family celebration scheduled for mid-July in Ohio; it was my parents' fiftieth anniversary party. We had a surprise party planned near Lake Erie, and the entire family was to attend. I had six brothers; I think we had twenty-eight kids among us, and one of us had a grandchild already. Additionally, my parents had eight siblings between them, and all their spouses and kids. Huge deal. Big family event.

Just before heading to Ohio, I had a company event, an executive retreat, in Florida. Wendy was invited, and so we also took the kids and their friends. Of course, that meant I could take my sailboat. Which was always fun, at least for me.

I was out on the sailboat alone, not thinking. Just being. It had been about a year since I had been on the boat. In fact, the last time I was on her I was on vacation. Funny, the CEO of my company called me that day last year in a mini-panic. There was a crisis, and he needed help. That's the job I had, it never stopped; there was no way out; no way to get away—even on vacation. It was parallel to my life with Jack; I was trapped in his world, whether I wanted to be or not. It had been four years since I took the job that required 24/7/365 availability on my part. I am not complaining about the job—I wanted it, and I was compensated for it. But looking back on what happened, it is not hard to see that work played a part in it. The stress and tension in the job was probably enough for an average man. That stress and tension, coupled with what was happening to me at home, was breaking me.

I didn't know what the answer might be—but short of a nervous breakdown—I wish I had found another way out.

I did not want to drink on the Florida trip. In fact, I pledged that I wouldn't. But the constant attention my brain paid to the pain in my hips always seemed to distract me from the stated purpose of not drinking. Besides, I was depressed. I had lost my sense of purpose, my sense of value. So much had gone wrong so quickly that it just didn't all get processed. I was fucked up and didn't even know it. What else could I do? I had a shrink; I had a therapist, I practiced MBSR, I took my meds, what more could I do?

I didn't enjoy the corporate event. My attention was not on corporate needs or objectives. Honestly, I am not sure if I had "attention." I was lost,

I was drifting, but this time I didn't know I was drifting, and I didn't care about anything.

The following week was the drive to Ohio. Everyone in the extended family was excited. It would be the first time we would all get together since my niece's wedding. Well, Jack was in jail for her wedding—so technically, we didn't all get together ever. This time he wouldn't be there again—and neither would David.

I expected it to suck. David was gone, and that would affect all of us equally. But my son was in jail again. He wasn't overseas serving his country or doing some hot research project for college. No. He was in jail. Again. I did not look forward to answering questions about him from my loving aunts and uncles.

They loved me so much. My entire life, my aunts and uncles loved me, as if I were their own kid. Not only would talking about Jack break my heart—it would break theirs too.

Then there would be the family pictures. Dozens and dozens of family pictures of my parents with every conceivable combination of child, grandchild, and great grandchild that could be imagined. All female grandkids, all male grandkids, all males, all females, my family, his family, with spouses, without spouses.

Jack would not be in any of the pictures. Each of my brothers would pose with my parents and their families with great pride and joy. I would watch as they posed—happy for all of them. Then our turn would come, and we would be one short—and everyone knew why. No pride. No joy. It would be this way for years. Anytime my dad would pull out the pictures of their fiftieth anniversary—he would be reminded that my son wasn't there and why. Every time my niece would look at her wedding album— no cousin Jack. Nope—jail again. I resented him for not being there— again. I had endured enough of this bullshit.

I drank that week. Every morning, every afternoon, every night. I half-heartedly tried to hide that I was drinking—but I didn't care if anyone knew. I wanted to be numb. I wanted to check out of this crazy hotel that had become my life. I felt like shit and drinking helped me feel crappy. Crappy was better than shitty—and so I drank.

It was this trip that resulted in my daily drinking habit. I think from the time I left Ohio in late July—up until my last drink on August 20, 2015—I drank at least 48 ounces of beer every single day. This was in addition to my prescription medications. Hell, I even drank before and after cross-fit.

Chapter 9 Concepts

1. IOP is an important time to establish habits that will carry the addict through to a lifetime of recovery.
2. The most important habit is daily attendance at AA meetings.
3. Guide your addict with balance—too much, too soon will result in tragedy.
4. The two most important things in a recovering person's life are spirituality and sobriety. Without them, nothing else matters—they must come first.
5. Relapse is likely. Be prepared for it.
6. Given that relapse is likely, be on the lookout for signs of it.
7. If you don't take care of yourself, you will regret it. You must have a strong support system that will ensure your mental and emotional health as you go through this. Life is not going to stop while you deal with this tragedy.
8. Nervous breakdowns don't just happen in one day. It takes a long time to get there.

Chapter 10

Intensive Outpatient Program

The successful person has the habit of doing the things
failures don't like to do.
~ Albert E. N. Gray

Intensive—Outpatient—Program
Read the words above—it should be all three.
Intensive: Focused, dedicated, committed, priority
Outpatient: Still a patient required for health
Program: Plan, progress, measured goals, timed

A Transition Back To—Well, a Transition Out of Rehab—There Is No Going Back

After spending thirty to ninety days as an inpatient at an addiction treatment center, most addicts are not ready or able to be tossed back into the world directly. Most benefit from and take advantage of a transitory program between rehab and independent living. Often this transition program is called IOP.

The possible combinations of features and attributes of an IOP are infinite. There is no "set-in-stone" menu that exists indicating the proper form of care following an inpatient program. However, there are certain attributes that are commonly found in many IOPs; we will discuss some of them in this chapter.

Before discussing IOP though, let me suggest that you take another look at rehab. Every situation is different, but it might be possible, or necessary, to extend your loved one's stay at the treatment center. You should discuss this case with the clinical staff and with your loved one. Sometimes 180 days is better than 30–90. Money, resources, and willingness will all drive this decision, as will the depth of your loved one's addiction.

Assuming your addict is going to leave rehab, here are some suggestions for IOP: Any initial or first-time transition program should be at least ninety days. During the transition period, the amount of time spent each week or each day on recovery activities should taper down from the highest at the beginning of the transition to the lowest at the end of the transition. How much recovery time should be spent each day will depend on the needs and circumstances of the addict. I would suggest that at the beginning of the transition, at least 50 percent of the addict's time be spent on recovery and recovery-related activities. The balance of time should be spent working, going to school, and rebuilding relationships.

Where Does Recovery Time Go?

Relapse Prevention (12–20 hours)

A formal provider of IOP services will offer a continuing education curriculum that the client is expected to follow. Often, the addict will be expected to attend classes, sessions, or seminars at the facility three to five days per week, two to four hours per day. These classes are facilitated by professionals who cover various topics of interest—like those from rehab. Of these, relapse prevention is the most critical for IV-heroin addicts.

Individual Therapy (0–2 hours)

During the recovery process, it is common that the addict discovers some neurosis or disorder that requires additional psychological or therapeutic attention. Weekly or biweekly therapy sessions are often incorporated to help the addict progress in resolving those issues, while reducing the likelihood of a related relapse.

Group Therapy with Addicts (1–2 hours)

Supervised and facilitated group therapy with other addicts who have various amounts of recovery time should be a critical part of the designed program. The facilitator would introduce topics of interest, and then the addicts share their personal experience, strength, and hope with one another. Often, newly recovered addicts benefit from the experience of more advanced addicts and from gaining exposure to others who have "walked in their shoes." It's comforting for the addict to know that he is not alone in the feelings and thoughts that he carries daily. These group sessions also allow the addicts an opportunity to grow their personal recovery support networks.

Group Therapy with Family (0–1 hour)

There are many damaged relationships as a result of the addiction. Continued healing and support can help family members regain trust with one another, while recovery takes hold. Additionally, hearing the experiences of other families is helpful and comforting as the addict's family members learn they are not unique in their damage and brokenness.

Ninety-in-Ninety AA Meetings (1 hour per day)

A critical component of long-term recovery is active participation in an AA or a Narcotics Anonymous (NA) group. The process of AA becoming an integral part of the addict's daily routine requires that he attend ninety AA meetings in ninety days. At the front of this effort, it seems like a lot to ask—and perhaps it is. But there is much to lose, and besides isn't it true that before rehab the addict did what was necessary to be high ninety times in ninety days? Initially, this activity is uncomfortable for many, however, in a short time, your loved one will begin to forge many new, sober relationships with people who are active in long-term recovery. Hopefully, during these ninety days, your addict will find a routine set of meetings, find a sponsor, and join a home group. If he is lucky, he will begin making honest progress in the twelve steps of the recovery program.

I cannot stress enough how important this part of recovery is. At the end of IOP—AA is all that is left—it must be strong. The house will stand better in a storm, when the foundation is well built.

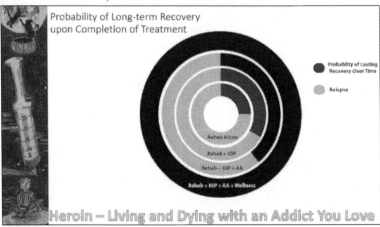

Figure 9: Probability of Long-Term Recovery.

Continued Monitoring and Medication

Obviously, the Vivitrol program continues and requires monthly visits to a physician for a drug screen and the injection. In addition to this monthly opiate screen, random drug testing should be conducted by the IOP provider. There should also be professional monitoring of all OTC and prescription medications taken by the addict.

Living Arrangements/Support

There are many options, ranging from staying in residence at the rehab center to independent living in an apartment. For IV-heroin addicts, a slow and conservative approach is probably best. Transitioning to a place of their own or, if necessary, back home, should be done patiently and gradually. Any major moves should be done with intent and some degree of planning. No brash decisions should be made concerning living arrangements. Here are some options to consider.

Stay at Rehab

Your loved one is already familiar with this arrangement; if it works, why change it?

Sober Living

There are sober-living complexes and communities in nearly all cities. These are occupied by recovering addicts who have decided to live clean and sober. These locations are drug- and alcohol-free and designed so that the residents support one another in recovery and a sober lifestyle.

Three-Fourths-Way House, Halfway House

These are difficult to describe. These are locations often owned and operated by recovery facilities but are co-located in normal everyday communities and apartment houses. They are occupied by recovering addicts and are somewhat supervised by the operator. As a part of the living arrangement, residents are expected to submit to random drug screens and to participate in a defined set of recovery activities, such as AA meetings or facility-arranged events. Other than those minimal requirements, residents come and go as they please within the bounds of curfew and quiet hours. The residents are also expected to remain employed, pay rent, and care for their living needs, such as grocery shopping, laundry, and upkeep of personal and shared space.

Back Home

Coming back home to live with parents is an option; however, keep in mind that part of the reason they are in this situation is due to their continued dependence on their parents and others. A temporary arrangement might be ok, but the goal must be independence. Therefore, there should be a definite deadline on when the addict should move out.

If married, the health of the addict and the stability of the marriage should be considered closely before moving back home. A volatile relationship might need healing before it is safe for the addict to return home.

On Their Own

Ideally, this would work well if they could live with other recovering addicts their age. Sometimes it might work if newly recovered addicts found roommates who shared similar life experiences. You might expect that the group could support one another and work together through the many trials and issues of sober and independent living. The downside in this scenario is that if one person slips—they all might slip. The end, in that case, could be tragic.

Employment

Hopefully, if your loved one has had difficulty finding a job, the rehab or IOP administration will offer employment support and placement services. These services might be as simple as résumé writing and interview skills; or as advanced as job placement and referral. Many times, there are opportunities with employers who understand the difficulties some clients might have with drug screens and criminal records.

Legal Issue Support

Employment referral letters from doctors and administrators will certainly help your loved one find work; but perhaps, more important, letters of reference and witness of character could be immensely helpful in any pending legal situation that your loved one was involved in before entering rehab. The treatment center and the IOP facility should both be willing to stand up for your loved one. Additionally, if he is active in AA, his sponsor and other recovering addicts will often stand in defense of a member of their group. These same people could be helpful during probation or parole situations or in working with a drug court.

Ideally, during three months of IOP, the addicts will fully develop everyday life skills. They will learn to live well, while maintaining a strict regimen of recovery activities. Overall, they should have six months clean, be employed, have an active network of clean and sober friends, and have their legal issues understood. Assuming they are attending AA regularly, five or six times per week, and their Vivitrol program is proceeding as intended, they might be at a point where independent living can be seriously evaluated.

Chapter 10 Concepts

1. As you consider IOP, make sure you look at all options available at your existing treatment center and from your insurance provider.
2. Be sure to include the most important habit—daily attendance at AA meetings, initiated with what is known as ninety in ninety.
3. IOP should definitely be done in the location where the addict will end up living.
4. IOP should be most aggressive at the beginning and taper down toward the end.
5. During IOP, as with life after treatment, recovery comes first. Pressures of job and finances need to be put aside in favor of recovery. If the addict doesn't learn that now, he certainly will not later.

Chapter 11

It's Not Over, 'Til It's Over

Out of suffering have emerged the strongest souls;
the most massive characters are seared with scars.
~Kahlil Gibran, The Broken Wings

My journey was certainly not over. Nearly all that I held to be true about life had been turned repeatedly and, in many cases, destroyed in the wake of what happened. I am no longer the man that I was on February 24, 2014. In many ways, God did "take me" when I begged him to. Both Jack and I died on that bathroom floor, and we both survived. It has taken me three years to achieve this level of awareness.

Before 2006, my views about depression and anxiety were fairly inflexible. I felt that too many people were being prescribed expensive medications to deal with normal and healthy levels of sadness and worry. I had studied and practiced methods that enabled me to manage my "state" and pick my mood. I was fairly good at overcoming adversity.

However, between fall 2006 and spring 2007, I was having difficulty focusing on everyday tasks at home and at work. I visited my family doctor, and he prescribed Zoloft to temporarily aid me while I dealt with the initial impact of Jack's drug habits. I was already running 30–50 miles per week and was practicing yoga. There was no room for more exercise. I consulted with loved ones about their personal and medical experience with antidepressants, and they urged me to try them. So I did. I was impressed with the relief the medication provided. The tension in my body was relieved, and I was able to focus a little better at work. I remained on Zoloft until 2010.

I admit that my prejudiced attitude toward depression, anxiety, and the meds used to treat them changed dramatically. Therapy might have worked for me then; I'll never know. Perhaps I wasn't quite ready for therapy at that time.

I was therapy and medication free from 2010 until the early months of 2014, when I went back on Zoloft and added Klonopin and Xanax. I also started therapy and practiced MBSR at that time.

Except for minor incidents of what I would refer to as PTSD flashbacks, like the one in his bedroom after finding syringes, I did not have a significant episode of a panic attack through all of 2014 and 2015. I was fearful most of the time, rarely did I feel safe or secure—no matter where I was. I developed some strange habits. One was to never sit with my back to the door—for fear of someone sneaking up behind me. For quite a while, people had to be careful when waking me, because if startled I might strike out. I spent a lot of time in the fetal position, because it was the easiest way for me to relax. I tended to stay at least arm's length from strangers; I had become uncomfortable in crowds, and I avoided public places unless I was drinking.

I had become apathetic about everything and everyone. I didn't see the point of trying hard anymore—what was the point? I had done everything the right way, and it got me to a fairly shitty place. It was difficult to give a damn.

In 2014, I owned no guns. In fact, since leaving my dad's house in 1984, I owned no guns, and I hadn't fired one since leaving the military in 1991. By the end of 2015, I had collected five guns. Somehow, I had become convinced that I was going to need them. I bought a gun for every conceivable self-defense scenario. I had a concealed carry, a close-range home defense revolver, an accurate semi-automatic pistol, a nine-shot semi-automatic shotgun, and an AR-15. Despite having grown up with guns and being in the military police—I never had any need for guns.

Now all of a sudden, in 2015, I owned five. Buying them was an obsession. No one could talk me out of it—my mind was set on having them; they had become a major priority. I think at some level I believed my safety and security were in jeopardy, and guns were going to help me feel more secure. Hell, I wouldn't even go to the movies unless I was packing. Please remember—I was never really in jeopardy—I just thought I was. Or my mind did. Thanks to an awful lot of coaching and hard work—I have since sold all five guns. I am disarmed. Hopefully, the person who shoots me at the front door in my nightmare isn't reading this book. I hope he buys it—but doesn't read it.

It is horrible to live in constant fear. It is not easy to describe it—but an overall feeling of dread dominated my life from February 2014 until recently—almost three years. Fear of what? I don't know. I can't say that

I was running from anyone or anything, in particular, I was just not safe. That is the best I can say.

It is reasonable to say that in the spring and summer months of 2015, I snapped. Until then, I was dealing with PTSD, anxiety, and major depressive disorder. By the time I returned from my second 2015 visit to Ohio in my new truck, the one I had got after Jack totaled the first one in April, I was in the throes of a nervous breakdown. The thing about these breakdowns is they are not an instantaneous failure, where you know it happened and something needs to be done. In fact, I didn't know I had one; I was still fighting to survive, to return to my old self, the self I was before February 24, 2014.

Three weeks after leaving Ohio after my parent's fiftieth anniversary celebration, I lost my job. It was August 20, 2015. That was also the day of my last beer—the last drink of any kind. I have come to believe that had I not lost that job—I would be dead now. There was simply no way that my life could continue in the way that it had been.

Not working provided me with the time and the capacity to figure out what was happening to me emotionally and mentally. It too took a long time. I was in a dark place and my brain needed time to sort and process through all that had happened. Sorting and processing became my primary focus. Work had been serving as a place for me to hide—to escape—and as long as I was there—I wasn't going to face the problems that were plaguing me—and I believe—would eventually kill me.

The holidays in 2015 were nothing special—probably not for anyone in the family. Jack missed them again, because he was in jail—and probably going to prison. Everything around the rest of us—especially me—felt artificial—not real. Life had become like a plastic houseplant. It looked real, but when you got close to it, it had no smell. When you touched its leaves, they had no warmth. It was a plant, but it had no life. It was fake, artificial, an illusion.

Despite that, it seemed like I was getting better. By January 20, 2016, I had five months of not drinking. I was immersed in meditation and mindfulness and was beginning to experience new forms of spirituality. I was eating well and sleeping well. I was improving nearly all my relationships and was initiating two new career paths. One was a heroin awareness foundation called The Heroin 411 Foundation, Inc. The other was a coaching and wellness practice called The Sandalwood Wellness Center. I was convinced that my calling was to help other families, especially fathers, avoid the traps of suffering that I fell into while my son overdosed, recovered, and relapsed. I wanted there to be more than just an online search to help them find their way through the dark path of addiction.

I ended up getting a few coaching certifications. I was focused on coaching comebacks. The idea was to help normal people suffering from setbacks plan and execute an epic comeback. I was particularly interested in helping executives in crisis, as they (we) tend to have a particularly hard time of letting go of the need to control everything and everyone.

Through January 2016, I was involved in what seemed to be an awesome project. My college roommate knew that I was having problems with addiction at home and that my family had suffered through an overdose. His sister's son was potentially a heroin addict. My roommate wasn't sure, and neither were his parents. He asked me if I would help—of course, I agreed.

I spoke with my roommate by phone and got as much information as I could from him before contacting his sister. Keith knew a lot about drugs, but not so much about addiction. In speaking with him, he knew that pills were involved. He was not certain about heroin; but he was certain that his nephew was not honest about his drug habits.

Keith suggested that I speak with another sister, Kay, before calling on the mother. Kay had a lot of experience with addiction. She too was fairly sure that her nephew was not honest and that her sister, the boy's mom, was being naïvely optimistic that Johnny's condition wasn't "that bad." It sounded all too familiar and dangerous.

Next, I spoke with Johnny's mother—Kim. As Kay had predicted, Kim didn't feel the issue was in need of a significant intervention at this time. She and her husband believed that Johnny needed to decide to quit and then use his willpower to stay clean.

We talked about the drugs he used and, of course, pills came up first. No one wants to admit to heroin use. So, I had to ask her if he used heroin. She told me that he did—intravenously. The whole tone of the conversation changed in that instant. Not just because of what I know, but because of a voice in my heart that told me, again without using words, "He is in trouble."

It was the same voice that used no words and communicated to me that Jack was dead in the bathroom while I was on the stairs in February

2014. Again—I don't know how to describe it, and, in a book, I only get to use words. It wasn't English; it wasn't a language—it was a sensation.

I offered that if her son was indeed an IV-heroin user, there was little chance that he was going to stop using; in fact, there was a good chance he would overdose. She was not immediately receptive to what I said; though I know that in her heart, she agreed with me. The problem was this was her son, and, after a series of bad breaks, he was finally getting his life together. He was making positive moves in his life.

Johnny had a plan! He was moving to Columbus and enrolling at Ohio State University. He already had a place to stay, and the family was excited for him. When I asked what his plan was to stay alive—she told me that he had that planned out too. Before I describe it, I want to make absolutely clear that **this was not a feasible plan. It was not feasible or safe. In my mind then and now, this was a plan to take up permanent residence in a 6-foot hole.**

Johnny had arranged, with his family doctor (not an addiction specialist), to begin a Vivitrol injection treatment program. All Johnny had to do was pass a drug screen each month and then receive his Vivitrol shot. There was no recovery program, no supervision, no 24/7 monitoring—nothing. Just a well-meaning family doctor administering what I was certain would become the shot of death.

I explained to Kim how Vivitrol worked and what the risks were. I became adamant that they NOT do this program. I emphasized that if they did—I could guarantee that Johnny would die. Thinking back—who was I? In their minds at the time, who was I? They had a plan and a doctor helping them. It would turn out, that the only thing that had saved Johnny—that week anyway—was that he had failed the drug screen (I do not know that his mom knew this at the time), so the family doctor didn't give him the shot. Johnny had to wait another week.

The first call ended. I remember talking again with Keith and Kay and expressing in the bluntest terms that Vivitrol administered with no program and no supervision was going to end badly. I believe that Keith and Kay both spoke with Kim and were pushing rehab for Johnny. The problem was he was enrolled in the upcoming semester and was moving into his new apartment. No one was willing to put his plans on hold.

I had another chance to talk with Kim, and we had a great conversation. Many of the addiction signs that had been readily available for her to see were now shining through the shroud of her intense, motherly desire for him to be happy and successful. I had a great deal of empathy for her and her family. It is such a tough situation to be in. I asked her if she thought it would be ok for me to speak with Johnny, one on one. It was a great idea, but she wasn't sure if he would go for it. He was twenty-six, and she wasn't sure he'd be cool with talking to some old college buddy of his uncles.

I got a text from Kim the following day—Johnny would speak with me! She had set up a time for me to call him and verified it worked for me. It did.

I was nervous talking to him. Everything I thought I knew about heroin addiction was going to be tested. There were not a lot of samples in my case study, but I figured all phenomena follow certain patterns that don't change much. I called Johnny.

Our conversation went well. I sensed right from the beginning that he wanted to talk; he needed to talk; he wanted to surrender. He reiterated everything that I had learned from his mom and aunt and uncle. I then shared my story—or rather—Jack's story. I was specific, graphic. Johnny probably felt it was too much gory detail.

I went through the whole story, the overdose, the detox, the rehab, the relapse. It certainly helped me build some rapport and credibility with him. Things were going well; so, I thought I would be bold.

"Johnny, why didn't you get your Vivitrol shot last Friday?" I asked, believing I knew the answer.

"Because I used on Thursday and didn't pass the drug screen," he said; my intuition was correct.

I went on to describe what happens to addicts who are actively using when they start Vivitrol. I went over cravings and how cravings feel and how the little voice of heroin keeps coming back repeatedly—"Just once more; one more time."

"Johnny, Vivitrol doesn't stop cravings, dude. If you take that shit outside of a treatment program, there is a strong likelihood that you will succumb to the cravings. Those cravings won't be satisfied until they feel the full effects of heroin. Vivitrol stops those effects—so the cravings want more—you take more and then you overdose and die," I paused.

Johnny wanted to leave his hometown; he hated it there. He had come to believe that the only people his age who still lived there were losers, and he didn't want to be a loser anymore. He thought that Vivitrol and a change of scenery would be enough for him to quit and get his life back together. He wanted to get out of the prison that heroin had locked him in.

"Did you use today, Johnny?" I asked

"Yes."

"Did you use yesterday?"

"Yes."

"Do you have dope now?"

"Yes."

"Dude, you know as well as I do what you need to do and it's not Ohio State! You can't quit! You will never make it through withdrawal. Stop fooling yourself—tell your mom you want to go to rehab—she is ready for you to ask!

"My dad won't want me to do it," he said.

"Johnny, c'mon, man, your dad is going to do whatever he has to, to keep you safe—to save your life! But he is not going to force you—it is up to you. You have to decide to do it, and then he'll support you. He knows what works and what doesn't."

"I don't know," he said.

We went back and forth for a bit longer without ever closing him on rehab. He was convinced he had so much vested in this current path he was on, that there was no other way. He did agree that his Vivitrol plan was risky. I begged him to not take that shot—no matter what.

"Don't take that shot, dude; no matter what, do not take that shot!" That was the last thing I said to him. It was Friday.

I knew from speaking to Johnny that he would fail the drug screen and not get the Vivitrol shot that day. He had already used that morning and the day before. I was scared. This kid was active and in a bad spot. His parents did not yet know how much danger he was in.

I called Keith, and the first thing I said to him was something like this, "Dude, Johnny is in trouble. You don't have weeks or months; you have days. He is going to die in a matter of days." Where was this confidence coming from?[30]

"What do we do?" he asked.

"Rehab. Keep him alive until you can get him to rehab," I responded.

"Will you call Kim?" he asked

"I promised Johnny that I would keep our conversation from his parents," I said.

---

[30] I am convinced it was spiritual.

"Dude, fuck that, call her."

I did. I spoke with both Kim and her husband, John, about what I believed to be true about their son. Understandably, they probably believed I was exaggerating and being overly dramatic. I did too! But a messenger that used no words convinced me that Johnny was in danger.

I told John and Kim to make sure they knew CPR. In fact, anyone who was going to be around Johnny had better know CPR. Obviously, if anything goes wrong, they should call 911 immediately.

"Make sure you consider how much time he spends in the bathroom—don't assume anything. Try to find Narcan; look online for it. Have it available, if you can. Find a rehab—one that can detox him—and get him there ASAP. If he does overdose, DO NOT allow the staff to discharge him from ER—break his legs if you have to. He cannot go back to the house if he overdoses."

I told them everything I could think of. They could tell that I was nervous and scared for them. I was the only person outside the family who they had talked to about this—the only source of info they had. I hoped in my heart of hearts that I was delivering the message I was meant to.

Kim was going to work on Johnny. She was going to try to get him into rehab. In the meantime, she asked if she could speak to Wendy about her experiences as a mom. I told her I would set it up.

Wendy came home, and we talked about Johnny and the situation unfolding. She was against me getting involved. She thought it was too soon and my emotions were too raw. I was finally making progress, and she felt that this could only harm me; I thought it could only help me. Regardless, I sincerely felt that Johnny was in trouble, and I needed to be helping him.

"Oh, by the way, would you mind calling Kim? She would like to get a mother's perspective on all of this," I said.

"I am not talking to anyone," she said.

"What?" I cried out.

"I am not getting involved. It's too soon. No!" She was decided.

"It's been two years! We promised that we would try to make sure this never happened to another family. No one should go through this alone; no one should have to search online for everything."

"No! I am not talking to her!" she said angrily, this time.

I lost my temper. I was in total disbelief. This woman gave everything she had to other people—what the hell? There had to be something else going on.

"I can't believe this! I can't believe how selfish you are being! They need us!" I screamed into the room she had just walked into.

Silence.

It was a long time before she responded to that. What was coming next was the most shocking statement that had ever come out of her mouth in almost thirty years together.

"Clearly, we don't see things the same way. I think it's time we both admit this is over, and we go our separate ways," she said firmly.

I was so astounded and taken aback by the past ten minutes that I just threw up my arms.

"Fine. I am not fighting anymore," I said. "Tell the kids; I don't want to dance around this for months."

She gathered the children during the weekend, and we told them we were getting a divorce. Although going through the motions felt artificial—like a fake house plant, like 90210, once we told the kids we were divorcing the idea became real to me.

On Monday, I received a call from Johnny's dad.

"Hey, Bob, it's John. Listen, Johnny just overdosed and when you were telling me what to do the other day I wasn't listening. I am hoping you can go over everything I am supposed to do now," he said calmly.

"What! What? Is he alive? Where is he?" I shouted into the phone.

"He's at the hospital with Kim. As far as I know, he is gonna be ok. Kim saved him. Like you said, he was in the bathroom too long; she broke the door down with a dumbbell and dragged him out," he said.

"Oh, John, I am so sorry!"

"She had to do CPR until the EMTs came, and I think they gave him that stuff." He was so calm when he told me.

"John, I am so sorry. Is Kim ok? I asked.

"I think so. I am going to see her at the hospital after I get home and change my clothes. To be honest, I am going to have a couple of drinks before I head up there. But I know there are things I need to do when I get there," he said.

"Yeah. Drinks are a good idea. So, the hospital is going to want to discharge him, once he is stable. Tell them no. Do not take him home again. If the EMTs gave him Narcan—he is gonna want to use when he gets back. If he has dope—you'll do this all over again. Get him to detox."

Keith was calling me. I let it slide to voicemail. John got back to his house and thanked me for everything. I was happy to help—though I thanked the voice. I wished John all the best.

I listened to Keith's voicemail. It was thirty-nine seconds long, and by the end, he was crying. He wanted to let me know that Johnny had overdosed, Kim saved him, and he was eternally grateful that I had helped save his nephew's life.

In a single instant, every event that Keith and I ever experienced together flashed through my memory. Was this moment destined to happen when we first met back in 1985? This was all so weird. I listened with raw emotion as my old friend finished his message. I visualized the terror Kim had just experienced trying to break down that bathroom door—not wanting to see what was waiting for her on the other side. Dragging his body out . . .

I lost it. I started to cry, and I couldn't stop. At first, I could reflect on how ridiculous this was; but soon I was overrun. As I started to hyperventilate, part of my mind was wondering what the hell was happening, while the other part was driving me into a full-blown PTSD flashback. It was February 25, 2014, all over again. I was emotionally in the same place—completely covered with despair, dread, regret, fear, and sadness. I saw the blue face of my son's dead body, and it seemed as though Kim was there with me. I felt so bad. Paralyzed.

I could not catch my breath. I was going to a dark place. I shot Wendy a quick text to not come home. I let her know I was losing my grip and was a mess. She did not need to see me like this—especially since we just announced our divorce.

I tried to find my psychiatrist's number. I couldn't. I couldn't find Adam's either.

I got a text back from Wendy. She told me to hang in there; she would be home right away to help.

"I belong there with you," she wrote.

When she got home, she came right up to where I was sitting and wrapped her arms around me, as I sobbed. I was sitting at the kitchen table, so I buried my face in her belly, as I cried. My tears, my snot, and my drool were all over her sweater, as I tried to get a grip. She rubbed the back of my head and reassured me that everything was ok. I was safe; Jack was safe. I was here with her, and it was going to be ok.

She called my psychiatrist and asked what to do. The ER was an option. The doctor told her to start with two times my prescribed Xanax dose and see if that calmed me. I hadn't taken Xanax before; she had to look for the bottle. It was time to break the glass. I took two Xanax, as she walked me to my meditation cushion. She actually sat with me. She sat with me and continued to remind me to breathe and that I was safe. Eventually, things started to calm down.

Once I was breathing normally, she left me alone on my cushion. I was impressed with the Xanax. It took away the physical components of my fear and anxiety. I was able to sit and reflect—more emotionally than mentally—on all that had happened to me since February 2014. Everything that had happened—all of it—seemed so vivid in my mind. It seemed like it was happening to someone else—but I was watching it. It's hard to explain. Maybe I was that someone else.

2017

I didn't fully appreciate that I was no longer the person I always thought I was—the person of February 24, 2014. The person I grew up with—the one who was there with me through thick and thin was gone. He died. He left me alone and afraid, because his world no longer made sense to him. The rules—if there even were rules—were not fair, and he could no longer figure out how to win. And for that person—winning was what it was all about.

I have waited a long time for that guy to come back. I have put many of the last thirty-five months on hold waiting for him. It was only just recently that I realized he is not coming back. I have to move forward from here—without him. I have to create something new—someone new.

Chapter 11 Concepts

1. If you are not well, things can get a lot worse.
2. Have someone in your life who knows you well, keeps you honest with yourself. You will not notice major emotional trauma on your own until it's too late.

Chapter 12

Relapse

You will not be punished for your anger,
you will be punished by your anger.
~Buddha

Don't be angry, don't blame, avoid guilt, avoid regret.

Relapse—It Is Inevitable—Be Prepared—It Is Bound to Happen

If your loved one is an IV user of heroin, it is highly likely that even after all the trauma and tragedy, the tear and fears, the money spent, the prayers said, the promises made, the all-star performance at rehab, that he will eventually, once more, answer the call of the former lover and succumb to the seductive net.

The lover's voice says many things, kind and unkind—in the mind of its addicted partner. And though I have never heard the voice myself, I believe the voice is ironically subtle—at least at first. "Just once more; just one more time."

That's all it has to say to pique the addict's attention. From there, if left unattended, it will fill in the remaining narrative. "Once more won't kill you; you can do it, once more and then stop; it's only one more time."

As long as the addict gives the voice any consideration at all, the "once more" dialogue will continue to grow in intensity and frequency, ever reminding the addict, it is only one more time. "You and me, one more time."

For many, it can become a never-ending dialogue that consumes the entirety of the addict's consciousness. The base message doesn't have to change; the focus is "one more time," not a long-term relationship, just a one-night stand. The mind begins playing the "greatest hits" of experiences—the best highs with the best people and the best dope. The disease knows that "just once more" is the most tempting message. It is not asking for a relationship or reconciliation. It is just asking to be with the lover one more time—to part ways on a good note—on a high.

Eventually, the assault on the addict's mind overtakes him, and he again craves his lover. Thoughts consume him until he meets his lover once more. They join, just like the old days, and regardless of the experience, it leaves him with only one final request. "Someday, maybe, one more time?"

The addict might feel guilty for his failure, for his lack of control. Maybe guilt drives him to use. Or maybe the experience wasn't so bad; he lived and seems to have all of his recovery powers restored. But he doesn't close the door. "Maybe, someday," he whispers, in the back of his mind—regretting it immediately.

That is all the lover needs to hear, knowing full well that in the not-so-distant future, the subtle sound of a whisper will again be more than enough to seduce him once more. And so it goes. So enamored with the seduction, the addict does not even recognize the extent of his fall. Thoughts of rehab and relapse prevention are crowded from his mind by the loving return and presence of his reason for living. Hopefully, someone from the outside can remind the addict of his demise. Remind him of his lover's deceptions. Remind him of how it uses him and then abandons him when things get tough.

When confronted about relapse, anger and rage are usually the first responses. As if we, who have stuck by this person through thick and thin, are now somehow trampling on sacred ground.

"How dare you interfere with my private life, my love life," are the words transmitted through the facial expressions of a confronted addict.

It is possible that every conceivable hurtful and harmful thing that can be said about the person intervening is thrown into the air. At this point, your loved one is gone; he has returned to what he truly loves most. The person you worked so hard with to avoid this occurrence is no longer here. The active addict is back, and this is not easy to accept. Unfortunately, you probably need to wait for his lover to directly remind him of its evil ways. When it leaves him hopeless, helpless, at yet one more bottom, you might find the one you love. Until then, you can only watch with dismay as he slowly decays away in a deadly trap.

Again, I have no personal experience with what happens. But it does seem to resemble a sick and unhealthy romantic relationship from my perspective. I do know that the subtle seduction of heroin works patiently. It can wait; as long as the addict draws breath, one year, five years, twenty years, it matters not. It still has a chance to be the last thing on his mind when he draws his final breath.

Most addicts do not go willingly; from a certain perspective, they don't go consciously either. They are unconscious. It seems like the addict is placed on autopilot. He is tricked into flipping the autopilot switch to "on." It might take weeks before he even realizes what he has done. Almost always, though, when called out on his failure, the addict lashes out with anger and resentment.

For those of us who witness this insanity firsthand, it is almost impossible to accept. We worked as hard as he did to recover, and he let us down. He spent all that money and made all those promises only to relapse and lie about it.

Sometimes, the anger is replaced by guilt. Once an addict is caught, remorse will eventually arise. When it does, there is only one way to relieve the pain—the warm embrace of the lover. For some time, it will seem as if you had never spoken to each other about heroin, or addiction, or staying clean. The anger and resentment will begin to grow in you too—and, at some point, it will be replaced by guilt and remorse. Soon, you will be faced with another fork in the road. Should you help? Or should you let go?

The voice in your head becomes as insane as the voice in his. Sometimes I think it is the same voice speaking to both you and the addict. "Leave him alone; it is his own fault," says the voice, hoping you will abandon him.

"If you leave him alone, he will die," says the codependent enabler.

"If you help him, you are an enabler, a codependent," the voice of heroin reminds you with a hint of guilt.

It is crazy. Trying to figure out how to react to a relapse while it is occurring is not easy. Again, I suggest that you decide in advance; what are you and your family willing to do in the event of a relapse? Having thought it through after recovery and before relapse, while you, the addict, and your family are rational, will allow better decision making. Don't wait until you are angry and resentful—because that cycle never ends. Relapse is something you are going to have to face—be ready.

Tells: See Appendix 3, Is My Kid on Opiates?

What to Do Now

Hopefully, you are in a support group, such as Al-Anon or Families Anonymous. Dealing with feelings of guilt, fear, worry, and sadness is far easier when speaking with people who have been there before you—and who love you. These people will also serve as a trusty sounding board for you to bounce your options on. Should you help? If you help, how much? Under what conditions?[31]

Despite your anger, you need to consider what obligations you made to your addict and family previously (if any). Did you establish boundaries and expectations with your addict? If so, were there consequences for a relapse? Hopefully, you realize that you must live up to them now. You have to do what you said you would do. You must enforce the boundaries. If you don't, you lose credibility with the addict, and you become an ally of his lover, that is all too happy to remind him that you don't enforce any rules. That he will be able to get his way later. Heroin has enough power— you do not need to supercharge it by not living up to the bargains you made.

Likewise, if you agreed to help the addict through additional relapses and rehab visits—then you need to live up to your commitments. At some point, the addict (and his lover) must know that you are a person of your word. You say what you mean, and you mean what you say.

Regardless, the addict made a decision to relapse. Fully aware that there would be consequences. You and your family must not contribute to his illness any longer. It is not ok that he relapsed. It is never ok.

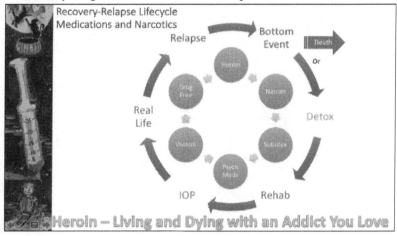

Figure 10: Recovery-Relapse Lifecycle.

Hopefully, you are not shocked. Although your addict might think, at times, that he has some special superpower, and that the statistics

---

[31] Remember, love is unconditional; help is not.

surrounding heroin addiction do not apply to him, you cannot fall subject to such illusion. You know that addicts always lie. They never tell the truth. You also know that if your gut tells you that your addict relapsed—he did. No additional evidence is necessary.

So Now What Do You Do?

You start over. Only this time, you are armed with experience. You can approach this incidence with less fear and more practicality. You should have much more realistic expectations. If you previously wrote a plan for relapse, dig it out, it is time to use it. If you didn't, you need to start planning for overdose, detox, rehab, IOP, decay, relapse. This is probably not easy to accept, at this point. I know when Jack relapsed—even though I expected it—I could not accept it. His mother did not accept it, until it was impossible to not admit the obvious. It just doesn't make sense that a person who is lucky to be alive would go back down the path that killed him. It is similar to a battered woman who continues to go back to her abusive lover. It makes no sense.

If you do not know what to do, pray until you do. In certain respects, you too are starting all over. Emotionally, you have relapsed and will need to revisit the recovery lifecycle—overdose, detox, rehab, IOP, decay, relapse.

Anxiety Management between Your Addict's Relapse and Recovery

The period following a relapse and prior to attempting recovery is filled with anxiety for you. So far, I have not found a method that eliminates the fear and worry associated with not knowing whether his next bottom will be his last. However, I have discovered a method that makes it all bearable. MBSR is a practice that has enabled me to reduce the paralyzing impact of fear and panic. It takes time and effort. But it is worth it. Mindfulness and other wellness development suggestions are discussed in Chapter 14 on wellness.

There are also medications that can help you. If anxiety is an issue for you, do not hesitate to visit your family doctor or a psychiatrist. Both can provide you with temporary relief from anxiety and depression with nonnarcotic medications.

Questions You Will Face

1. How much money would you spend to keep your child alive?
2. What if that is not enough?
3. Can you live with yourself and your money when he's gone?
4. What if you spend it all and he is still addicted?
5. Can your spouse/partner live with you if you don't risk it all?
6. Can your spouse/partner live with you if you spend it all?
7. Is it your responsibility?
8. Is it your moral obligation?
9. What does your spiritual teacher say?

I don't know these answers, but you and your family need to work on these questions in advance—because a time of panic, guilt, and pain is not the time to try to figure this out.

Chapter 12 Concepts

1. Heroin is hard to beat. It has been done, but it is hard. Do not take it lightly.
2. The seduction of heroin will never cease working on your addict.
3. Know "The Tells." See Appendix 3.

Chapter 13

Living While Your Addict Is Dying

The most painful thing is losing yourself in the process of loving someone too much, and forgetting that you are special too.
~Ernest Hemingway

YOU have been through hell, YOU must recover, or YOUR mind will never let you out.

Anxiety, Fear, and Worry between Relapse and Recovery

Maybe you realize it, maybe you don't, but this journey does not have an ending. You are as ensnared in this evil plot as much as he is. There is no way out. If he survives—you will always be afraid that he will relapse when he is clean, or overdose when he is active. If he dies, you might forever wonder what you did or didn't do or could've done to change the outcome. While he lives, you struggle with anxiety; if he dies, you deal with regret and depression. There is no way out—the recovery-relapse cycle is a circle. This is bad news. As long as you choose to stay on his addiction circle, you will forever suffer.

Is it possible that you might have *caused* his addiction?

Did you do something wrong when he was a child or a teen that *caused* him to begin sticking needles in his arm?

Have you believed, or do you still believe, that somehow you can *control* him or his addiction?

Are you more powerful and influential in his physiology than heroin?

Do you maybe have a super power over heroin addiction that millions of parents and spouses/partners through the ages always sought but never found while they suffered through their lives?

Do you think perhaps you can *cure* his heroin addiction?

Somehow, someway, if you pray hard enough, love hard enough, work hard enough, will he be *cured*?

Even worse, maybe like me, do you think that the fact that he isn't *cured* is because you didn't pray hard enough, love hard enough, or work hard enough?

These questions represent the obsession (addiction) that many of us have when watching our addicted loved ones destroy themselves.

Cause. Control. Cure.

"I must have done something to *cause* this."

"I should have gotten involved earlier; I could've gotten this under *control*."

"If only he would listen to me, I know I can get him off this stuff (*cure* him) for good."

Those of us who still believe that we can *cause, control,* or *cure* heroin addiction can use these phrases before, during, or after any known usage and during every single relapse. Unfortunately, as long as we cling to the belief that we have any ability to *cause, control, or cure* heroin addiction, we are bound to the same endless circle of overdose, detox, rehab, IOP, decay, and relapse that the addict is. Not only is there no way out of witnessing our loved one's demise, but there is also no way out of the suffering associated with our own.

The *cause, control, cure* beliefs are deeply rooted in our psyche. It is almost instinctual for parents and spouses/partners. They are difficult to overcome. Often, you will hear parents say, "I know I didn't *cause* this addiction."

Intellectually, they mean it. But the intellectual level is superficial, as compared to the instinctual and emotional level. The deeply rooted beliefs that you have about yourself, about your loved one, and about the relationship that you have had through the years are complex and intertwined in the core of your innermost self. I do not believe, that by simply confessing your inability to *control* his addiction, that you are any more capable of freeing yourself from the bondage of these beliefs than a manic-depressive can free himself from the depths of despair by stating his refusal to remain sad. It doesn't work that way. I wish it did; believe me.

If you are honest with yourself and willing to work hard toward surrendering your beliefs about *cause, control, and cure,* you will find a way out from the seemingly "no way out" situation you find yourself in. You can find peace and serenity regardless of the decisions your addict makes, and despite the consequences that arise as a result of those choices. This takes effort, patience, and an unyielding commitment to take your life back. The way I see it you have two choices:

1. You can live miserably, because of decisions he makes, despite your best efforts (to *control*) to help him. You can stay on his path, trapped in his circle, with no way out. Or . . .

2. You can live a meaningful life with purpose in peace and serenity, knowing that whatever he does—he chooses to do. You learn to accept, at the core of your being, that his choices are not your fault, you cannot *control* his outcomes, and you cannot *cure* his sick thinking.

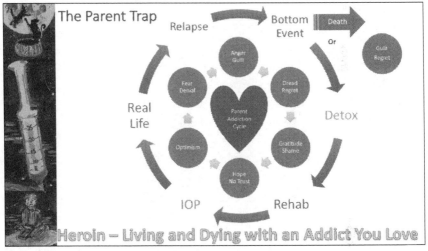

Figure 11: The Parent Trap

It is possible for you to live in peace, with a clear conscious, even if you are watching him die. This does not mean that you must stop loving him or that you give up on him. It simply means you can separate your life's causes and effects from his.

There are a variety of recovery programs for friends and families of addicted people. In these programs, you will find others remarkably like you; people with tragic stories and difficult struggles, just like yours. And many of them have recovered from the vicious, emotional torment associated with loving an addict. You will learn that addiction is a family disease—and it is. Everyone in an addict's life is affected as the addiction runs its course—and everyone is sick, once it does.

Programs, such as Al-Anon, Families Anonymous, church and community support groups, and others, are focused on supporting one another as they recover from the family disease of addiction.

I suggest that you immediately begin working with one of these groups. It will change your life and give you life at the same time.

You could continue to work with the rehab staff. Often, they will have opportunities for group or individual therapy at a nominal cost for alumni. If your rehab had "family night," you should continue to participate. Gather around you a group of people who know firsthand the path you travel, so that you have support when you need it, and so you can provide support to others when they need it.

The Sandalwood Wellness Model, described in the next chapter, has many proven suggestions to help improve the overall wellness of people suffering from loss or disappointment.

You must be prepared for the inevitable questions.

What more could you have done?

What if you spent more money on treatment?

What if you went to visit him?

What if you only had . . . when he was younger?

These questions and the associated guilt and regret will only result in your own illness. Search, if you must, but there are no answers to these questions.

You cannot answer the question, "How much would you spend to save his life?" because the question is designed for you to fail, regardless of how you answer. When you hear that question, it is the dark side of your ego driving your belief that you have control over the life of another; that you have the ability and the resources to be in control. And the coercion comes when the blame and guilt start rolling through your saddened mind.

Only when you give all this up to a higher power will you begin to find peace. I urge you to find that higher power now.

Remember, you have done your best under extraordinary conditions to keep your loved one alive. Once he learned how to recover, you were totally off the hook. Once he decided to use, he was on the hook, all by himself. You are relieved of all obligation.

I know it is hard to buy into what I am saying. You might need to hear it all 10, 100, or 1,000 times before you change your innermost self. But trust me—it is done every day by people just like you. Find an Al-Anon group and get started now. There is much living to do—don't wait to start.

Chapter 13 Concepts

1. Locate and start attending Al-Anon.
2. Know that you didn't *cause* it; you can't *control* it; you can't *cure* it.
3. Seek a way to permanently break out of the recovery and relapse lifecycle.

Chapter 14

Living Well

Even if life gave you at one time everything you wanted—
wealth, power, friends—after a while you would again become
dissatisfied and need something more. But there is one thing
that can never become stale to you—joy itself.
~Yogananda

In many situations, a heroin addict "finishes" formal recovery in one year or less. Following that first year, it is often observed that the intensity and enthusiasm for recovery begin to subside, and ever so slowly, the addict begins the slow and subtle slide back into old habits. This slide is so gradual, day-to-day and week-to-week, that it is hardly noticeable to either the addict or to his loved ones. It is like watching the erosion of rock—it looks the same—even though it is constantly changing.

As time progresses, the addict's ability or willingness to reject heroin's seductive voice as an ill-fated temptation is dampened. The resistance to its frequency and volume is reduced, and, in time, however long it takes, the voice of heroin begins to grasp at the addict's consciousness in such a way that thoughts of anything else—including recovery defenses, sponsors, or steps, are no longer available consciously. Inevitably, the addict relapses.

Hopefully, he has an opportunity to start all over again—detox, rehab, intensive outpatient program (IOP), and real life. How many times does it take? I don't know. I do not personally know any IV-heroin addicts with more than three years clean.[32]

For the addicted, it seems to me that completing the recovery cycle of detox, rehab, and IOP works as intended. These programs provide the addict with a firm foundation of recovery and sufficient tools to remain in recovery for some period following treatment. However, it does not seem obvious to me that these programs are extensible into the far future. From my perspective, they do not result in a permanent foundation of

---

[32] I know one non-IV user with nine years clean.

sober and clean living. Something more is needed after completion of IOP to support an addict throughout his lifetime.

For family members, I think the same is true. The shock and trauma associated with discovering that a loved one is addicted to a deadly narcotic can be a low bottom for many of us. Family members make this sad discovery in a number of ways.

Perhaps their loved one was jailed, maybe he suffered an overdose and survived, or maybe the addict came forward begging for help. In any case, even if the addiction was known and this discovery is a relapse, there is a certain level of shock and trauma that affects the family members. When it does, they are at the end of one recovery cycle, and, hopefully, at the beginning of another.

In a certain sense, when you decide to help your loved one for the first time, or again, you too need to detox, rehab, and IOP. Although you enter recovery devastated, early on you will begin to feel a sense of hope and optimism. Eventually, you might even feel a sense of relief that your addict has made it! He is recovered and safe. Your focus then begins to drift to other areas of life, and perhaps you begin to miss warning signs of a potential relapse. Or, maybe you accept some behaviors that your loved one returned to. Heroin is a patient killer; the changes in your addict will happen over such a long period, it will be hard to notice.

Eventually, you might realize how different your loved one has become. Regardless, once relapse is certain, it is inevitable. Your recovery cycle is coming to another end. Soon, you will be devastated yet again, and your whole life will be upended. Similar to your addict, you must work hard after IOP, with a program in place, to help mitigate and avoid the steep emotional slopes of recovery and relapse. Otherwise, your life and the lives of those around you will be miserable. This is one of the saddest side effects of heroin addiction. Not only is the addict's life and his personal relationships destroyed, but your life is also at risk. The impact of a heroin addict in your life cannot be understated and should never be underestimated. Heroin can and will destroy you—even if you have never laid eyes on the substance.

What can be done to extend the recovery cycle for both you and your addict? This chapter proposes a way of living that will increase the likelihood of long-term recovery and minimize the likelihood of relapse.

Take a look at the Recovery-Relapse Lifecycle (Figure 12).

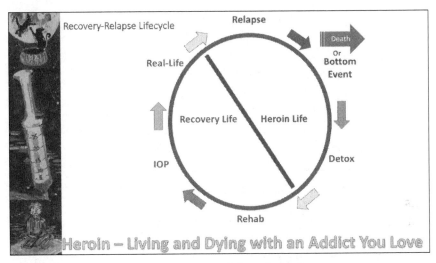

Figure 12: Recovery-Relapse Lifecycle.

It is true that many addicts relapse and even overdose right out of rehab. Hell, my son relapsed *in* rehab. The information that I will present would not be much help to such addicts, as they would have relapsed before beginning. My aim in developing this program is to help addicts and loved ones develop a style of living that is of such high well-being that the recovery cycle can be extended beyond three years into permanence.

I am a strategic interventionist and life coach. I am not an addiction counselor—I have not studied addiction beyond Alcoholics Anonymous and Al-Anon. Both programs, AA and Al-Anon, serve as the cornerstone to post-IOP recovery. This is true whether the proposed program here is implemented or not. In my view, there are no substitutes for the twelve-step recovery programs. They must be the major recovery building blocks. But outside of daily AA meetings are twenty-three hours of living. These twenty-three hours should be lived with as much balanced well-being as possible. Otherwise, what is the point?

It seems to me that "real-life" becomes unacceptable to many heroin addicts. Heroin offers an alternative, or a substitute to "real-life." Heroin abuse makes life a little easier to accept—until the "bottom event." Then heroin life becomes unmanageable, and there is no obvious suitable substitute. This is where a recovery program enters. It offers a substitute for the alternative "heroin life," which has become a travesty. Recovery life works well and prepares the addict to return to "real-life," which he ultimately does. Throughout time, the intensity of recovery decays and is replaced with "real-life," which might work well for a while, but it potentially becomes unacceptable once more, and the addict relapses and returns to the alternative "heroin life." The circle is endless.

I know of heroin addicts who have been to inpatient rehab fifteen times in twenty years. There are families who have spent more than a quarter of a million dollars trying to save an addict from death. Each visit to the intake office offers renewed hope and optimism that this will be the last time. Then each relapse crushes not only the hope and optimism—but the source of hope and optimism—the human spirit—the souls of men and women.

I do not have any hard statistics, but the addict and the loved one go through the recovery cycle of bottom event, detox, rehab, IOP, and "real-life," only to re-enter the relapse cycle of heroin life, relapse, and bottom event. Something needs to be added in the "real-life" phase of the cycle to extend and eventually make permanent the recovery life cycle.

The wellness model I offer is based on personal experience and years of trial and error. The development of the model is ongoing; however, at its foundation, it works. It enables individuals to understand, pursue, obtain, and preserve a high level of wellness. More important, personal progress and development never end. There is always "just one more step" that people can take in personal well-being. Finally, it doesn't contradict anything that is true. It is easily integrated with any growth or spiritual program that an individual might pursue. I can show it to you, but you should discover its usefulness on your own.

What Is Well-Being?

Well-being can be defined as the absence of suffering. Any model, or life program, should focus on reduction and eventual elimination of suffering. This model aims to that end. For addicts and those who love them, a continuous reduction in suffering should result in a better "real-life" experience. A sustained improvement in "real-life" should result in an extended period between relapses for the addict (Figure 12). For the addict's family member, the program's result should be recognized as the mitigation of high emotional peaks and low valleys, as the addict cycles through the recovery and relapse.

Wellness Program

The Sandalwood Wellness Model consists of six zones of well-being. These are best represented as six cells of an ever-expanding and developing honeycomb as shown in Figure 13.

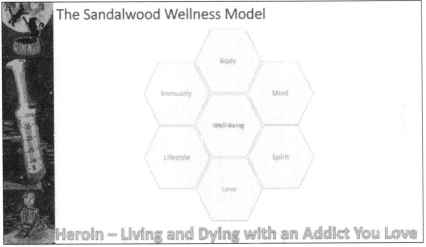

Figure 13: The Sandalwood Wellness Model.

The Six Zones of Well-Being

- Physical wellness
- Mental wellness
- Spiritual wellness
- Relationship (love) wellness
- Immunity and defense wellness
- Lifestyle wellness

Each cell contributes to or detracts from the overall wellness of a human. A well person, or a healing person, should balance the amount of time, effort, energy, and focus invested in each of these areas. Each zone must be fully well for the person to be optimally well. If one zone becomes weak or ill, all other zones are negatively impacted. If one zone is emphasized more than others, and "grows" faster than the others, the resulting imbalance disrupts the wellness of the person.

Wellness should not be confused with success or health. Wellness is at a different level from success and health. The idea is that a whole human should rest in wellness, despite his or her relative levels of health or success. Many people allow poor health or lack of success to affect wellness in a negative way—but that is a choice—not an affect. However, a fully well person is capable of extraordinary health and success when maintaining a high level of overall wellness. The takeaway here should be that a person with cancer can still be well, and a person living in poverty can also be well.

The intent is wellness, well-being. We aim to reduce suffering. By reducing suffering, we can forge a path toward happiness, joy, peace, and serenity. Are these not the ultimate objectives we all share? What would we trade now, if we could find peace and joy in everyday life? Is there anything we wouldn't trade? As we continue, think about these questions. What if there were no suffering? What would we call that state of being?

Personally, I can tell you this. I have done everything in my power to become happy. By happy, I mean having a high level of joy, serenity, and peace of mind on a consistent basis, regardless of what is happening around me. I followed the "path to success" to the letter. I went to college and became an engineer; I married the girl of my dreams, went to work at a Fortune 500 company, had four kids, went to graduate school, joined the executive suite, and bought a big house, five cars, stocks, bonds, and cash accounts.

At every turn, I waited for happiness to permanently settle in my being; it never did. My ego always told me I had to do "one more thing." *You'll be happy after the next promotion, then the next bonus, then when the mortgage is paid off, then when you retire*—and that's when it hit me. I had spent my entire life "doing what I was supposed to" and here I was—on the threshold of retirement—still not happy.

I told myself, the ego is wrong! It is lying to me, and if I don't change something, I will be thinking that maybe when I'm dead, I'll be happy.

How insane is that? What a waste of a lifetime! MY LIFETIME! I can assure you of this, if happiness is what you are looking for, you will not find it in any of the rooms of an eighteen-room house. You will not find your happiness in another human, in a European sports car, or in the corner office of the next greatest company in the world.

There are many ideas and definitions about what wellness is. Here are a few of mine.

Wellness is—

- the continuous development of awareness of one's being.
- the discovery and acceptance of the truth of one's being.
- a whole-being effort to apprehend and reduce suffering.
- a journey, not a destination; one can always go further.
- the joyful pursuit of joy; the happy pursuit of happiness.
- an appreciation of the paradox that obtaining anything is also the loss of something.

There is not a social structure, culture, political movement, or secret policy that will improve an individual's happiness. All suffering occurs within. The *reduction* of suffering occurs within. Therefore, happiness occurs within. Once we stop looking externally for the elusive concept of happiness, we might reach the conclusion that it is not "out there." If so, maybe we can begin looking at the only place that is not "out there"— that place is "in here." It's inside you, or even better, it's integral to you.

The model we use metaphorically is a honeycomb. I like the honeycomb because of the interdependence of its design. The wall of every cell is dependent on the wall of another cell. The entire structure is dependent on the well-being of each independent cell, and the individual wall of each independent cell. An individual's wellness is dependent on a balanced investment in each area.

Not only can we use the honeycomb to model an individual's wellness, but we can also use it to model the wellness of a whole society. The wellness of every person is represented by a group of cells, and groups of cells are integrated together in perfect interdependence. No person's wellness can become too big or too small compared to any other without harming the wellness of the whole. It is an interesting concept to meditate with; but we are not building a social model here, maybe in a future book.

The honey-making process is also interesting to consider in the metaphor. A honeybee vomits into the cell of a honeycomb. Then, by fanning the cell with its wings, accelerates the evaporation of the fluid and what is left behind is sweet and wonderful honey. For those who are addicted, turning vomit into honey makes quite a bit of sense.

Honey never spoils. The honey that was buried with King Tut is as edible today as it was when he died. We would prefer a sweet and everlasting recovery from our addiction.

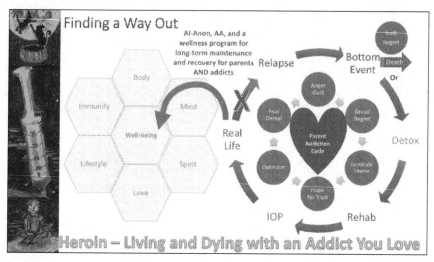

Figure 14: Finding a Way Out from the Recovery-Relapse Lifecycle.

It takes a ton of work to make honey, and also for an addict to stay clean and sober. First, the universe (higher power) has to provide the flowers; the bees cannot do much without the cooperation of the universe. An average bee can visit 5,000 flowers per day; it takes 2 million flowers to make a single pound of honey. A single bee can only make 1/10th of a teaspoon of honey in its lifetime! To produce any substantial amount of sweetness, the bee needs help from other bees, and so it is with the addicted.

Our wellness is dependent on our careful and balanced maintenance of our honeycomb. We must behave with an awareness that our wellness is interdependent with the wellness of everyone around us. Our recovery can be sweet and permanent, but it takes a lot of work on our part, and we will need the help of other addicts and from the universe. I believe that if we can maintain a state of wellness—we can remain in recovery. We can break away from the relapse, recovery, relapse, recovery lifecycle, and restore normalcy to our lives (Figure 14). In our recovery, we enter the program not feeling particularly well, like vomit. When we come out, we feel sweet, and we want that feeling and that state to last permanently.

Developing an approach to improving and maintaining each of these six zones of well-being is the key to developing individual wellness. Wellness is ultimately happiness or a lack of suffering.

When considering the addict and his loved ones, both are likely to be weak in all six areas. Years of battling addiction, each other, and a need to be in control have likely wreaked havoc on the addict and those he loves.

The first question I usually get when I introduce this model is, "Where do I start?" And the answer is simple, yet, elusive. "It is not *where* you start; it is *when* you start. When is now!"

In any moment, a human can make a decision—a new choice. That decision is the beginning, and that beginning is now! The decision is the onset of willingness, and once a person becomes willing, anything is possible. Start now!

A common next question is, "How can I possibly do all of this?" Again the answer is simple; "You can't. Not today anyway. But each day you can do a little—and eventually you can achieve quite a bit." It took me forty-eight years to become miserable. I cannot expect to become happy in a few months.

There is much that must be changed in how you perceive yourself, others, and the world. But remember—change is the goal. Even the slightest change in thinking is an achievement. Wellness is the *pursuit* of, not the *achievement* of. Work slowly, diligently, with intent. It won't be long before you see yourself in a whole new light, living in a world you would never have recognized three years ago.

Mindfulness

You will notice a recurring theme as each zone is discussed. That theme is mindfulness. For now, let's use "awareness" as a working definition of mindfulness. By awareness, I mean the act of being completely conscious, in real time, of whatever you are doing, saying, sensing, or thinking. Awareness does not include judging, contemplating, considering, or criticizing; it means noticing, letting go, and noticing. Whatever the phenomenon is, notice it, let it go, and notice what happens.

At times, when observing your thoughts, you might notice that they often, or always in my case, come in the form of a voice. In other words, you likely think in a language. Sometimes, the "voice" is having a conversation in your head. Occasionally, you might find yourself participating in the conversation and other times you might not pay attention to most of what is said. Often, the voice will skip around from thought to thought, from conversation to conversation, for no particular reason. It has this need always to be "doing something."

When you are mindful, don't try to interfere with the "voice" or the thoughts that are moving through your consciousness. Just watch them. Don't judge them or criticize them; certainly, do not criticize yourself for any thoughts you notice. Simply notice, and let them pass. If you feel an overwhelming urge to react to a thought, just say quietly, "Isn't that interesting?" and then let it go. Sometimes it helps to gently turn your focus to your breathing.

People often believe that a mindfulness practice requires sitting meditations and other formal activities. These practices certainly add to the overall, long-term experience. However, when you are getting started, it can be much simpler. There are many activities that we perform day to day, that we notice slightly more than the act of breathing. You can start by being aware of what is happening as you do these things. Take a close look at brushing your teeth, washing the dishes, and driving.

When you brush your teeth, notice how the bristles feel as they cross your gums; how many individual bristles can you feel? Taste the mint of the paste; feel the coolness of the rinse water. When you wash the dishes, notice the temperature of the water; is it higher or lower than 98 degrees? Feel the suds on your skin, as the bubbles pop—can you hear the suds? Try to notice the subtle sensations that you started taking for granted years ago. As you drive, notice where your mind goes. Bring it back to driving and try to notice how long it takes to drift off on its own again. How often are you "really" driving?

During your day, take a moment here and there just to notice where you are, what you are doing, what you are thinking. You might be surprised at how much you have been missing, as your undisciplined mind roamed aimlessly from thought to thought.

Mindfulness is an essential element of the healing process for a variety of reasons, and by practicing it, you will open new and exciting opportunities for you and your consciousness. For now, we will just focus on one main important benefit. When we are mindful, or aware, we are in the present moment. When we are mindful, or aware, we find it difficult to regret the past or fear the future, because we cannot be anywhere but present.

In any given moment, when you are mindful, and you find yourself living in this instant of your life, you will come to realize that you are safe—there is nothing to fear. For just this one single moment of life, everything is perfect. You have food, shelter, and clothes. Maybe, if we can find peace in a single moment, we can learn that we can string several moments together—and, in doing so, create a minute of peace, then an hour of happiness, then a day, then a week, and so on. But to get there, we must decide to begin, and then we have to notice. A minute of noticing, then five, then ten, and soon you might find yourself calmer than you have been since your childhood.

Unless you are under a threat—anxiety, anger, fear, and worry, cannot be present in the now. Mindfulness can help ease the stress and anxiety that so many of us feel when we dwell in the past or forecast the future.

One last note on mindfulness, there is only an instant in which you are actually living. The instant that just passed is gone—it is now in the past—and you cannot live it again. There is another fifteen seconds from now that you have absolutely no control over. It will happen regardless of what you think or do. In fact, you cannot even predict what you will be thinking in that instant. Once it arrives—it becomes your present—but only for an instant, and then it to slips to the past. Before you know it, that once future second will be fifteen seconds ago.

It is here now, by the way! Is it what you expected? Yeah, that moment that I mentioned fifteen seconds in the future, it just passed, and now it is fifteen seconds ago. I sometimes look at the future, present, and past like an old-fashioned movie film. It's all on a big reel, and it is continuously slipping through the lens of my consciousness. I only get a split instant to spend with each frame—and then it's gone.

The future frames are on the feed reel and are queuing up in front of me. If I don't want to miss the next frame—I ought not to try to cling to the last one, or worry about the next one after that. I should always focus my lens on the frame that is with me now. Consider that you can only do something in the present moment. You can't do anything in your past, nor can you do anything in your future. Everything that you have ever done was done in the present; everything you might ever do will only be done in your present. So, let's get into the moment.

Physical Wellness

We believe that the body should be maintained in a state of wellness; not for the sake of the body, not for the ego, not for sex appeal, but because of how the body can positively affect the mind.

Awareness of your physical nature is an important aspect of wellness. Most people are probably more aware of their bodies and aspects of their bodies than they are of any other part of their beings. The bad news is that you are not your body.

Despite my understanding that I am not my body, I do believe that the body serves me, the universe, and others. We could not exist in the human manifestation without our bodies, because that is where we are at the moment—we ought to take care of it and learn how it can help take care of us and others.

You have probably realized that your body and mind are closely linked. Some of you might also have awareness that your spirit is closely intertwined with your body and with your mind. Each of these dimensions of a human has a definite impact on the other two. We might not always feel the impact or notice it, but it is always there. As we advance in our understanding, perhaps we can learn how to create certain spiritual, mental, or physical sensations by leveraging one or both of the other two.

If you think about it, nervous thoughts of danger, or an upcoming public speech, or a performance can quickly generate sensations in the body. Butterflies in the stomach or a nervous twitch are common physical reactions to a nervous situation. A strange and unexplained spiritual experience can startle you and result in goosebumps and perhaps a chill down your spine. It's a physical reaction to a nonphysical stimulus. The reverse is also true; certain physical activities can result in mental or spiritual responses. You have probably developed a certain appreciation for the interconnection of mind, body, and spirit.

Self-help author and philanthropist Tony Robbins teaches extensively about the dependency of emotions on physical motion. In other words, how the body affects the emotional mind. In a simple demonstration, Tony has his students stand tall and stare at the ceiling with a big, stupid smile on their faces. He then has them hold their arms out to the side, and while smiling attempt to feel sadness. It is difficult to feel sad while looking up. Then, Tony has his students drop their heads and slouch. They close their eyes and frown, looking toward the floor. From that position, Tony challenges the students to feel happy. Again, it is challenging to achieve the requested feeling.

The body and the mind are closely connected. So a great question is, "Can we use our bodies in such a way to generate desired feelings, while also developing it to help us avoid unwanted feelings?" Tony's simple exercise demonstrates that there is a clear connection between the body and the mind.

Addicts use drugs to alter the states of their minds. As you progress through this chapter, remember, the aim is to learn how to mitigate the desire to use drugs and to provide substitute activities that are pleasant and safe.

Activities to consider when looking at physical wellness include running and yoga; both are essential components for this way of life, especially for addicts. They are also complementary activities. Runners need to lengthen their bodies and calm their nervous systems; yogis need a cardio component to improve overall wellness. But I didn't choose running and yoga because of how they relate to each other. I chose them because they provide the opportunity to build physical wellness in a fashion that will support and enhance the wellness levels of the other five cells of the honeycomb.

Running

In a moment, I am going to make a statement that any human can run. I know that this statement is not always true. In those cases, where it isn't true, please substitute some other cardio-based activity where time and intensity can be easily varied. Some ideas include swimming, cycling, spin cycling, rowing, and elliptical training. Some people might need to consider alternatives that include wheelchair racing or similar activities.

There are numerous benefits to living a running lifestyle, and all of them are valid reasons to become a runner. Already, some of you are saying to yourself that you can never be a runner—hopefully, you are noticing that voice, mindfully, in your head and then letting those thoughts go. Ladies and gentlemen, we humans were built to run. We are designed to run, and we have evolved eventually to be able to run long distances slowly with little difficulty.

If a human has difficulty running, there is a reason, but it is not because "we are not made to run." This is not a book about running; there are thousands of those. If you need to learn how to run properly, I strongly urge you to consider *ChiRunning*[33] by Danny Dreyer and the Pose Method of Running[34] explained by Dr. Nicholas Romanov.

Let's assume that my assertion that anyone can run is correct. Given this is true, why is running important in this addiction context?

Endorphins

First, especially for heroin addicts, running promotes the body's production of endorphins, which are, quite simply, morphine produced by the body. The word "endorphins" consists of two parts, *endo*—meaning from within the body, and *orphin*—meaning a morphine-like substance. The main purpose of endorphins is to mitigate pain; they also produce a feeling of euphoria or a "runner's high."

Endorphins attach to the opioid receptors, just like the morphine molecule, and inhibit pain signals through the central nervous system. They also contribute an increase in dopamine levels, which produces a feeling of achievement. An endorphin release or "rush" is commonly referred to by long-time runners as a reason they continue to run.

Endorphin rushes are not going to be nearly as euphoric as an orgasm or a good heroin high. But they are a naturally occurring result of a healthy activity that contributes to physical and overall wellness. As you become a regular runner, you will notice how far or how fast you must run to experience an endorphin rush.

---

[33] Dreyer, Danny. (2009). *ChiRunning: A Revolutionary Approach to Effortless, Injury-Free Running.* New York: Fireside Books.
[34] Romanov, Nicholas. (2014). *The Running Revolution: How to Run Faster, Farther, and Injury-Free—for Life.* New York: Penguin Books.

Take your time building your running program. You have the rest of your life to find the magic, and, once you do, you will want to reach a little further. Don't overdo it—in fact, don't overdo anything that I recommend. The journey is far more impactful and beneficial than the destination. Every step, of every training run, is just as significant to your wellness as the step you might one day take over the finish line of a marathon.

I once thought this was the most ridiculous thing I had ever heard. But I had to take it seriously, because it was said to me by my mindfulness teacher. After sitting with this thought, I came to believe he was correct. My running is no longer drudgery—every step is as good as the final step of the Boston Marathon; I know, because I have taken that step three times.

Breathing

The second positive attribute to running for wellness is breathing. Breathing is an instrumental part of wellness, and you will see it in nearly every cell of the honeycomb. Breathing is a focus activity for mindfulness, because it is an easy sensation to follow, and it occurs only in the present. When running, you will breathe more deeply and more rapidly than you normally do—this results in a higher concentration of oxygen in the blood and the brain. An oxygenated brain feels good and provides an overall feeling of wellness. Breathing also results in a more rapid transfer of waste products from the cells to the blood to the lungs and then to the universe.

When you become aware of your breathing, your mind focuses on the present. Your mind is removed from thoughts of the past and fears of the future. While running, you will often find yourself in the present, in the now, observing only your breath.

As a beginner, finding the present through breathing is sufficient. Gaining an ability to stay in the present for a matter of minutes while running will take practice, but getting there has tremendous benefits in a mindfulness practice. As your running improves and your mindfulness practice advances, you will learn to shift your awareness to other sensations, such as the springiness of your feet or the swing of your arms.

The repetitive nature of running provides endless opportunities to become aware of how your body moves, feels, and functions during the course of a long, slow run outside in the fresh air. Remember, awareness is the only objective, if you have a thought, notice it, let it go, without judgment, criticism, or condemnation. We are gaining wellness by moving the body and watching the mind. Running is a tool to get there.

Yoga

Yoga is an extremely useful activity that will aid you in watching your mind. Learning to watch the mind is a tremendous skill to have when building a clean and sober life.

Yoga has many definitions and translations. For us, it means to join, to connect, to become one. You might ask what are we joining or connecting to. Connecting "to all," I might answer. Some might focus on the mind-body-spirit connection; others might focus on a connection with all beings, some might focus on a connection with a higher power or the universe. Ultimately, we want to improve and enhance these connections, and these relationships.

Yoga is one more way to assist us in that objective, but it alone is not sufficient. None of these activities are enough on their own. As with most things, practice is the key. There is no destination; there is no time that you will say to yourself that you have arrived. The moment you get where you think you are going, you realize that there is a little farther you can go. There is always a little deeper, a little farther, a little more. The universe is infinite in time and space; there is no end to it; so travel as far as you might, there is always farther to go—more to learn, to see, and to "see."

Gate, Gate, Paragate, Parasamgate[35]

As with running, a significant part of the yoga practice is breathing. Breathing will always enable you to leave the past and the future and arrive exactly at the present. The present is the only place, time, and dimension, where you truly exist. You do not exist in the past; you do not exist ten seconds from now. You only exist in the present moment and at no other time. If you spend all your thoughts on your past or future, how can you ever come to know yourself? How can you get to know anyone, if you are never in the present where they coexist with you? Focus on your breathing, and it will bring you to "*the now*."

Although I mentioned that you are not your body, yoga will enable you to discover the connection between your mind and body. This

---

[35] Part of the Buddhism Heart Sutra that I interpret as, "Further, Further, Go a Little Further, Go Further Still."

sensation might take time to arise, or it might happen in your first practice. It might last for only a micro-second, or it might last for several seconds. Regardless of how long the sensation takes to arise or how long it lasts, once it does, you will recognize it when it happens.

For me, I get a physical sensation in my nervous system—from my brain—through my spinal cord—and then through my limbs—I actually feel or sense my nerves as cords that are signaling my body to move or balance in a manner consistent with the pose ordered by the mind. It is a wonderful sensation. After yoga, my entire physical body enjoys a low-level vibration, as my mind eases into a deep sense of energetic relaxation.

Physical wellness, for the purposes of this book, is developing and maintaining the body so that you can use it to positively affect the mind. The body is a wonderful tool for this purpose and when properly used can provide addicts and their loved ones with benefits that will help break the relapse cycle.

Mental Wellness

I have spent sufficient time describing the informal practice of mindfulness. Remember, I defined mindfulness as awareness, and that the purpose of awareness was to notice. As you practice informally, you will begin to recognize "how" your mind responds to stimuli, what thoughts recur, and how thoughts can grow in intensity, like a snowball rolling downhill. We notice, we acknowledge, we let go, without criticism or judgment, of the thoughts or ourselves.

Formal Practice

In addition to your informal mindfulness practice, I suggest you also begin a formal one. This should not seem scary, overwhelming, or as if you are being recruited to some weird cult. I am again only suggesting that you notice, in real time, what you are experiencing, thinking, and sensing. I ask that you sit up, with a straight spine, and breathe. Focus your mind on your breath, preferably at the point where the cool air enters your nose. Focus on that point of your nose and breathe normally in and out.

If you have difficulty focusing on your nose, try focusing on the rising and falling of your chest or belly. Breathe in, breathe out, rising, falling. Sit like this for five minutes, two to three times each day.

Informally, I discussed being aware of brushing your teeth, washing the dishes, and driving your car. I asked you to notice and focus on each sensation you have during these activities. If you have a thought, notice it, and let it go without criticism or judgment. Return your focus to the sensation.

Formal practice is the same idea. In this case, the activity is breathing. The sensation is either cool air passing your nose, or the rising and falling of your belly. Thoughts might enter your mind, and you will simply notice them. Let them go without judgment or criticism and return to focusing on the sensation of breathing. If you have difficulty with certain thoughts, it might help to acknowledge them by saying quietly, "Isn't that interesting?" Then let it go and return to the breath. Don't be concerned if your mind wanders; it will. *Noticing* that it wanders *is the practice* of mindfulness. *When you notice, you are doing it right!*

Beginners often ask, "Well, what is supposed to happen?"

The answer is simple. "Nothing." Right now, all you want to do during your practice sessions, whether formal or informal, is notice, let go, and return to your focus. We are practicing awareness. Our desire is to become more aware, more often, of the life within us and the life around us. As we become more aware, we can begin to make certain distinctions that eluded us previously. But to make distinctions, we must first become aware.

Presence

The formal and informal mindfulness practices will increase your awareness. They will also help you begin recognizing the present moment in contrast to the past moment and the future moment. When I first introduced mindfulness, I explained that you cannot live in the past or the future. There is nothing you *can do now* in the past or the future. The only instant in which you exist is right now.

As you practice awareness, you want to learn to accept that the past is lifeless; it does not exist. Likewise, the future is lifeless; it does not exist either. Only in your mind, by creating thoughts, can you generate guilt and regret about the past, or fear and anxiety about the future. To make matters worse, you dwell on the past and imagine the future in *the NOW!* If your attention is always distracted by thoughts of the past and future, when do you experience the life you are living in the present? You miss the present (your life) because your attention is on the past or future.

Mental wellness is pursued in the present moment. Well-living beings recognize that we live in a series of present moments, and it is on those that we should focus our attention. Breathing only happens in the present. Therefore, it serves as an excellent sensation to help us return to the present moment, to real life.

Differentiation

As awareness increases, you will begin to sense the differentiation between what you do and experience consciously and what you do and experience unconsciously. By unconsciously, I mean activities and experiences that occur without your full awareness, without your full attentions.

Common activities where you might be unconscious include standing in line, taking a shower, and participating in a casual conversation. The awareness you are developing is helping you become more conscious and attentive to what is happening in your present moment. You should strive to spend every moment while standing in line, taking a shower, or in a conversation, fully aware and fully present. Your mind is becoming more disciplined.

Your awareness is reducing the mind's opportunities to randomly ramble through the day about all your mistakes in the past and all your worries about the future. Differentiation between *consciously living with intent* and unconsciously going through the motions is an important skill to develop. One day, when your mind is creating an avalanche of negative thoughts, you will notice it immediately and stop it from dragging you into the pit of despair. Live with intent!

Consciousness

I just discussed consciousness as a form of awareness in the previous section. In this section, I will be a little more precise.

You sense or probe the outside world (outside of you) through five senses. In fact, a primary purpose of the body is to serve as a portal through which you have experiences. The world produces many phenomena and many of those we can experience through sight, sound, smells, tastes, and touches. We can experience these items only inside our minds and only after they are converted to electrical signals that our brains can process. All five senses behave in the same way—but I will walk through a hearing example.

Three things must happen for you to hear a sound. First, an energy wave in the audible human range must occur. Then, that energy must reach your ear, where your sense organ converts the energy wave into an electrical signal that is transmitted to your brain. Finally, your *hearing consciousness* must accept the electrical signal and process it into a thought.

Sight, smell, taste, and touch all work the same way. There is an external event that is captured by a sense organ. That organ converts the event into an electrical signal for the brain. Then the sense consciousness for that sense accepts the electrical transmission and creates a thought. It might be hard to accept, but everything that you experience only occurs within your mind as electrical pulses bouncing around inside your head. From this perspective, NOTHING exists outside your mind.

There are also thoughts that arise independently from any external stimulus. Many of these can be classified as thoughts about what has already occurred (memories) or thoughts about what might occur (dreams). But there are also thoughts that seemingly come from nowhere. Thoughts that aren't based on any personal experience or the experience of any other being. These creative thoughts are believed to arise from a shared "infinite intelligence"—from a source we can all tap into.

Dr. Wayne Dyer explains this concept as well as anyone in many of his books. The point is, humans walking on the Moon, voices traveling through the air across the country, electrically powered lights, and time travel all started as thoughts that happened to arise in the mind of a human. Where did these ideas originate? Why? The sixth form of consciousness is *thought consciousness*—the conscious recognition of thought.

Understanding the basic concepts of consciousness is an important steppingstone to developing mind wellness. As you practice awareness and contemplate your experiences, consider how or why a certain thought happened to arise. Did it start with one of the five senses? Did it arise from a memory or a dream? Is it a new creative thought with an unknown origin? Play with these ideas to discover what is true for you.

Ego/Self

This is one of the most complicated topics that I will cover. Covering it well in a few pages will be challenging, but this section is crucial in the long run. I hope this basic introduction will raise your curiosity to investigate these concepts further.

One of the most significant realizations that a person can develop is the truth about who he or she is. This is incredibly difficult for beginners to do and it takes a lot of practice. But to continue advancing in overall well-being and mental wellness, one must seek the truth.

Who are you?

You might have been practicing mindfulness for a few days. You have been watching your thoughts and letting them go. Let me ask three questions,

1. Who is it that is noticing your thoughts?

2. Who is it that is creating the thoughts that are noticed?

3. When you are thinking, in a language, who is speaking and who is listening?

For most people, there is a profound awareness that there is separateness between the entity that is creating thoughts and the one noticing them. Do you think that you, the true you, is the thought generator, or *the noticer*?

Most people respond as the noticer. Who or what then is the voice or the thought generator? We will refer to this voice as *the ego*.

The ego is an entity that has been fully created by you. You and your parents started building the ego from the moment you were born. The building and occasional remodeling have continued unabated throughout your entire life.

The ego is your personal brand, it is your image, and it is your identity. Brands have certain characteristics that help differentiate (separate) them from other brands. They project certain attributes that the world needs to understand when making choices. Brands develop reputations that must be lived up to. They must possess a certain quality, a certain value, and project a certain emotion or image.

The most defining characteristics of brands are timeless. They do not change. Brand management is always protecting the brand and maintaining the image. But you probably know—that the brand does not exist. It isn't real. It has no physical nature. A Mercedes is a car. A car exists—Mercedes does not. Levi's are pants; pants exist, Levi's do not.

When I say Chevy, you immediately have a certain idea. If I then mention Mercedes, you have a different idea. You will naturally begin to compare and contrast between Chevy and Mercedes. You might have driven neither, but you still form perceptions about Chevy and Mercedes. The same can be said about Marlboro, or Budweiser, or the Ivy League. Immediately when those brand names are mentioned, certain ideas enter your head, and often the ideas you have are the ones the brand managers want you to have.

In the case of you—*the ego* is the brand; it is what you identify with internally and what you project externally. Usually, your name is the brand name too. The ego is the brand that you created and manage for yourself. You project it; you defend and protect it. When you say the words—me, my, mine—it is the ego you are referring to. Any attack on your ego, you interpret as an attack on you. The problem is—like Mercedes, Chevy, and Levi's—except in your mind, the ego does not exist. It is an illusion.

Who were you when you were conceived? As you grew in your mother's womb, who were you? The week before you were born, who were you? You were a person, a human, you existed. Where is that person? What if you had been born in a different country with different parents? Would you be the same person you are now?

Even at the moment of birth, you were not "whatever your name is now." In fact, the first thing said about you was likely your gender. "It's a girl!" That was your first label. The first of millions of labels that you and others would put on you through the years. The healthcare staff then probably described you with weight, length, and general health indicator. You might not have had a name for a day or so. So, who were you before your name was stamped on a government certificate?

Previously, when I introduced myself to people, I would say, "I'm Bob Hobbs." And by saying Bob Hobbs, I was representing something. In fact, to me, it represented everything about me. Everything I had ever done. When I said my name, it was if my entire life history were instantly available for my new acquaintance to download. If you asked me, "Who are you?" or "Who is Bob Hobbs?" I would start with a personal and family profile. I would ensure that you knew I was the oldest of seven boys; I was the son of a Catholic steelworker, and I played football and went to college. You would get a full history to help you understand who I am. But now, I understand that what I have done, is not who I am. Bob Hobbs—is a series of sounds uttered . . . those sounds are not who I am. Today, I no longer introduce myself with, "I am Bob Hobbs." Today, I say "My name is Bob Hobbs."

The ego defines itself by everything you have done, and it will fight all efforts you put forth to discover the truth of who you are. The running conversation in your mind, *the voice*, regarding everything you should have done and everything you need to do is the ego. Left to its own, the ego will completely fill your mind with endless, contradictory conversations. It will never take responsibility for anything; it will blame you for everything; and then, because it is so wonderful, the ego will offer to bail you out of trouble one more time.

Another benefit of finding your way to the present is that the ego cannot exist there. The ego's power comes from your belief that it is protecting you from fear of the future and regret of the past. You do not need it in the present.

The ego, also known as "the self" in many teachings, creates rules about how it will live to maintain its brand image. It desires greatly to be respected and appreciated in the world, so it also creates rules about how the world operates. When the world operates by the ego's rules, the ego is happy. The problem is that the world the ego created does not exist, so when the ego's rules are not followed, the ego becomes upset.

Anxiety, worry, fear, anger, and defensiveness are common reactions to a world not behaving in accordance with the will of the ego. Excuses, such as "It's not fair; I don't deserve this; and I got screwed," are common initial reactions to a world that defies the ego's rules. All this is an illusion. The ego does not exist, and the world created by the ego does not exist.

My ego, like many, created a world where I could be decisively successful. I believed that good, hardworking people always got ahead. My ego let me know that I was well-above average in the good, hardworking department. I expected greatness to befall me. Even with minor setbacks, everything balances out for the better in the end. Eventually, I would get a fair deal, and I would get what I deserved.

As you would expect, I suffered many setbacks along the way, as the ego made excuses, modified the rules, and moved on blindly toward what we deserved and would eventually get. I considered some of the setbacks to be significant on a relative basis—major travesties. All of this was shattered when I held my son's blue body in my arms. It has taken almost three years to begin to understand what happened to me that day.

I try to explain to people that the ego I had that day was destroyed, in that moment. In many ways, I have been living a life without a full ego, in a world that requires I have one. For three years, I have had a hard time living in an adult world that requires a brand. Imagine trying to sell a car without a brand! I lost my brand—I am just a body.

I have often been lost, wondering what to do. Because I relied on my ego for everything, I continued to wonder. The good news is that I have had an opportunity to discover the possibilities of living a truer life—truer to me and truer to the universe in which I am an integral, inseparable part.

Your ego is telling you how to be happy according to its rules. You will spend most of your life doing the best you can to appease your ego and the egos of your loved ones. You will also be constantly reminded of how well you are performing relative to others. Mostly, it will compare your material possessions and professional accomplishments to others and then make you feel guilty for not living up to your potential.

In the most insane mind game, the ego will blame you for not living up to your obligations under its world order. It will make you angry at a world that does not follow its rules, and it will make you guilty for failing. Then, like a superhero, it will offer to swoop in and solve all your problems. Many people go through life never discovering that the ego is an illusion. If you are reading this, you have a chance to break from this madness. It is only through awareness and noticing, that you will find how.

Mental wellness requires that you investigate who you truly are. Learn to identify when the ego is working in you and on you. Work to develop the ability to draw a distinction between the ego and your true being.

Most suffering arises when you experience a loss of things that you are attached to. Things can be material items or the desire to have those items, relationships, thoughts, identities, beliefs, or values. Loss does not just mean having something and losing it; it can also mean desiring something and not obtaining it.

Humans also suffer excessively due to their attachment to the "self." The idea that this separate existence is going to one day die causes most people significant fear and anxiety throughout the course of their lifetimes. Death is an area to explore as you gain experience.

Keep in mind that your death is a certainty. The time of your dying is not certain—it could come at any time. At the time of your death, nothing you have, and no one you know, will be able to prevent your passing. You did not give your consent when you entered this world— you had no choice in the matter. You will leave under the same conditions—without your consent, and probably at a time not of your choosing. This is such an important part of your humanity that you ought to consider it; you ought to bravely discover from within, as much as you can about this inevitability. As you accept death for what it is, much anxiety will dissolve.

When you suffer, it is not the absence of a thing that causes you pain. You have lived up until now without that thing. It is the attachment to the thing that causes your suffering. The clinging to the idea of having it, the strong desire of possessing it, left unsatisfied is what causes your suffering.

An oversimplification can help explain this concept. All you need is food, shelter, and clothing. If you have these three basics, there is no need to suffer. But when your shelter is only 1,500 square feet, and all your friends have 3,000 square feet, the ego might begin to work on you.

You deserve at least 3,000 square feet. You might start driving through neighborhoods, looking at brochures, and talking to real estate agents. Each step you take increases the desire to have what you deserve. You become attached to the idea of living in a bigger shelter. But, for some reason, it is just not possible now. Your attachment, to the idea of the larger space, becomes so strong that it causes you some degree of suffering—a feeling of lack, a feeling of unfairness, or a feeling of envy. You might even become so completely consumed by the idea of getting the bigger place that your obsession begins to affect your loved ones. Are you really suffering? In the real world, are you in danger? Of course not. It is not the object that you have, nor the object that you desire that is causing your pain; it is your attachment that is causing it.

You might also become attached to certain ideas that demonstrate your success—to you and others. A bigger house, a faster car, plastic surgery, fancy schools, country club memberships, power, influence, are all items you might pursue to measure and show your level of success. You become attached to the idea that if you do not get these items, then you are not successful, and if you are not successful, you cannot be happy. Does the absence of these items cause any pain or distress? No! Your suffering is due to your attachment to these items, not the items themselves.

When you start to accumulate things, you need to maintain them. You begin investing time in taking care of things that you already spent time acquiring. One of my teachers talks about shoes. He reminds us that shoes were made to serve us and to protect our feet as we walk on rough terrain. We only have two feet, yet some of us have 100 pairs of shoes.

Some of these shoes we might only wear once per year, yet we remain attached to each pair, as if we have some special relationship with them. We take care of our shoes, we clean and polish them. Who is serving whom here? As we accumulate more shoes, we decide we need a shelf to properly store our shoes, so we buy or build a shelf, a shoe shrine, if you will.

Our spouse or partner might not feel any urgency to provide a shelf for shoes, so the project is delayed. We become frustrated and maybe even angry, because our loved one is not getting a shelf for our shoes. We have a fight, and it turns into a painful argument about the shelf. The shelf for 100 pairs of cleaned, polished shoes, that we wear once per year, to protect our feet from the rough ground. Why are we suffering here? Why is our spouse/partner suffering? Who serves whom, when we have attachments?

Me, my, mine. Any sentence that contains any of these three words is sure to be followed with something you are particularly attached to. Be aware when you use these words and consider the level of attachment that you have to whatever you refer to.

Suffering can be substantially reduced when we begin to recognize our attachments and what they truly are. As you become aware of things you are attached to, pick one or two, and try to eliminate the excess items from your life after contemplating what it truly is to you. Eventually, continue to eliminate items that have captured your desire for no particular purpose. Practice this so that you can eventually free yourself from attachment and from the suffering that it brings.

Your Will

The culmination of all that you want in life is in totality your will— the will for your life. When you make decisions about how you are going to spend your days in pursuit of your objectives, you are executing your will. In the last few sections, I have introduced concepts such as unconsciousness, ego, and attachment. These items, left untamed, are creating a "will" for you based on illusion. As you practice awareness and other suggestions offered in this chapter, you will discover a pull, tug, or call that draws you toward something different. This draw is not coming from the voice of the ego; you might not recognize its source.

You have a specific purpose for being. You are here for a reason, not of your making. The true meaning of your nature can be manifested, as you come to know and strive to fulfill your true purpose.

Meaning and purpose are spiritual concepts that we will leave for the next section on wellness. I will close this subsection with the idea that you will find peace, once you align your will with your higher power's will.[36]

Education/Knowledge/Learning/Discovery

You should keep your mind's attention on growth. Today, there are so many ways to become educated; it is amazing. YouTube alone has enough hours of academic instruction that it could become a university. There are books, online courses, live seminars, community colleges, and spiritual centers available like never before. There is no excuse for rational people to avoid an education.

But, I acknowledge that there are far too many distractions in the world of today. Heroin and other mind-altering substances are a distraction. There are social media, more than 400 TV channels, multiple movie and streaming outlets, video games, and so much more. All these activities distract us from becoming our best selves. Every one of them feeds the ego, promotes attachment, and enables complete surrender to unconscious living. It is far easier in the short-term to be mindless, distracted, and unaware. We enjoy not having to do anything. We enjoy living in an illusion. We will never find what we are looking for in any of these distractions, and as life continues, we become less satisfied.

---

[36] See next section on Spiritual Wellness.

The ego loves that you are willing to surrender your life to its need of power. If no one watches the hen house, the fox will steal the hen. Make an effort to avoid distraction. Instead, be aware; be mindful.

Spiritual Wellness

This book is focused on helping those of you who have a heroin addict in your life learn to live well, regardless of what the addict chooses to do. It also offers suggestions that will assist you in helping your addict in recovery. It describes a relapse-recovery lifecycle that both the addict and you live in and eventually become trapped in. Many times, both of you feel imprisoned, and it seems there is no way out. The addict cannot escape the snares of heroin, you cannot escape the fear, anxiety, guilt, and regret associated with witnessing the addict's demise. The addict follows heroin; you follow the addict. Both are sick and require long-term recovery options. You must find a way to break out of the cycle—regardless of the addict's behavior. Hopefully, the addict finds a way to break away from the madness of heroin addiction.

Everything offered here can be utilized by both you and the addict. Finding a way to live well is the essence of our human journey, and discovering the true path to what we desire is living-well. Living-well means wellness, which as I have discussed means the joyful pursuit of joy and the happy pursuit of happiness. It means reducing suffering— with the implication that joy, peace, happiness, and serenity are always present when suffering is not.

In almost all cases, the cornerstone of recovery is the twelve-step program developed by Alcoholics Anonymous in the 1930s. You will likely find that the principles of AA are integral to the rehab and IOP phases of treatment. It is expected, following treatment, that the addict will be fully immersed in an AA program, as this will serve as the basis of recovery going forward. The wellness program that we are offering here is not a replacement or substitute for AA. It is meant to provide you and the addict with a way of living that builds on wellness, so that relapse becomes less likely.

Al-Anon is also a twelve-step program, designed by the loved ones of Alcoholics Anonymous in the 1950s. From my point of view, it has two great features that will assist you. First, the fellowship of the program is going to help you understand your role in the addict's addiction, and help you recover from the misery you are living in. Second, the program closely mirrors what your addict is doing in AA, so you will develop a common understanding of what he is doing in recovery.

From here on out, when I mention AA, assume I mean both Alcoholics Anonymous and Al-Anon.

AA is the cornerstone of recovery. You will learn that AA is a spiritual program and that recovery depends on a spiritual experience. Many people struggle with the idea of spirituality, or a higher power, or God. People who have lived through the hell of addiction find it particularly hard to depend on a higher power to save them, as many believe that the higher power let them down. If you struggle with spirituality, I urge you to approach AA with an open mind and heart. Be patient; you don't have to adopt anything. You only need to notice.

A big reason so many people are "put-off" by spiritual concepts is because they confuse them with religious ideas. Those of us raised in a Western culture have been trained to believe that God is a bearded, robed, human-looking, old man walking on the clouds above Earth. He loves us completely until we mess up—then he becomes angry and threatens eternal damnation.

Many are taught that the path to everlasting peace is suffering here as humans. Most of the religious rules we follow were developed throughout the centuries by men. Usually, these men were more interested in money and power than our personal salvation. Religion has given many of us a slighted view. We must believe what religions tell us, or else we will burn forever. We learn to fear, rather than to love.

Spiritual living does not require any understanding of religion. It does not have rules, priests/elders, buildings, or ancient books.

Spirituality is something completely found within you. All you need to know is already inside you, waiting to be discovered. With this in mind, I again urge you to let go of all your fears and perceptions and seek the truth for yourself.

By the time an addict reaches recovery, he is prepared and willing to do anything, but when the spiritual "God thing" is introduced, he might back off, confusing it with his ideas about religion.[37]

The problem with this reaction is that it is based on our perceptions of God and our perceptions of ourselves, as formed in our minds through the teachings and traditions of institutions run by other humans. Rarely are these reactions based on who we truly are, or what we individually have found within ourselves.

Spirituality is not based on the teaching of any institution. Spirituality is a personal exploration of what is true about you. Through that exploration, the discovery of God, the universe, the Tao, or a higher power is inescapable. I believe you will find that God is not an old man in the clouds waiting to punish you for all eternity. Rather, God is love, life, light, and cannot be found outside you. God can only be found within. If you contemplate this, you might come to recognize that everything you perceive is within.

For now, let's just assume that spirituality is not religion. Humans can discover a higher power without religious institutions.

Before I describe my personal perceptions of God, please consider *who you are*. Try not to consider your name, your personal or family history, or your experiences. I think, in the end, you will find that you are not any of those things, and they cannot describe the essence of your being. Perhaps you can begin to accurately describe yourself or maybe you can't. It's ok if you can't; it is just something to explore and discover. You can begin the discovery process by experiencing the present. Only in the present—when your ego is absent—will you begin to identify with who you truly are. You already know, the only place where you can find *who you are* is in the present, because you do not exist anywhere else.

It is important when entering a discussion about the universe or higher power or God that you have an acceptance of the idea that only

---

[37] Note: When I refer to "God" in this book, I am intending to be inclusive of all thoughts of the universe, a higher power, or however the reader chooses to identify that concept.

your true being can know this concept. Only your true being can know you. Your ego cannot know any truth, because the truth will destroy it.

The eleventh step of Alcoholics Anonymous states these words:

> *Sought through prayer and meditation to improve*
> *our conscious contact with God as we understood*
> *Him, praying only for knowledge of His will for us*
> *and the power to carry that out.*

"Prayer and meditation" are the paths to close "conscious contact." Conscious means contact without your ego—not through your ego— directly into the consciousness of your being. "As we understood Him" allows for your understanding or comprehension to change and evolve.

It's obvious that as you better know *who you are* and better know *who God is,* your understanding will change. You cannot expect to hold to old ideas of the universe as your awareness expands. Don't fight ideas that are introduced to you during meditation. All ideas are valid for investigation. They are leading you somewhere. Sit and explore your ideas.

Exploring "His will for us" is how you will discover your purpose for being, the meaning of your life, or your reason for being here. God gave us free will—we can follow the will of the ego, if we choose, but when we do, we often end up unhappy and dissatisfied. We continue to wonder what we must do to find peace and joy and happiness. I challenge you to find *God's will for you* and to align your will with what you find. When you do, you'll find your life drastically changes for the better.

Who Is God?

1. I cannot tell you who God is. No one can. Even if I knew God, I could not describe God in any language. No language is big enough, no name is descriptive enough, to describe to a finite human mind the infinite majesty, the eternal essence, of God.

2. In my few spiritual experiences, where I have experienced God's presence, as soon as I recognized God's presence, it was gone from my awareness. Not because God left, but because I tried to grasp the idea of God in my mind or soul.

3. God is everywhere, and God is nowhere; God is in everything and in nothing. God is infinite love, infinite light, and infinite

intelligence. Humans do not have the capacity to fully grasp the truth of God. Much of God's existence is a mystery as we cannot grasp infinity.

4. In my investigation, I have come to believe that God is an infinite being. *All being* is encompassed by God. God is comprised of *all being*. *All being* is comprised of God. God is infinite. *All being* is infinite. If God is an infinite being, then *all being* is part of the infinite being. Like waves are part of the ocean, they are waves, and they are ocean, at the same time. A bucket of ocean water is still ocean, and the ocean is still ocean. All beings are part of *all being*. *All being* is part of all beings. *All being* arose from nonbeing at the same time, in the same place, from the same stuff. This idea might be difficult to grasp, and it is unique, but as I consider it more deeply, it makes sense.

5. We desire relationships, because we desire communion. We desire communion, because the essence of *who we are* wishes to be rejoined. If our egos didn't stand in the way, all beings would become one with all being. There would be no perceived separation.

6. God is always with you, and you are always with God. Your sense of isolation and separation is caused by the ego's desire to be in charge and in control.

7. God does not need to forgive, because God does not recognize imperfection. God's creation is perfect, as God is perfect. The ego was created by you—not by God. Acts of the ego are not known to God, for God only knows the true you, the you God created, the you that is divine, as God is divine.

8. God is loving and only loving. God does not punish. God will not harm you any more than dog lovers would harm their dogs. The dog is just being a dog. It might make a mess of a great many things, but it is just being a dog. The dog lover only sees the dog being a dog, doing what dogs do. A dog lover would not punish a dog for being a dog. The dog lover is patient, loving, and enjoys the dog as it is. God only sees you being you. God would never punish you for being what you are, because God is patient, loving, and enjoys you as you are.

9. God cannot connect to your ego. God does not know your ego. Perhaps your soul is your divine nature. Maybe your spirit is the

"you" whom God can speak to. Perhaps your soul is a place; a sacred room where you can meet God.

10. Your spirit dwells in the soul, and perhaps the Holy Spirit does also. The Holy Spirit communicates with you and your ego in helping to guide you back to where you came from. Some people pray to the Holy Spirit or this inner guide for guidance about how to behave in various situations. Coming to the now and reaching out to your inner guide is almost always a spiritual experience.

11. Your true nature is one with God and one with all. When you're calm, and manage to quiet the ego, you will hear your true nature calling, reaching out. You might not recognize it for what it is, but it is your spiritual self. Often when I sense mine, I get goosebumps. It is an awesome feeling to connect to the universe in this way. For me, bliss would be finding a way to stay connected after noticing that I was connected.

12. The ego stands between you and your truth. Some believe that the Jewish idea of original sin was Adam's creation of his ego, his perception of his body and identity separated him from God. Through the generations, humans have forgotten their origin, their inheritance, and their true nature. They have come to believe that each person is separate, as the body is separate. Their sense of loneliness, their fear, and their isolation will arise from this illusion of separation. Enlightened teachers, such as Buddha and Jesus, disposed of the ego. They became awake to their truth, enlightened to their nature. Each of us must strive individually to find truth about ourselves.

13. In AA, there is a teaching about fear. It states that fear is what happens when we take control of our lives away from God, when we place ourselves in God's place, as the ruler of our universe. By giving your life and will to the care of God, you begin the process of replacing your fear with love. Regularly, we should state that we choose love instead of fear. If only to remind ourselves of our truth.

I have had almost mystical experiences where I was communicated with via a mechanism other than a voice. Meaning, I was told what to do or shown what was happening in a form other than language. I believe that those communications, those nonverbal, short duration, but extremely vivid and detailed messages were direct communications from God. Had I listened to the ego on the morning of my son's overdose, I would have gone to work and my thirteen-year-old daughter would have found her dead brother in the bathroom after school. But God intervened, without speaking a word, and sent me up those stairs into that bathroom. Why? What was the purpose of that intervention?

It is one of two reasons. One, God wanted me to suffer from the memories of that morning for the rest of my life. Two, God wanted to transform my life from one of chasing material items to one of saving lives. I saved my son's life that day. I helped save another life two years later, when I worked with my roommate's nephew, and now I am writing this book with the expressed intention of helping to save more addicts and, equally as important, the lives of parents struggling with what to do.

God's Will

God's will. Until February 25, 2014, I had no idea what God wanted me to do. I asked nonchalantly, almost insincerely, for God to just tell me what to do, so that I could be happy. Truth be told, I didn't really want the answer, because I would have to "give something up." Maybe God told me, and I wasn't listening, or maybe I wasn't ready.

During the past three years, God transformed me. I am still trying to accept and get used to the new me. By writing this book, I am aligning my will with God's will. I cannot tell you the results yet. I still don't know, but if one life is saved or made better by this effort, then that life might go on to do something amazing for God and people.

I just got goosebumps, and as soon as I acknowledged them, they were gone.

Relationships (Love) Wellness

If your ability to love or be loved is not well, then you are not going to be well. You don't know where your spirit is. You don't know where your soul is or where your mind is. But we refer to them as if they are physical entities. I have jokingly asked every doctor I have ever met if they ever found the soul or mind when dissecting a cadaver in medical school. They smile, and, of course, say no.

When it comes to emotions, we refer to our heart as the store of our feelings. Like the soul and the mind, it is an imaginary heart. Sometimes we point to our actual, beating heart when referring to our emotional heart, but they are not the same. When we lose a love interest, we say we have a broken heart, and when we fully love another person, we say we have a full heart. Obviously, we are not referring to our cardiovascular heart, but the heart of our emotions, the heart we share with other beings.

It is this heart I will use in this discussion.

Relationship wellness and well-being is a measure of our heart's ability to give and receive love. When we open our hearts to others, we are open to receiving their love and returning our love to them. When our hearts are closed, we can neither give nor receive love.

Usually, when we live with an open heart, we are experiencing mostly positive emotions all the time. However, when we open our hearts to others, we become vulnerable. Our vulnerability exposes us to harm that can be inflicted by our life situation or the life situation of someone we love. Sometimes the experience becomes so painful, *that our heart breaks*. When we hold on tightly to the feelings experienced in the past, in an effort to recapture the good times, we might close our hearts. Temporarily closing your heart assists in the healing process of a broken heart, but prolonged mourning results in loss of wellness and a susceptibility to attack. This is because when love is absent, fear takes charge.

Optimization of our relationship wellness requires that we maximize the time that our heart is open to receive and return love, while minimizing the time that we close our hearts to others. Our hearts usually close after they have been hurt, damaged, or broken. These conditions are caused by the vulnerability we have when we live with open hearts. When we become hurt and close our heart due to emotional pain, we are cutting off the infinite source of healing, which is the infinite source of love.

We must learn and practice loving all beings unconditionally. See Appendices 2, 4, 5, and 6 for additional information about relationships with family members, friends, neighbors, colleagues, and others.

Why Love All?

All being arose from nonbeing. All being—regardless of your interpretation of creation—originated from nonbeing, and was once joined as one single being. In fact, all being is still joined as a single being, but the egos we each created coupled with our identification of self, and with our bodies, have caused the illusion of separation. We behave contrary to our own interests and the interests of the whole, as if we are each separate, fully independent bodies, all traveling to a destination of our choosing.

To minimize closed hearts, we must maximize our time in *the now*, where the ego ceases to influence us. When in *the now*, we find it much easier to love unconditionally, regardless of other's faults, because the ego cannot judge when absent.

We must strive to become aware and to notice all beings, known and unknown, as divine members of the divine whole. We must strive to see past their egos and into the essence of their beings. What we find there is pure beauty, pure light, and pure love. God is love; we are love. We long to be reunited as one being, as one love. The ego is the barrier. Love and light dissolve the ego, and, despite its resistance, it cannot exist in the light.

The ego is not going to be eliminated immediately, not for most of us anyway. So, in the meantime, how do we make progress toward unconditional love? Well, first we need to work in *the now* as much as possible. When not present, we need to be aware of how the ego is influencing our loving nature.

We need to recognize the true nature of whom we are and who others are. With that recognition, we should develop certain habits or philosophies about how we will treat others, so when the ego begins to confuse us, we can fall back on a habit to guide us through troubled times.

In *The Five Love Languages*, the author[38] says every ego (he says person, but he is referring to ego), requires love in five forms.

---

[38] Chapman, Gary. (2015). *The Five Love Languages: The Secret to Love that Lasts*. Chicago: Northfield Publishing.

Uniquely, every person requires more love from one form than from the other four forms. The love we give and receive should be balanced, but we should be aware of what type of love is best received by those we care about. In moments of turmoil, it is likely our loved ones will respond more positively to their primary love language, than to any of the others. There are free tests online where you can have fun learning about yourself and your loved ones. Find out what they respond to best, and learn to use it to show your love and affection as much as possible.

A good example of applying *The Five Love Languages* is the following: Suppose a woman's primary love language is "acts of service" (#4). When her husband is trying to ask for forgiveness, he might try to *give gifts,* which is a noble effort on his part. However, because the woman prefers acts of service, his buying gifts is an inefficient way to show his love. He would be better suited making dinner, rather than giving gifts.

Sometimes the husband might be disappointed because his wife does not respond as excitedly toward his gifts as he had hoped. Had he known that simply making dinner is all that was required, he could have saved time and effort and gotten better results.

Another popular set of strategies was developed by Dr. Stephen Covey. In his book, *The Seven Habits of Highly Effective People,*[39] several habits speak directly to better relationships and how they can help you become more effective.

Covey also introduced the idea of an emotional bank account. In this metaphor, he described that there is an emotional bank account for each person in every relationship. Like a real bank account, you make deposits into and withdrawals from your account held by the other person, and you hold an account that the other person deposits to and withdraws from. Covey suggested that people should never overdraw their accounts, in fact, everyone should constantly make deposits. Deposits are simple—kind words and kind deeds. Withdrawals are unkind words and unkind deeds. If people maintained positive balances in their accounts, their relationships would be awesome, and seldom a source of pain, or lack of wellness.

Covey's third habit is "put first things first." It is usually thought of as a productivity management strategy. But I view it as a primary

---

[39] Covey, Stephen R. (1989). *The Seven Habits of Highly Effective People: Powerful Lessons in Personal Change.* New York: Simon and Schuster.

relationship builder. What are first things? Hopefully, not your job! Likely, they are people and relationships: God, spouse, partner, kids, relatives, friends, community, etc. The idea of *putting first things first* is that you schedule your life around the most important things, and then you add other things. Too often, we schedule what is urgent first, and rarely is that a relationship, well, not until the end of the relationship anyway.

Covey's fourth habit is "think win-win." He describes that in any relationship when there is a task, negotiation, or argument, we too often think that we must win, without realizing that if there is a winner in the traditional sense, there is also a loser. Do you want to be in a relationship with a loser? Nobody does. In romantic relationships, I have learned that every situation will end in either win-win or lose-lose. Win-lose and lose-win do not exist, because when our partners lose, eventually we lose too. You cannot win if there is a loser. So, do not ever pursue that outcome. Find a way where everyone wins, or don't start the confrontation. Win-win or go home.

My favorite Covey habit is number five: "seek first to understand, then to be understood." This is empathy, where we become fully present while listening to another. It is refusing to respond until we fully understand what the other is trying to communicate. Then, we enter the gap between stimulus and response. We wait and exercise integrity in the moment of choice, and then we respond empathetically and respectfully.

Additional Relationship Wellness Tips

1. Put people first. Don't try to squeeze your relationships into your schedule. If they don't come first, you are doing something wrong. Always have relationships with other winners. This means you are a winner too. No one can be a loser in winning relationships. Always seek win-win outcomes to all problems and disagreements.
2. Respect the other person's opinion. Be empathetic. Listen and think, before offering your thoughts and ideas. Whenever possible, use the other person's ideas to solve problems and give them the credit. You are in this for the love and support of the relationship, not for the credit of solving problems. Keep in mind your ego will tell you otherwise.

3. Give your time and effort to those who are younger or less experienced than you. Always seek opportunities to develop another human toward their maximum potential. Coaching and mentoring in the community is a common practice, but at work, there are younger people who need mentorship as they grow in their careers. Never withhold your help to those who can benefit from it. Give of yourself; you will be rewarded.

4. Never *lend* money to loved ones. If someone needs financial support, and you can help, then *give* without an expectation of return. Too many relationships are destroyed over money. There is no need to fight about who owes who what. You'll find that once the borrower is back on his feet, he will repay you. Somehow, he will repay you, and it might be something you need more than money. Love comes to mind.

5. Don't hold grudges and grievances in your heart. Forgive all, daily, including yourself. Never let your ego be the judge of good and bad. It is almost always wrong, mainly because of the poor assumptions it makes. Forgive all, including debts. Even if you feel taken advantage of, be glad you have the means to be taken advantage of. Forgive.

6. Choose to be kind and loving, rather than right, especially in social media if you use it. Buddha spent forty years teaching his message face-to-face, and not everyone got it. Jesus spent three years teaching, and even his apostles doubted him. Don't expect people to change to your point of view because you put a clever post online. They won't. Be kind. Forget being right. Being right only matters to the ego. Being loved, being kind, and receiving love and kindness are far more rewarding than winning an argument.

7. Be present. Strive to be present with people you enjoy. If your mind wanders, simply notice and look your friend in the eye to look for her true nature while in the present moment. Fight the urge to plan how you are going to respond to her comment. Your answers will come naturally when you are in the now. They will be far more meaningful than anything the ego can produce.

8. Drop your anger and resentment at the beginning and end of each day. They harm only you, no one else. Too often we think that we harm the person we are angry at, but not necessarily so. What is

true is we harm ourselves when we are angry. Let it go, twice each day.

9. When you feel anger rising, take a breath and *let it go*. Before you say a word or make a body gesture, breathe and release. Road rage is a great example. When you get cutoff in traffic, do you get angry? Do you cuss the person? Flip him off? Do you try to position yourself to prevent him from doing it again? Do you think he cares if you are mad? He has probably been driving like that for miles today. He doesn't care if you're mad. He is probably glad he can piss you off so easily. Your anger in road rage is only felt by you. Unfortunately, everyone with you in the vehicle is affected by your emotional change. There is no point to it. Breathe and let it go. If this is difficult for you, consider that the person might be rushing to the hospital, or maybe his mom or dad is dying, and he is trying to get there to say goodbye. There might be a valid reason for his driving. Regardless, we are always better off if we make way and let him go.

10. Meditate on the idea that all beings came from nonbeing. Consider that we all originated from the exact same place and the exact same stuff at the exact same time as everyone else. We are part of the universe that is ever-expanding and, as waves move on the ocean, we move with the universe. We are not separate from the universe. Wherever we are going, we are all going together. We are all one. We are all a holy part of the universe. We are joined, connected, and divine.

11. Love without condition. You can only receive love, if you give it away. Why enforce conditions, formed by the ego, when someone deserves your love? In doing so, you put conditions on the love you receive. Keep an open heart, recognize the divinity in all. Embrace the idea that everyone is struggling to shine through the cloudiness cast by the ego. Don't be impatient with them. Love them and encourage them to continue to find light in themselves and in others.

12. Meditate regularly with lovingkindness, compassion, and sympathetic joy. Sit quietly and accept the love cast on you by your loved ones and by the universe. Feel it shine on you and then cast it back onto those you love and into the universe. Cast your lovingkindness, compassion, and sympathetic joy on all beings,

including your enemies, strangers, acquaintances, and 7.5 billion humans on this planet. Give compassion to those suffering—feel their pain. Take some of their suffering upon yourself, as you get stronger at meditating. Celebrate the success of others—especially those in your life you envy, especially your enemies and people who got the fortunate breaks that you seemed to miss. Celebrate with sympathetic joy the good fortune of all.

13. Always give. Seek opportunities to give the most intimate and vulnerable pieces of yourself—the parts the ego tries to hide from the world. What the ego tries to conceal is likely what you are meant to reveal. It is likely that it is the real you behind the curtain of the ego. Give—trusting that it will all come back to you, multiple times.

Everyone Has an Ego—Two People, Four Egos

I encourage you to investigate what the ego is and how it affects you and your relationships, both from your point of view, and from the point of view of others. For now, let us assume that your ego is *your perception of who you are.* Let's also assume that everybody has an ego.

A person you are developing a relationship with has an ego, or a perception of who they are. Their ego has certain rules about how the world *should operate*, and how other people should function *in that world.*

When you meet a person, your ego begins to build an image or identity of him or her. It tries to identify how the other person will behave in certain circumstances. Initially, your ego wants to ensure that your personal safety is not at risk when you are with your new acquaintance. Rapidly, your ego creates a profile, an identity, and a perception that best fits the other person. As long as you are in a relationship, your ego is continually refining its perception of the other person.

Your ego expects the other person to abide by rules it has associated with the perception it created. Your ego is almost always upset when the other person does not behave by those rules. In your mind, your relationship's success is dependent on how well your ego gets along with the mental picture it has created for the other person.

The other person does the same thing. She has a perceived identity of herself—her ego. When she meets you, she begins creating a perception of you—her idea of your ego. In her mind, the success of your relationship is based on how well her ego and the perception she created for you get along with each other (Figure 15).

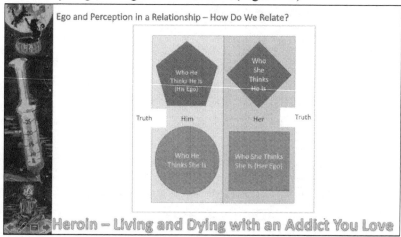

Figure 15: Ego and Perception in a Relationship.

Think about this! There are two humans trying to develop a social relationship. Each person has created a perception of themselves—two egos—and a perception of the other person, effectively two more egos.

When your friend is having an argument with you, it is not you or your ego she's arguing with. Her ego is arguing with her perception of you. When she gets upset, it's not because you don't behave properly or consistently with your values and beliefs, but because the perception she created for you is not behaving the way she believes it should. Her mind has created rules that her perception of you is supposed to follow.

In every relationship between two people, there are four egos involved. Not one of them is real. Let's look at a conversation.

When you speak to your friend, your ego, your perception of yourself, is speaking to your perception of your friend.

When she hears you, she hears her perception of you speaking to her ego, the perception she has of herself.

Your ego is never known to her. Her ego is never known to you. Both egos are illusions. Is it any wonder we have so much difficulty finding true and unconditional love? The fact that we do not know who we truly are makes getting to know the truth of another human impossible.

Can you accept the idea that your ego is an illusion that you created? Can you accept the idea that your perception of another person is also an illusion? In other words, it's an interpretation of who you think they are, but not who they truly are. Can you accept the idea that you don't know yourself and you don't know them, and the reverse is also true? If so, shouldn't we always give each other the benefit of the doubt?

Think about it. Why argue with a person you don't know? Why argue as a person you don't know? There are strong odds that you are incorrect in your evaluation of the other person and his or her motives. You are only guessing, perceiving, and assuming. More important, remember, you—the true you—did not create the perception of the other person—your ego did. The ego only serves itself—so how could you ever trust it to accurately evaluate another person?

The fact is that the ego will set up a perception of every person it meets, so that it (and you) has an advantage or an excuse. The ego will not lose—and neither will the other person's ego. Relationships are weird! Give everyone the benefit of the doubt; learn to love unconditionally, because any conditions you might place on another ego are almost guaranteed to be false. Other people are divinely created beings, just like you, from the same stuff, the same place, and the same time. They are you—you are them—all are joined as one with the universe.

The key to relationships is your ability to give and receive love. Anything that stands in the way of this must be minimized and eliminated. It is up to us to learn how to live in such a way that we can love in every possible condition—to give and receive love unconditionally.

Immunity and Defense Wellness

As hard as you work on building wellness, there are forces acting on you to tear it down. This is not a conspiracy theory. There is no evil genius plotting your demise. Rather, it's just the nature of life. You cannot control the weather or the climate where you live, but you do have influence over many of the inputs affecting your being.

Poisons, toxins, and Trojan horses (something trying to secretly undermine you) can usually only be introduced to your mind-body-spirit complex with your consent. If you're living in an unconscious state, you might not appreciate that you have control over the external influences entering and attacking your wellness.

This section is about defending your wellness from attacks. Your best defenses are awareness and intent. You must be aware of the forms the attackers take as they attempt to weaken and destroy your wellness. As you notice attackers, you must have a strong intent to repel them, and then strengthen that part of your system where the enemy attacked you, presumably because it was weak.

You must defend the vulnerable areas of your wellness in the three areas of mind, body, and spirit. Each of the three areas has common attackers and common offenses. Naturally, each area has specific strengths and weaknesses that need to be considered. Before I cover the specifics of each area, here is a general idea of the most common attacks.

The mind, body, and spirit are all susceptible to weakness and attack. Weakness comes from the following four common sources:

- Stress and tension
- Exhaustion
- Separation (via *compare and contrast* with others or your ego)
- Lethargy and indifference

The four primary attacks on your wellness are:

- Too much (overindulgence)
- Too little (self-denial)
- Toxic inputs
- Temptation

There are also five basic defense mechanisms that the mind, body, and spirit share. These all require intent from you, so that they can be strengthened or implemented in defense of your wellness.

- Awareness
- Discipline
- Consistent practice (habits)
- Rest
- Sandbags

Four Common Sources that Weaken Your Immunity

There are four sources that weaken your wellness immunity to attack: stress and tension, exhaustion, separation, and lethargy and indifference.

Stress and Tension

Yes. This is the same stress and tension that you talk about with colleagues. It is the stress you hear about on television commercials, and the tension you might discuss with your family doctor. This is the stress and tension that is a known killer and a known destroyer of well-being. Too often, Americans have become used to the idea that stress and tension are normal parts of our lives. We accept them as a part of who we are. My friend, this is an absolute lie. It is a fallacy. I don't know how it started, or exactly why so many have bought into it, but you are not intended to live a life of stress and tension.

I can tell you with all certainty, that it is not the *true you* who accepts stress and tension as normal. It is the ego. Your ego has accepted this deadly way of life, because it is easily influenced by the egos of others, while pursuing sources of happiness that ultimately provide only discouragement. For many reading this book, we try to alleviate our stress and tension with drugs and alcohol. What we are doing is insane—we accept more stress and tension, followed by discouragement, and then we cover it up with mind-altering substances, so that we can accept more stress and tension. Isn't the ultimate outcome obvious?

Stress and tension will weaken your wellness. It will deter your intent to stay well and distract your awareness. You must become aware of what sources of stress and tension are common internally and externally and then mindfully work to reduce those sources from your life.

Exhaustion

It is natural to be tired. And it is natural to rest and relax when we become tired. It is unnatural to become tired to the point of exhaustion. In this, I mean chronically tired. Tired all the time. Again, our culture demands, for the sake of our ego, that we work and play ourselves to the point of having nothing left. Because we are chasing our ego's goals and objectives, and because all the other egos around us encourage us to do so, we are all too willing to drive ourselves to complete and total exhaustion.

When we become chronically tired, we lose our ability to focus and concentrate. Our awareness dims and our will to intentionally notice weakness in our ability to remain well is diminished. Living in a state of exhaustion increases the probability of error. Many of these errors can be fatal. Obviously, driving and doing other activities that require quick reaction time are more dangerous when we're exhausted.

All our defenses are lowered when we are not rested. The likelihood of giving in to temptation is higher. The probability of becoming unconscious is greater. Spending too much time here will result in lower overall wellness and the potential for successful attacks against you.

Separation

There are always situations where you might fall victim to separation when you compare or contrast your situation with that others. Every single time you do, you give the ego a voice to speak into your consciousness and remind you that it can do better, that it can solve what bothers you.

Notice that until you compared or contrasted, you lacked nothing, but by simply opening the door to the ego, it has already given you a challenge, which doesn't really exist. Unless you notice it and dismiss it, the ego will begin offering solutions that will drive you away from well-being. Always protect yourself from the isolation of compare and contrast. Separation always weakens your defenses and makes you susceptible to attack.

Lethargy and Indifference

Sometimes due to exhaustion, or due to a need for variety and entertainment, you might invite lethargy and indifference into your mind-body-spirit construct. This is similar to a military general tiring of battle or becoming indifferent toward its outcome, thereby allowing his soldiers to leave the perimeter, providing the enemy with easy assault and victory.

Lethargy and indifference are not the same as surrender—though surrender might come. Lethargy and indifference are usually only a temporary loss of focus. Overall, the general does not want to lose the battle, nor do you want to lose your wellness.

Momentary lapses in judgment result in many of the world's tragedies. One split-second can make all the difference in many aspects of the way we live our lives. Awareness, noticing, and presence are hard to keep up on a continuous basis, but can be easily called on to protect you when lethargy and indifference attempt to reduce your defenses.

Four Primary Attacks on Your Wellness

Although there might be many attacks on your wellness, I only want to discuss the four primary attacks that are common against each of the mind-body-spirit constructs. The four attacks are too much, too little, toxic input, and temptation.

Too Much and/or Too Little

Before the Buddha's awakening, he was a prince. He had everything a man could desire. But despite that, he still came to know suffering. He concluded that too much leads to suffering. His first inclination was to go from having everything to having nothing. He spent many months fasting and denying himself. He was so intent on finding a way to live without suffering—he almost died. Having everything did not block suffering. He soon found that having nothing, or too little, did not block suffering either. The Buddha then investigated the *middle way,* and it was in this time that he became enlightened.

Too much or too little of anything, good or bad, is an attack on your wellness in all parts of life, and in all six zones of well-being; we must pursue the middle way. Do not confuse this with moderation—too much or too little moderation is too much or too little of something. We are not seeking moderation; we are seeking wellness.

We might run too far before we are ready and become injured. The injury will sideline us and we will not run while we heal; we run too little. We might become obsessed with our spiritual practice and forgo our loving relationships, or we might spend all our time working with others, and forget to care for ourselves. Balance is essential in all things, in all activities. There is no need to hurry, you are not going anywhere. The journey is joy, the journey is happiness.

Journey or Destination

Enjoy the journey. Don't be so driven toward a destination that you miss the experience involved in getting there. A common metaphor that describes the joy of the journey versus the drive to the destination is the motorboat versus the sailboat.

Motorboats are designed to move rapidly across the water to arrive somewhere fast. From a sailor's perspective, they are loud, their gas fumes are annoying, and they cause disruptive wakes in the water. In getting to their destination, motorboat captains miss most of what the waterways offer. They are only concerned with where they are going and getting there. The motorboat captain is satisfied with arriving, not in boating.

Sailors, on the other hand, are in no particular hurry to go anywhere. In fact, when there's no wind, they don't mind going nowhere. Often, they just leave their slip, sail around the local waterway for several hours, and then return. Sailing requires that the captain is intimately involved in the journey. To move at all, he must properly capture the wind. To move quickly, he must know how to exactly trim his sails for the available wind. The tide, the current, and the depth of the water, all play a role in how he captains the vessel. His journey is quiet, the air is fresh, and he is present. Because he is present, there is little in the journey that escapes his consciousness. He might reach his destination; he might not. It doesn't matter particularly, for he is satisfied in allowing the journey to unfold just as it will. His joy is in sailing, not in arriving.

Toxic Inputs

There are toxic inputs waiting to attack every single layer of your wellness. These attacks from the outside are trying to find their way in. Mentally, spiritually, physically, you must always defend from toxic inputs entering your being. Once they enter, they will work actively with the ego to destroy your wellness.

Toxic inputs to your body are easy to recognize and understand with a little reading. But do not underestimate the power of mental toxins, such as social media, and spiritual toxins, such as another person's ego giving you doubt. Any toxic input can destroy the wellness of its entry point and the whole honeycomb of wellness. Strict awareness and discipline is required to defend against toxic input attacks.

Temptation

The fourth attack is temptation, which can come from anywhere. It can slither into your mind while you are peacefully meditating, or it can flash through your sight consciousness on a television commercial. It is usually subtle. But when it enters your mind-body-spirit construct, it can become a powerful persuader. Guarding against temptation is a major skill to develop in defending the wellness you are building.

The ego, sources of weakness, and attackers on your wellness will never cease in their efforts to return you to a state of unconsciousness and delusion. You must always be on guard for signs of attack. For that reason, your best barriers toward defending wellness are also the best offenses to building wellness. Those include the following defense mechanisms.

Five Basic Defense Mechanisms

I have already discussed that the ego does not exist in the present moment. When you are in *the now*, you are experiencing life as it is. There is no past or future. There is no time. If you remain in the present, the past and future dissolve. There you can find glimpses of infinity, eternity, and of universal intelligence. The best defense against an enemy might be to be where it isn't. The ego is not in the present. Five defense mechanisms include awareness, discipline, consistent practice, rest, and sandbags.

Awareness

Awareness of weakness sources and attackers is the best defense against them. Simply noticing a threat can often dissolve it. Sometimes, you might need to take a definitive action to remove the threat of the attack from harming your wellness, following your awareness of it.

Discipline

Discipline is also required of you. When you become aware of a threat to your wellness, you must have the discipline to remove yourself from the threat or remove the threat from your surroundings. This is not always easy and might require a written commitment to yourself.

Dr. Stephen Covey wrote about the gap between a stimulus and a response. When we are unconscious, the gap is so small it hardly exists. As soon as an unconscious person receives a stimulus, the reaction is almost instantaneous. As we become conscious, we can begin to extend the gap. We can stop being instant responders to our stimuli. As we lengthen the gap, we have time to make better choices. Dr. Covey said that we must exercise integrity in the moment of choice. The moment of choice is the gap—and the longer it exists following a stimulus, the more integrity we can offer in making our choice about how to react. Our response doesn't need to be one of instantaneous, ego-based reaction. We can use the moment of choice to enter a moment of presence, connect to our source, and react according to our truth, rather than according to our ego.

This discipline of reacting only after recognizing the moment of choice, entering the present, and choosing based on personal integrity will always result in better outcomes. More important, in the case of defending wellness, it will serve as a brilliant barrier against what wants to harm us.

Consistent Practice

A consistent practice is a major defense against weakness and attack. Daily practices and habits developed for building and maintaining wellness are also building defenses and immunities preventing its loss. This might seem obvious, but I am not talking about the practice itself or the growth it produces. I am talking about the habits and the conscious decisions made daily to enhance wellness. These decisions build immunity and help prevent susceptibility to loss of wellness.

Rest

Physical, mental, and spiritual rest is obviously an antidote to exhaustion. Rest is what we do as part of a wellness routine, not in response to being tired or exhausted. We can be proactive in our rest, storing capability to persist in whatever area we are challenged. Rest does not mean just sleep; it means to come to a rest—to stop.

Sandbags

Sandbag is a term I use to describe specific defenses we build around our wellness to ward off attacks that we know or feel we are uniquely susceptible to. For example, some people might be susceptible to online pornography. They might put website blockers in place so that these webpages are not easily accessible. These blockers are sandbags built to defend against a known susceptibility. People who have no interest in online pornography would not need to build such defenses.

Another example might be Facebook. Some people might have a problem with constantly checking Facebook updates. If so, they might disable Facebook on their mobile phone, and only login at home for limited amounts of time. This is creating a sandbag when removing Facebook from the phone, and another sandbag to limit their online time.

The Defense of Mental Wellness

Defending the wellness of your mind will require that you identify those inputs that cause you distress, either directly or indirectly, and then eliminate or mitigate their impact. Some of these inputs might require complete abstinence. Others might be allowed on a limited basis. Keep in mind, certain life events might require a temporary abstinence of a certain input—life changes. Accept it.

One personal example for me is national political news and commentary. I started business school almost twenty-five years ago, and a professor told us that good Americans read the opinion editorial pages of either the *New York Times* or the *Wall Street Journal* every day. It was 1993 when I first subscribed to the *Wall Street Journal.* Once I started reading the op-ed page, I was hooked. I couldn't get enough political commentary. Through the 1990s, cable news networks brought more political opinion to me at night. There were times when I could not stop watching. When 9/11 happened, I was completely hooked to 24/7 cable news and became mentally and emotionally attached to all that was happening for many, many months. It became so important to me, that I would become quite agitated if I missed an event or an important story.

Life circumstances helped wean me from the 24/7 nature of my news addiction, and I was back to just the daily op-ed before long. In 2012, I found myself becoming angry and agitated at the state of political discourse in the country. It seemed to me that the US Constitution was being trampled on, and I was getting quite aggravated. I started watching cable news again, and I became attached to the idea that I could somehow defend the US Constitution from my couch.

I watched the news and then posted Facebook entries regarding the constitutionality of the various items that bothered me. My obsession became so bad that I was continuously thinking about the loss of constitutional freedoms and an all-too-powerful federal government. I was emotionally upset, and it started to show up in my body.

Finally, a friend asked me why I was taking all that news so personally. His question rattled me from my unconsciousness about my news obsession. He suggested that if I wasn't going to run for office, or do something about what was bothering me politically, then I should just let it go. Stop watching the news. It was like he threw a bucket of cold water on me. Wait, could I actually stop watching the news and be normal? It was a crazy, yet obvious, observation. I quit. My stress level and blood pressure dropped substantially—just because I let go of the news!

Everyone has a story like this. I always hear new examples. Common ones include certain television shows, especially those that carry a plot over from week to week, or the aforementioned news and associated political movement. Pornography is more common than I had thought, and it can be disruptive in all three dimensions of mind-body-spirit. Debates and arguments on social media are also a cause for unnecessary suffering. Entering a conversation online with the intent of winning a debate or argument is a sure way to open the door for losing your wellness. These activities activate the ego and strengthen it. When the ego wakes up, it will remind you of everything other people have that you do not. When the ego starts, you can quickly spiral from a state of wellness to a state of despair.

If the ego gets you to feel guilty about something you have yet to achieve, or something you did to prevent the achievement the ego believes you should have by now, you could be headed quickly to dwelling in a space filled only with negative emotion. Guilt, regret, anger, resentment, fear, and worry all start to creep in. These emotions feed off one another and can create a frenzy. Months of solid work on building wellness can be destroyed in minutes, if you dwell with these emotions for too long.

Often, when you are reminded of your shortcomings, your ego will offer to bail you out of your negative situation once again. Sometimes *monkey mind* is what happens next—like a monkey swinging randomly from limb-to-limb, tree-to-tree, bar-to-bar—your mind, because of your ego, swings from topic-to-topic, solution-to-solution, with little resistance or abatement on your part. You are no longer noticing, you are participating—you *become the monkey*—you become the ego once more. Awareness *and noticing*—these are the antidotes to the *monkey mind*.

A common trick the ego will use to take control of you is *compare and contrast*. It does not care who or what it compares you to; it will try anything to get your submission to its influence. Like a dog wanting your affection, the ego will keep coming back at you with anything it can, until you give it the attention it requires. "Your house is small. Look at that guy's house. Look at that runner there, you are a fat ass, and you could not run around the block. Remember when you had the most money in the family? You used to be so smart."

All this comparing and contrasting will work you over, hoping that you forget who you are, and that you will submit to a *feeling of lack,* that somehow don't have what you need to survive. How can you possibly be well, if you do not have the most?

Old attachments are hard to break. Especially when it comes to ideas about how we should have performed in this lifetime. The ego helps us form a vision of what we are going to become in this life and it reminds us of our progress. We become attached to this idea, as if it were real. I am this or that. I am going to become this or that. We become attached emotionally to these images. They are hard to break, because deep inside, in a complex, intricate dynamic, we think that what we are attached to is who we are. If we don't achieve this objective, then what is our identity? What are we destined to become? These things are our birthright. Dropping the attachment to these ideas seems like quitting or giving up.

Almost all suffering is tied to attachments. Compare and contrast, covetousness, envy, and jealousy are all on-ramps to the ego's *attachment freeway*, which leads directly to suffering. We must develop defenses against these attacks. The defenses must be continuously monitored by awareness and reinforced by noticing.

Here are some suggestions for mental defenses, including forgiveness, rest, mental growth, discovery and exploration, spiritual immunity, and body wellness immunity.

Forgiveness

One of the quickest and easiest methods to escape the ego's guilt trap is forgiveness. Forgiveness frees you from all debts that you believe you are burdened with, as a result of being human. Think of all the things you feel guilty for as *debts*, and then simply forgive the debt. Do the same for those you think have harmed you, and forgive their debt. Let it go.

So much guilt, anger, and resentment can be dissolved by simply living as a forgiving soul. The ego will always hold influence over a person who clings to grievances. Let them go, and you block one path of attack the ego has on your wellness.

Rest

Mental rest is as important as physical rest. The challenge is resting the mind, while preventing the ego from filling the void. For beginners, it is best to rest the mind during meditation and mindfulness practice.

Rest is enhanced and strengthened when you have a consistent mindfulness and meditation practice. A calm, disciplined, and rested mind is less susceptible to an attack than a noisy, ego-driven mind.

Mental Growth

Learning and knowledge development are growth strategies that strengthen people mentally. Stimulating the mind through learning raises its resistance to weakness and attack. People have different interests and ways of learning. Reading is a common method of learning, but attending seminars, watching videos, and taking courses should also be included. An appreciation of the arts, music, theatre, dance, and visual arts are also learning mechanisms that can add immunity to wellness of the mind.

Always be careful of content, as some might not be appropriate for the strengthening of defense and immunity. The affect that content has on you is completely unique to you. If the content or method you choose to learn from causes agitation or discomfort—reconsider your choices.

Discovery and Exploration

Discovery and exploration tease the imaginative spirit. Always plan to do something unusual for you. If you are a beach person—try the mountains. If you are a country person, try the city. Get out of your comfort zone occasionally to excite your curiosity of what is possible for you, for others, and for the world. Strong, imaginative, and creative thoughts promote stronger wellness and reduce the threat of attack.

Keep in mind, as you consider these suggestions, we are dealing with recovery. You and your addict have had your minds occupied by some terrible obsessions and driven by extreme anxiety and regret. You are trying—through recovery—to drain all the negativity associated with addiction out of your mind. You want to enhance recovery by filling it with clean, fresh, positive ideas, thereby diminishing the space available for negative ideas. Fill your mind with helpful concepts and you will not have room for an attack.

Spiritual Immunity

In modern, Western culture, your spirituality is under constant attack. The outside world has 24/7 access to you via nonstop news and media cycles, on-demand entertainment, and all forms of social media, all of which are delivered directly to your sense consciousness via myriad devices that are always in your possession.

The mobile phone is the Trojan horse to the walls around your spirit. It entered the city as a convenience device and allowed you to be in touch with the ones you love, while providing safety and security via calling 911 in the event of emergencies. Little did you know that inside the horse were armies of attackers seeking to destroy your well-being. As with narcotics, when it comes to the media form that will ultimately destroy you, you will be the one to choose it. Innocently at first, you play a game, log into social media, or follow a celebrity feed. Before long, you will make more eye contact with a glass screen than you will with other humans. This is not meant to rail against the phone industry or its partners, but rather a reminder to you, that the city of *your being* is yours. The walls are built and guarded by you. The gates are opened and closed on your command and your command alone. If the Trojan horse is allowed inside your city's gates, it is your fault; you allowed it. Awareness and presence; these are the defenses against being tricked by a Trojan horse.

Attacks on spiritual wellness do not come in big, bold messages. Spiritual attackers have learned through the centuries that many people's ideas and beliefs of the spiritual realm are deeply rooted and reinforced by generations of family tradition. Boldly proclaiming that you are wrong and need to instantly change your beliefs has never worked. In fact, it most often results in a stronger defense against the spiritual attack. No one is going to tell you or your ego what to believe. Even if they sound reasonable, you are more likely to dig in and stand your ground.

The attackers have evolved. Their attacks are now subtler, and they are more patient. Rather than trying to cut down your *oak tree of belief* and convincing you to burn it, they have learned to plant seeds. During the course of however long it takes, they will plant seeds at the base of your oak tree. Without your direct awareness, they will deliver water and fertilizer to their seeds. Occasionally, they will shine bright sunlight on the ground, and you will feel good because of the warmth provided. Through the years, the attackers will tend to their plants, as they take root and begin to grow. The oak, the stronghold of your belief, is no longer the sole focus point in your spiritual forest. New, younger plants are growing and crowding the central themes of your ideas.

The new plants growing in your forest aren't that bad, you tell yourself. You don't particularly like them—but no need to get rid of them. You allow them to stay. The attackers continue to grow the plants and soon it's hard to see your *oak tree*. What once stood tall and proud as a symbol of your core beliefs is now difficult to see. No longer can you wander to its base and sit in its shade, while listening to the birds, nesting in its branches, sing songs of the universe to you. The new plants have blocked access. You can no longer directly experience the *oak* of your core.

You are left with the new plants. At one time, they were harmless seeds and saplings, so you unconsciously let them grow. As they matured, you weren't particularly fond of them, but you saw no need to decisively remove them; they were harmless underbrush beneath your wonderfully strong *oak tree*. Now the new plants are all you see. These new plants are all you have. So subtle was their growth, you hardly noticed. Your tree was becoming less significant, but it was a subtle decay. You didn't notice from day-to-day. Now all you have are the plants that diminished your tree. You might accept them as yours, because now you have nothing else. In time, you'll think back about the tree; it will seem so distant, so foreign.

I was born in 1966. One example that I have witnessed in my lifetime is the drastic change in what is acceptable to broadcast on television. The changes that have transpired are quite remarkable. In just a few short years, the entertainment industry has moved from not using ANY foul language on TV, to showing graphic violence, nudity, sexual activity, and outright attacks on the core values of millions of viewers.

Unremarkably, what became acceptable on television has also become acceptable in real life. The changes have been implemented systematically, in my opinion, subtly, patiently. Now as I watch the mass adoption of multimedia via mobile phones, I wonder what seeds are being planted and what pillars of spirituality, like the oak tree, will be overgrown with the patient will of the attackers. I also sit and wonder whether our children will ever have their own oak trees, because the attackers are already in their forests before the oak has even a chance to grow.

I have used these metaphors to help you realize that those who wish to weaken or attack your wellness are not going to introduce themselves as the enemy and take a chainsaw to your core. They are going to come in disguised as a helper, and they will get to you most often through a subtle form of deceit. When you are unconscious, these little things do not seem worth your effort to dispose of, so you let them go. In time, you will come to regret such acceptance.

Be on guard, always, for those who wish to modify your spirit. Whatever it is that you come to know, should always come from within. Don't accept what others tell you; investigate for yourself in the present.

The spiritual attackers can come from many different sources. The media, people, and institutions are all entities that might try to weaken you. Temptation, due to ego and attachment or compare and contrast, can also dampen your spiritual efforts. Internally, guilt and doubt, likely triggered by a memory or a fear, are often "on guard duty" when the Trojan horse enters your city. When you are tired, or suffering from stress and tension, you are more susceptible to attack.

Practice

Consistency is an immunity-forming habit. By consistently practicing mindfulness and meditation, you reduce the duration where unconsciousness can exist. I believe that repetitively breaking the ego's hold on your consciousness will reduce its influences.

Strive to meditate twice per day for extended periods (twenty minutes) and adopt a formal, mindfulness practice at least three times per day for five minutes each time. The formal activities, coupled with informal awareness, will limit the ego's ability to recapture you. As you continue to break up the periods of mindlessness, you will find you are more naturally awake without conscious effort.

As for addicts, breaking up the times of unconsciousness is absolutely critical to long-term recovery. By staying aware, by noticing, and by allowing thoughts to pass without judgment, the tempting allure of heroin's seductive voice is diminished. Stay here now!

Forgiveness

It is hard to forget, and that makes it hard to forgive. We can offer forgiveness to those who have harmed us and to ourselves for harming our ability to find the truth. But for almost all of us, even after having forgiven, we still hold a resentment or a grievance against others and suffer in guilt.

As I mentioned before, you should treat the grievances you hold against others and yourself as you would treat a debt. It's easy to forgive a debt; you simply let yourself and others know that they don't owe you anything, not even an apology. Forgiving the debt does not necessarily restore the relationship to the same status that it had prior to the offense. It only relieves the burden of debt from the offender. Minding and mending the relationship is a separate issue that follows forgiveness.

Your wellness is fully dependent on your willingness, ability, and practice of forgiving yourself and everyone around you. The only thing you offer yourself and others is your love. Your love for all should be unconditional. Why would you withhold what is so freely given to you? You have certainly heard of this teaching: if you want something, give it away, and you will receive it many times over. The most fundamental thing you have to offer others is your love, and when you get to the root of what you truly desire, you will find love is all you need.

Open your heart, your mind, and your soul to love; do this by living in complete forgiveness. A loving, forgiving, and open heart is closed to all attacks on wellness.

Spiritual Rest

Learn to rest in your higher power. Rest in the presence of infinite love. Investigate the truth of who you are and who your higher power is. You might find that it is love, and you are of it, and you are love. All beings are love. There will be times when you tire of seeking, when you just want to turn it all off for a while.

Most humans achieve this sensation by watching television—the average sixty-year-old American will have spent fifteen years of their life watching the boob tube. Fifteen years! My hope is that you have investigated the negative affect that TV has on your life, and you are instead filling your life with wellness. Instead of becoming numbly unconscious in front of the TV when you become weary, try to sit with your higher power and rest in the love for you. Rest with this love, knowing who you truly are, that you are safe, and that no matter where you go, your higher power is with you and you are with it.

Resting in your higher power's presence will powerfully restrict the attackers from destroying your spiritual wellness.

Body Wellness Immunity

You are not your body, but your body affects your mind and your spirit. Running, yoga, and breathing are wellness-building activities that I have suggested you use to develop a higher level of awareness of how your body affects your mind and vice versa. Discussing body wellness immunity should be easy to understand and probably quite familiar to you.

Preventing illness, weakness, and injury to the body is not especially important for the sake of the body itself. From experience, you know that you become less disciplined about issues of mind and spirit when you are physically ill. Naturally, your attention and concentration shifts, from mindfulness and consistent spiritual practice, to healing and feeling better.

When you allow your mental or spiritual guard down because you are sick, attack is imminent, and the likelihood of the attack's success is high, as your defenses are low. Addicts need to be especially aware of the propensity for relapse during times of physical illness. To reduce the opportunity for attack, you must maintain a high state of defense. Do what you can to avoid illness to diminish the opportunity for relapse.

Air, Water, Food

It is said that humans can live four to five weeks without food. We can live four to five days without water. And we can live only four to five minutes without air. Breathing is critical to wellness, yet we ignore it, because it is on autopilot. Your yoga practice and running habit are helping you learn how it feels to breathe. Several times each day, you should also take a moment to breathe deeply with intent. Remind yourself what it feels like to breathe deeply, to hold your breath, and to exhale fully—I mean fully. Obviously, don't smoke; smoking is poisonous breathing.

Dilution is the solution to pollution. The physical benefits of hydration are well documented and easily researched online. It is common sense, but many of us still refuse to drink the daily recommended amount of water. Instead, we opt for more toxic drinks, such as coffee, soda, and energy drinks. At some point in your life, I hope you have an opportunity to experience the wonderful sensation of living in a fully oxygenated and hydrated body. There is a noticeable difference in how good you feel when you are properly hydrating and breathing.

How much water should you drink? A good rule of thumb is half of your body weight in ounces. If you weigh 150 pounds, your base line is 75 ounces. Of course, if you have physical activity that dehydrates you, you need to make up for that loss, in addition to your baseline level.

We talk about clear, clean water, but how often do we talk about clean food? This is not a push for an all-organic diet. Decisions, such as that, are your choice, but I want to discuss the concept of eating clean. There are plenty of resources on the topic of eating clean, and you can investigate what works best for you. I will make suggestions on what works for me and people I work with in this area.

There are several staples of the American pantry to consider eliminating from your diet. I will start with this list:

1. White grains
2. All dairy
3. Alcohol
4. Sugar
5. Processed foods (anything in a box)
6. Fatty red meats
7. Bad fats (shortening, vegetable oil, mayonnaise)
8. Excessive alcohol or caffeine

Previously in this chapter, we discussed the error of *too much* and *too little*, and how you should seek the middle way. You should implement this principle when choosing what you eat and how much you eat. What I have found for myself, I offer you as a starting point. From there, modify what you do, based on what works and what you learn. Remember, our goal is wellness. We are seeking a basic way of living where we can be well and stay well.

I found that **white grains** destroy the natural processes of digestion. It starts with the balance of good versus bad bacteria in your digestive system. The same bacteria that cause yeast infections in women exist in your intestines, and when you consume white grains, you promote the overgrowth of the bad bacteria relative to the good bacteria. Overall, physical wellness is negatively affected by the imbalance, and many digestive issues can result. If you don't believe this, stop eating white grains and watch the change in how you feel.

Dairy products promote overall inflammation in our bodies. I can feel the effects everywhere. Most notably, for me, are aches and pains in my joints. When I stop consuming dairy products, my body feels better overall. Running promotes inflammation, especially at first, but it is much more prominent when dairy products are in your diet. Try thirty days without dairy products. It is almost assured that you will notice a measurable, positive difference.

Sugars don't process well through your body. They change structure at the molecular level, and the results are not wellness promoting. The most significant impact on me is emotional; sugars can make me feel great when I consume them, however, as they are processed, I can slip into deep levels of sadness. The ups and downs due to sugar were offering attackers opportunities to reduce my wellness when I was down. Once I stopped eating sugars, my moods leveled out and my overall wellness increased.

Eating **processed foods,** usually found in a box, is dirty eating. The number of substances in a box of cereal is unknown. Having the ability to read the ingredients requires a degree in chemistry. I have no idea what's really in there. Avoiding this form of fake food in favor of eating whole, natural food, will help you feel better. You will have more energy, more stamina, and general feelings of well-being. When you feel better, you're less likely to fail to defend against attack.

There is more than enough information to be found online about the problems associated with consuming **red meat, bad fats,** and **excessive alcohol or caffeine.** If you truly wish to be well, and stay well, avoid these substances. Remember, you are what you eat.

Medications

Many of us are medicated for some illness or condition. Adhering to your health plan with your doctor is important to maintaining your wellness. I do suggest that you learn what you can about each medication that you take, why you take it, and what the side effects are. As you begin to make changes with respect to your wellness, you might have an opportunity to coordinate with your doctor to reduce the dosage, or perhaps change or eliminate medications. Be cognizant of what your conditions are and how you change as your overall wellness improves.

Rest

Too many of us ignore rest as a wellness component. The seven or eight hours you spend sleeping are as important as any other hours you spend in a given day. If you are not sleeping enough, or are not sleeping well, your physical, mental, and spiritual wellness will deteriorate. Get the right amount of rest, and you will find that your productivity increases during your waking hours. If you are living a life where sleep "gets in the way," you ought to ask yourself why. What are you doing that is more important than being well? Can you be happy without being well? Don't sleep too much or too little; sleep how much you need to be well.

Aging

Aging is a natural process that every human has experienced since the beginning of time. No one has escaped aging—and no one has escaped death. Too many of us fear death and thus fear aging, because it draws us closer to death. However, death is nothing, like birth was nothing. You didn't choose to be born—you had no say in the matter. Likewise, you will have no say in your death. Accept this and you will improve your wellness.

Like death, aging is inevitable. You are going to age. Hopefully, you'll become an old—and very well—person. You can influence how well you age. Simply adopting the suggestions here will go a long way in supporting your aging. Embrace the process. Know what your body feels like as you age—age in *the now*. Learn about the characteristics of the various phases of getting old. Maybe you will learn that your bones might get brittle, your memory gets weak, or your skin gets wrinkly; whatever the characteristic, there might be things you can do to slow the process and reduce any potential impact it might have on your wellness. Don't be afraid to get old—and don't let the process determine your wellness.

Supplementation

Supplementation, or consumption of dietary supplements, is an often-misunderstood area of wellness. Many people will tell you if you eat well, you will consume everything you need. Others will tell you it is virtually impossible to consume everything you need from a good diet. I can't make an argument for you. Again, as with all things, this is an area you need to investigate and discover on your own.

I have great success with supplementation. Weight control, cholesterol control, blood pressure management, energy management have all been areas where lifestyle changes, coupled with exercise, clean eating, and supplementation have improved. My baseline supplementation consists of omega-3 fatty acids, amino acids, a probiotic, a daily multivitamin, and a mental focus supplement. The results I experience are consistent.

Omega-3 fatty acids positively affect my cholesterol, my skin color, and my hair. These are things I directly measure. The amino acids maintain lean muscle at times of calorie deficit, like during exercise or between meals. The probiotic promotes the growth of good bacteria in the digestive tract, while a daily multivitamin ensures I'm getting vitamins and minerals I need. The mental focus supplement provides a boost in energy and a higher concentration level. These are not benefits I read on the labels; these are actual results I experience. I suggest you consider supplementation.

If you overwork or overtrain, you are going to weaken the body and invite attack. Again, we are always seeking the *middle way* in all things. When you exhaust yourself at work on Tuesday, then Wednesday is going to be a low output day. If you run too far on Sunday, you might not complete your workout on Monday. There is a balance that you must find to level the peaks and valleys to consistently maintain your wellness.

Stress and Tension

Stress and tension are most notable when manifested in the body. The origins of these attacks can be fully mental, sometimes spiritual, but almost always, they arise in the physical body. The good news is, because they do arise in the body, regardless of origin, they can also be disposed of by the body. Regular practice of yoga and running will lower the overall baseline of stress and tension in your life. Sometimes, you might need a little more physical activity to help manage or reduce your stress and tension, particularly during difficult periods. Practice different forms of stress and tension reduction. Breathing, stretching, and massage are common practices, so find out what works for you. If you need to walk, cycle, swim, or meditate to reduce the impact of a stressful situation—do it when it arises; deal with it then; don't wait. If you wait, it can grow and weaken your immunity to attacks on your well-being.

One more note about body wellness—be proactive in monitoring your health. Have annual physicals performed that check your overall wellness. Keep your immunizations up-to-date. Have your blood and urine sampled to ensure your body is working normally and not harboring any illnesses that might weaken you. Have your five senses checked, as needed, especially sight, hearing, and reflex action to the touch sense.

Immunity and Defense Closing

This section started with a reminder that noticing and awareness are your best defense and immunity against attacks on your wellness. We have looked at the negative input on your mind, spirit, and body and described strategies to reduce their impact on your ability to defend against attack. Your goal is to pursue and maintain wellness as a way of living, to find what your true purpose is.

With that in mind, I'll end this section with this reminder: End every day with gratitude. Thank the universe for all in it and for any special accommodations made for you that day. Empty your mind of all negativity before falling asleep. When you awake, again be grateful for another day, and ask the universe to lead you to the place where you are meant to go. Set an intention for living well.

Lifestyle Wellness

Take a minute and think of all the major sources of stress in your life other than relationships. What comes to mind? Your job? Your house? Your car? Your bills?

It has been my experience that we chase things that we believe will make us happy. When we obtain these things, we often believe we are successful. More often than not, we become so focused on what we are chasing, that we ignore almost anything and everything else. We justify this approach as necessary. We promise ourselves that once this *thing* is obtained, we will restore our lives to normal. We will relax and, of course, be happy.

When we get close to our objective, we become excited. We vibrate with anticipation like children before a holiday. Finally, the day comes when we get what we deserve. We are so excited and so proud in the moments following our triumph. Sometimes our joy lasts for a few hours, maybe sometimes a month. But eventually whatever we just achieved becomes a part of the *new normal*. It is not so special anymore. Our joy and happiness fade. Now what? You have already burned some important moments of your life stressed out, as you pursued your dream. You can't get those moments back. You were happy for a while, but that wore off.

Often the object of our desire transitions into a source of anxiety. We have to care for it, clean it, insure it, pay for it, maintain it, and it's awful if any superficial damage occurs to it. That would cause great distress and anger, as we worked so hard to obtain something nice that we value.

There are many material objects that can fit into the above situation—cars, houses, almost any object with value. Cars and houses are good examples, because they are often a huge part of our identity and a huge part of our budget. Next to our relationships and our jobs, I would say most stress and anxiety is derived from our ability to obtain, keep, and maintain our two primary possessions—our house and our car. Many times, the stress about our job is wrapped up in needing to pay for the expenses associated with our house and our car.

Because our identity is often playing a huge part in where we live and what we drive, we are willing to use large parts of our budgets to have houses and cars that reflect our ego, our status, and our success.

We pay more than we should for both. The *potential* lack of budget to keep our house and our car causes unnecessary stress on us. But it's not just the money required for the acquisition that causes strain.

A bigger house, for example, requires more heat, more power, and more insurance. The systems in the house are all more expensive to replace and maintain. It takes more time to clean the house and tend the lawn. There's much more to worry about. You might worry about maintaining your house's value, hoping it is a good investment.

Remember all we need is a warm, dry shelter, but is that all your house is? Think about it. If you buy too much, you sentence yourself to financial worry with excessive care, maintenance, stress, and tension. Does your ego serve you well here?

I am not advocating against buying the house you want, your dream house if you will. I am suggesting, however, that you deeply consider the impact your decision will have on your personal wellness. Especially, knowing that eventually your new house will just be a house. Hopefully, you will get more joy and relaxation out of owning it, than anxiety, worry, and frustration.

Now think about a new car. The dialogue is the same as the house. Eventually, the new car becomes just *the car*. Every dent might get on your nerves. It gets dirty, it needs gas, it needs an oil change, the payment is due, and it's worth less than you owe on it. There are hidden sources of stress and anxiety wrapped up in many of our buying decisions. Because the ego is running the show, we often allow it to rationalize for us.

I will submit to you that a smaller house and a slower car are not going to make you happy either. Nothing in the material world can make you happy. However, if you opt for a smaller, less expensive, easier to clean, and easier to maintain car, you will find two things of value that might promote well-being. First, you'll have less stress, anxiety, and tension. Second, you'll have more time to work on wellness activities.

Minimalist Attitude

Develop an attitude and the discipline about having what you need and nothing more. Find your satisfaction level for your basic needs. Force yourself to notice what part of your decision-making process is the ego and then ignore it. Use sound judgment by exercising integrity in the moment of choice in all decisions. Your primary criteria should always be what will offer you the most wellness. What will enable you to achieve what you truly desire faster, what will enable you happiness and well-being, regardless of external circumstances.

Be disciplined. It has taken the ego many years to control your outcomes. It will not let go easily. Practice these "ego pleasing versus wellness developing" decisions in all that you do. Repetition is the mother of skill. Never put yourself in a situation where marginal changes in your financial status or health status cause undo anxiety regarding your house. Don't overextend (overdo) yourself to the point where one mistake or one life situation causes doom. The ego's satisfaction is not worth it. You know the ego is never satisfied; it is always going to ask for more.

Buy only what you can afford, less 5 to 10 percent. The bank is not the authority on what you can afford—you are. The bank's algorithms are based on it having collateral and a secured loan, not on your real monthly income and expenses. You decide what you can afford and then give yourself some margin of error. Knowing the bank's number will be higher, you can expect that other egos belonging to those people who love you are going to think you are insane. "You can afford more; the bank said so. Everyone does it this way! There is no need for you to cheat yourself."

Mark my words—you don't need to fall for it. You are not here to appease the ego and remain forever trapped in its loop of suffering. You are seeking joy, and joy is within you. Eliminate the sources of anxiety, worry, fear, anger, jealousy, regret, and guilt from your life and you will accelerate toward well-being. That is what you are truly after.

The same principles that apply to your house and your car should be established with all possessions. How many shirts do you need? How many pairs of jeans? The answer is fewer than seven! It is unlikely that you would ever reduce your shirts to one per day, but many people do. Do not possess things you do not need. When you do, you are submitting to the will of the ego, the will of something that does not exist.

Develop and grow more time, more wellness, more immunity, and more spirituality. By minimizing your investment of time and money in material items that appease the ego, such as cars, houses, and other belongings, you can reduce the stress, tension, and anxiety associated with making payments, cleaning unused space, and maintaining value, while investing in your true purpose.

Find your life's true meaning.

Essentialism

Would you rather do ten activities, 100 percent well, or one hundred activities, 10 percent well? Do you believe that multitasking results in more productivity or more wellness? Too many of us spread ourselves too thin. We are constantly on the run, on the move, always doing, never being. Keeping up with the Joneses used to be my father's way of reminding me of who I am. In today's society, it seems like the bare minimum requirement for acceptance.

We have become so busy that we have become addicted to busy. When we are not doing something, we become uncomfortable. We feel guilty. Somehow, the world has entered us into an insane race to nowhere. All the contestants are on a wheel, constantly maximizing their efforts to end up ahead of others, ahead of where they started, which is where they still are. We are racing to nowhere fast.

We don't even know consciously what we are after. It seems that we just blindly chase after the shadows of success, for ourselves and our kids, and every time we reach out to grab the shadows, they dissolve. But there is always another shadow to chase, and then another. We work hard to get nowhere. There ends up being little satisfaction in the work or the reward.

At work, many people take on more projects than can be completed. We believe that busy-ness is a better sign of value than productivity. We end up working too many hours, accomplishing too little tangible evidence of our abilities. Even the projects we do manage to complete are less than what we are capable of from a quality perspective.

Imagine if you completed twelve major assignments each year, and every one of them represents your best work. You take on three strategic projects each quarter, with the understanding of your supervisor that they will be completed on time, on budget, and with superior quality. The only catch is these are the only projects you will take part in.

You stop attending meetings that do not directly result in the excellent completion of your assignments, unless your input is necessary. Your communications are centered on just three tasks per quarter and twelve tasks per year.

How much less stress would you have, knowing that everything you are working on is achievable and can be completed at 100 percent of your ability? You provide your best work—every day. Nothing is hanging over your head—no side projects or requests to achieve the impossible.

In business school, we discussed an execution strategy called critical success factors or CSFs. These were three or four items that had to go well for the firm or business unit to be successful. All resources would be only focused on these three or four things. Nothing else mattered. It was a great academic exercise, but rarely followed in business. For whatever reason, business leaders have lost track of the meaning of priority.

Here is the definition of priority:

1. The state or quality of being earlier in time, occurrence, etc.
2. The right to precede others in order, rank, privilege, etc.; precedence.
3. The right to take precedence in obtaining certain supplies, services, facilities, etc., especially during a shortage.
4. Something given special attention.

It is clear that priority is singular. There is only one higher or one highest. When asked what your priority is, there can be only one answer. When asked what your priorities are, there is no answer. But somehow, a single priority became multiple priorities, as if you could have more than one priority. It doesn't even make sense. Think about it

"What is your priority?"

"Which one?"

"What do you mean, which one?"

"Well I have ten priorities."

"That doesn't make sense, which one is your priority?"

"All ten!"

"Never mind!"

It is ridiculous, but we see it every day. Rarely does anything get done as well as it could, because we are working, or pretending we are working, on everything at once. I suggest you begin developing a sense of *essentialism*. This is a life management strategy where you *do what is essential* and nothing else. In fact, you completely ignore anything that is not essential.

If an activity is not essential, it should be ignored. Every moment of your life is essential, critical, has meaning, and has purpose. Don't waste those precious moments involved in activities that are not promoting your overall wellness. Do not overextend yourself with commitments that will cause you or your family stress and anxiety. Invest all your time on living well and pursuing happiness.

Professionally ask yourself what's essential. Begin with, "What is the essential reason I work?" Then ask, "Why do I work here, at this place?" Then only do three or four things at a time and ignore everything else. Focus all your energy on excellence in pursuit of those three or four objectives. Work only when required to complete your three or four tasks. Spend the balance of time on wellness activities.

Don't try to multitask; it is an illusion. Don't overbook or double-book your schedule. Leave time on your calendar to move easily between appointments without ever being late. Who needs the dreadful feeling of arriving last?

Social and Political

At home, focus only on what is essential to you and your purpose. Hours watching TV, posting on social media, or pondering the daily news are never going to contribute to your wellness or your purpose. This is not a ban. I am not suggesting abstinence, but remember, there are essential activities that you must complete. If spending too much time on social media is impeding the completion of, or the participation in, what is essential to your wellness, then you should avoid it. Your happiness, peace of mind, and serenity exist in you—inside you. To get them to manifest in your life, you need to seek them out, and learn how to create the conditions necessary for their arrival.

Simplicity

Sometimes we complicate our lives and become frustrated. The mobile phone, the day planner, email, and instant messaging—those were all designed to make our lives easier. The idea was to get the same amount of work done in less time, with less stress, and less anxiety by using these technologies. That would leave us free to spend personal time working on relationships. Instead, we use the technology to pack more activity into less time, and we make ourselves available to the world on a 24/7 basis. Many of us cannot escape work. There is no true downtime. An invention that was supposed to improve our quality of life destroyed it.

This kind of intrusion is common in almost everything we do. Instead of focusing on simple ideas and solutions, we try to engineer some whiz-bang application that is too hard to implement and even harder to maintain. Sometimes this makes the situation even more complicated than the original problem was to solve. There are hundreds of examples, but "There's an app for that" is prevalent today. We buy applications that help us get from point A to point B, and they work great until you lose the signal or your battery runs out. Lost in the wilderness, even in your community, sometimes you have no idea where you are. If you can't read a map or use a compass, you're lost, subject to a battery or distant satellite.

Seek simplicity in all you do. Don't overly complicate your life with people or problems. Some low-tech ideas are simply using face-to-face communications. Talk to people in person—don't text. Tell them you love them. Who needs to buy gifts? Send handwritten notes that you care

Keep minimal, essential, and simple in your consciousness always. Keep all things simple. Don't overcomplicate your words in conversations. Don't make it difficult for others to understand or to connect with you. Instead, be open, be simple, and be easy. Take as few steps as necessary in any task; don't seek elegant or extravagant when simple is available, especially if the expense is anxiety, stress, or worry.

Leave your phone at home. You don't need to be connected 24/7. If you do, something is wrong in your life. Many times, I hear that a child or elderly person might need to call. They'll survive, trust me, but if this is a concern, then when you leave your phone at home, let your loved ones know, and have them call an alternate person in an emergency.

When you leave your phone at home, be simple, be old-fashioned. Try to personally connect with people you are with and the people you meet. Look into their eyes when you speak to them, and try to recognize more than their ego. Personally, reach deeper into yourself and them. Look for the soul, for the spirit, for the divinity within, which is common in all of us and yearns to connect and become whole.

Instead of watching a movie or playing a video game, stare at the night sky. Quietly, just stare at the immensity of our surroundings. Consider that the light you see from those stars might have been traveling to reach your eyes for five million years or more, and only now is it reaching Earth. There is no way to know if some of the stars you see are even there anymore. They might have died out thousands of years ago, yet their light from millions of years ago continues to shine and might continue to shine on us for millions of more years. Evaluate the contrast between space and matter, between light and dark, between near and far.

The universe you observe is only whole and infinite with you in it. You are as much a part of its awesome beauty as the brightest star. There is so much more meaningful entertainment in the sky and the ocean, and the earth, than Hollywood could ever produce. But you must connect with it. You must connect with yourself. In the simplest of places is where you will find the wonder of you. Be quiet, be calm, be still, and be discovered.

Find the path toward *wellness in simplicity*. Live easy. Live well. It's not hard; it's *simple*.

Financial

From a wellness perspective, money is a trap. A primary reason for this is that egos keep score by measuring money. The ego with the most money is the most successful. The ego with the least money is a loser.

What if I told you that the happiest people in the universe live on an isolated desert island and don't have a clue about money? They have life mastered, yet we look at them as ignorant to the human experience.

In the section on Minimalist Attitude, I suggested that you live below your means to minimize anxiety, stress, and tension associated with managing large, valuable assets. You probably thought that the title was reflective of my view on owning the minimum necessary. If so, you missed the point. The point with *minimalism is to minimize the impact of materialism on you emotionally, spiritually, and physically*.

When you live below your means, you will feel more confident professionally in doing your highest quality work on only essential projects. Again, you probably interpreted essentialism to mean doing only what is essential from an activity perspective. If so, again you missed it. In my view, *essentialism is focusing on your spirituality, on your true purpose, on discovering your meaning*. When you are burdened with excessive projects that can never be completed, you cannot successfully discover who you are. This discovery is what is essential.

Financially, too many of us seek financial freedom and too few achieve it. This is because we come to believe that financial freedom means we are rich and have more money than we will ever need to live a life of doing whatever we want. We believe that doing whatever we want will give us happiness. We spend our entire youthful lives pursuing the idea that one day we will have financial freedom. That we will have earned it, that we deserve it. Most travel this path; few get there. For those who don't make it, not only is there a young life wasted trying to be free in the future, but now *they are* old and not free. This might be the biggest disaster an individual can realize. The carrot and the stick—the stick always beats the crap out of you and you never get the carrot.

I propose that you become financially free as soon as you decide that you are. You can leave the rat race at any time by simply deciding that you are out. Stop letting your ego decide what you need. Stop competing in contests that are meaningless and unwinnable.

Prince, Elvis, Philip Seymour Hoffman, John Belushi, and Jimi Hendrix all had fame, money, and freedom, yet they all died tragically and young. I read recently that studies have shown that increases in income, more than $70,000 per year, do not result in increased happiness or joy. Isn't that interesting?

Maybe financial freedom isn't based on some amount of income or some balance in the bank account. Maybe financial freedom is a lifestyle choice. If you always live below your means, aren't you free from financial anxiety, worry, and stress? Only when we reach for items on the edge of what we can afford, for what is beyond our needs, do we enter the place where worry and anxiety prevail. Only when the score-keeping ego reminds you of your status, relative to your peers, are you compelled to stretch beyond what you need.

You willingly enter the bondage of slavery when you take on debt. First, you become a slave to the ego, and its unlimited desires. When you stretch beyond what you need, to what the ego believes you deserve, you become a slave to the ego. You put on chains and shackles when you borrow money to satisfy the insatiable ego.

Once you take on debt, and the string of payments begins, you might never be able to afford anything again. Debt takes monthly money, and after servicing the debt, there isn't enough to save for the next item on the ego's wish list. So, we submit to more debt. The cycle continues and eventually consumes our budget and our sanity. Stress, tension, and anxiety related to money are so prevalent in our society, yet we continue to service our ego and then service our debt. When we can no longer borrow to provide for the demands of the ego, the ego tortures and tags us with labels, such as loser and failure. It takes no blame for your financial condition but will offer you solutions to get out of your predicament.

But the ego's goal is not to get you out of your predicament; its goal is to get more resources for you to serve its infinite desires. Every item you buy and every dime you borrow reduces your freedom and flexibility. If you indenture yourself to your ego and debt, you will spend the rest of your life pursuing the ever-elusive status of financial freedom.

What if you say no to the ego?

What if you say no to borrowing?

What if you proclaim that freedom is a divine part of the universe?

If you live below your means, and if you focus on simple and essential living, you will not submit to the ego. You will not place yourself in servitude. The benefits are overwhelming, but what if the only benefits are having no anxiety, tension, or worry about money as long as you live? Isn't that enough motivation to say no to the ego?

What if another benefit was to never argue about money? You and your loved ones live in financial harmony with one another for life. Is that enough to say no to the ego?

Imagine if you could change jobs or careers whenever you desired without the worry of financial consequences. Suppose you could travel wherever and whenever you wanted or that you could write a book or start your own business. Aren't these activities byproducts of financial freedom? Honestly, why can't you have them now?

What if you had the flexibility to move every few years? You can live wherever you want. What would life be like if you didn't fear job loss? Wouldn't life be so much richer, so much fuller, without all the anxieties we place on ourselves while servicing the ego and financing its needs with money we haven't earned yet?

You know where the answers are. They are here, in *the now,* in the present, where the ego cannot exist. When you are in *the now*, the ego cannot tell you the score, it cannot decide your future, and you cannot feel guilt, shame, or lack. When you are truly in *the now*, you have everything you need—minimal, essential, simple, and free. These are the lifestyle characteristics of beings who live well.

Live well now! Not in the future, only now—for well-being does not exist anywhere but now. The ego persuades you to believe happiness is ahead. Religion compels you to suffer now for a later reward. Both are misleading you. They know too that you are fooled. They know you are likely to follow their instructions, but by the time you realize their deceptions, it will be too late. Find yourself now—in the now. Choose to live well in a state of well-being, and more truth will be revealed to you.

Keys to Living Well for You

1. Al-Anon
2. Wellness program
3. Active participation in addict's recovery (as invited)
4. An initial overdose/detox/rehab/IOP plan
5. A plan for eventual relapse (overdose, detox, rehab, IOP)
6. Boundaries—an understanding or agreement with your spouse/partner, your family, and your addict on how far you are personally willing or able to go with your support (love is unconditional) through recovery and relapse cycles
7. Private therapy, if needed
8. Active care of other relationships affected by the addict's behavior
9. Continuous education in the area of heroin addiction
10. Service, mentor, teach, and educate others, so they can prepare for the realities of heroin addiction

Keys to Living Well for the Addict

1. AA—sponsor, meetings, step work, home group, service work
2. Wellness program
3. Active participation in the recovery of nonaddicted family members (as invited)
4. An understanding of the recovery-relapse lifecycle and an admission of its impact on loved ones
5. An understanding of relapse and relapse prevention and an admission of its impact on you and your loved ones
6. Respect for the boundaries established by loved ones
7. Private therapy, as needed, for underlying issues
8. Vivitrol maintenance
9. Continuous education about the heroin epidemic
10. Service, mentor, teach, and educate others, so they can learn to avoid your pain

Chapter 14 Concepts

1. Be aware; be mindful.
2. Find your life only exists in the now.
3. Find your true purpose, your true meaning.
4. Focus on a program of wellness. Unless you are well, you cannot be happy, successful, or healthy. Without wellness, you will even struggle with love.
5. Live simply.
6. Search inside yourself, and nowhere else, for the truth.

Epilogue

Learning to Break-Out of the Cycle

Yes, there are two paths you can go by, but in the long run
There's still time to change the road you're on.
And it makes me wonder.
Your head is humming and it won't go, In case you don't know,
The piper's calling you to join him.
~ Led Zeppelin, "Stairway to Heaven"

This book has been writing itself in my mind for almost three years. I'd love to report that in 2017, the nightmare was over—but it isn't. Jack just turned twenty-five years old and lives in a halfway house near Atlanta. He was released from jail in June 2016 and relapsed in August. So far, he shows little interest in working a recovery program.

Following Johnny's overdose in January, quite a few things happened to me. The psychiatrist made Xanax a daily medicine instead of emergency use only, and he added the maximum dose of Cymbalta to the already maximum dose of Zoloft and my daily Klonopin. I was a walking drugstore. People asked me what it was like, and I'd tell them to imagine an old bloodhound on the porch of a country house. The family says, "Hey" on the way out in the morning and pats the old dog on the head. When they return, they pat him on the head again. All the while, he just sits there—vaguely remembering chasing sticks and loving life. That was me. I didn't feel—I just was.

Wendy and I didn't discuss the divorce again—whether we were going to or whether we were not. But we still weren't seeing eye to eye on much. We were both lonely; both looking for a way to make sense out of everything that happened while wondering what the hell went wrong. We were both drifting; neither had a purpose. As good as things had gotten in January—they were never worse than they were in April.

I had gotten sick of not knowing what I was feeling. I needed to be med free. I was becoming more confident in my sobriety and my spirituality. I had finished the Twelve Steps of AA and was meditating as long as three hours per day. I decided to quit all my meds—without the doctor's support or assistance. It took some time, but by July 2016, I had stopped all meds. Klonopin, Xanax, Zoloft, and Cymbalta were all out of my system, and the prescriptions were canceled. I was free, and it felt great—scary, but great. There were periods of brain zaps and other side effects that were tough. Once they were gone, things started to clear up.

In May, I completed my second, life coaching certification. I was following the lineage of Milton Erickson, Jay Haley, Tony Robbins, Choé Madanes, and Mark and Magali Peysha. Strategic intervention is an extremely efficient and effective method to help parents of addicts take action and get themselves and their families out of danger as quickly as possible. I enjoy coaching.

Wendy and I have started the long road of reconciliation. There are so many dimensions to what we have experienced and endured. Only time and God's loving compassion can heal us. It has been working so far.

My story continues to unfold. We are not yet out of the woods. However, there's been a tremendous change in all of us. It might seem like a negative outcome, but it's not. Sometimes the light of honesty shines on parts of our souls that we are not particularly proud of, but with the light shining, we at least can see what's broken, so we can fix it. The fixing takes time; we are still fixing.

For all of us, there is a tremendous amount of hope and optimism. The country is becoming more aware of the heroin epidemic, and help is on the way. Pill mills and pain clinics are under scrutiny by law enforcement. Enforcement of our borders and immigration laws are promised by the new presidential administration. As the flow and distribution of pills and heroin slow, we can be hopeful that the number of affected families diminishes rapidly, and that the needed resources to care for the addicted become available. I remain optimistic that the heroin epidemic will be behind us soon.

For those of us caught up in the throes of addiction and recovery, there is a way out. There is a way to break out of the recovery and relapse lifecycle for both the addicted and the family member. The process might not be traditional, and it might take a few iterations to become permanent. However, the seemingly hopeless nature of my personal situation is subsiding. I can see the light again, and I have every reason to live life to its fullest. The healing process for me has required a tremendous amount of honesty. Most of it is not related to addiction or alcoholism.

Only in seeking who I truly am and searching for my true meaning am I able to realize that most of my forty-seven years before Jack's overdose were not real. I was living a life I thought I should live, rather than the one I was meant to live. It's taken three years to get to where I am now. There was a lot of housecleaning to do, but as the clutter of my mistakes is whisked away by the wind of honesty, I am prepared to fill my life with meaning—the meaning given to me by the universe.

I am meant to be joyous, while seeking joy.

I am meant to be happy, while seeking happiness.

There is a reason; there is a purpose.

There are only two things I require in my life: spirituality and sobriety. I cannot have one without the other. So, my life now is organized around keeping and maintaining these two essentials. Deep wounds exist in all our hearts and souls, but healing is at hand. Personally, The Sandalwood Wellness Model that I designed has helped me maintain a sense of well-being that previously eluded me. I hope it continues to work—for all of us.

Appendix 1

A Proposed Addiction Lifecycle—Something for Parents to Think About

This appendix provides parents with a proposed cycle that kids might experience, as they approach a deadly addiction. This is only my personal hypothesis based on observations and personal experience. It is provided to raise a parent's awareness at certain addiction milestones that children pass through with the hope that a parent could intervene before overdose.

Willingness. Increasing willingness. Independent will. A child has to become willing to try something dangerous. How does this willingness come about for some but not others? In early childhood, children believe everything they are told. They have no reason to not believe what they are told or to doubt anyone who tells them anything. As long as there is no violation of trust, a child will believe what a parent tells them.

Eventually, though, a child discovers that his or her parents are not always truthful. Maybe Mom tells a little girl that the boo-boo on her knee will stop hurting soon—and it doesn't. Or maybe Dad tells his son that he is fast, but the kid loses every sprint in physical ed. The small stories we tell kids might make them feel better about a boo-boo, damaged pride, a broken heart, or a failed entrance exam in the short-term; but in the long-term, these stories might impact a child with doubt regarding honesty.

Of course, there are the stories we tell children about the Tooth Fairy, the Easter Bunny, and Santa Claus. Sometimes children have a traumatic reaction when they learn of our fables. And perhaps when they learn the truth from a friend at school—the friend instantly takes a place of higher credibility over the word of Mom and Dad. These are subtle things, small things. None on their own is enough to cause a kid to become a heroin addict. But sometimes, maybe children will be more prone to doubt things that Mom and Dad tell them—and more likely to believe ideas shared with them by their friends.

I can't speak for all parents, but I for one dealt in a few absolutes—or close to absolutes. When it came to lying, smoking, drinking, drugging, dealing, and sex, I painted a grim picture of what might happen. I think that many of us do. I was able to fulfill only one absolute—if you lie to me—I will punish you.

I told my son that if he rode a skateboard, he would hurt himself. His friends convinced him, eventually, that I was wrong; after all, they rode skateboards and didn't get hurt. Somehow, all our father-and-son history started to work against me. He rode a skateboard and did not get hurt. His friends were thrilled that they proved me wrong. He rode again—no injuries again. It became clear to him that his friends were telling him the truth, and I was hiding something from him, as if there were some secret source of joy and pleasure that I was withholding from him. Of course, eventually, he did get hurt on his skateboard, but by then my credibility was way down. His buddy's credibility was way up.

Think about the next time the kid is offered something that I had forbidden him. After the skateboard situation, do you think he would be more or less likely to take another step? More or less willing? I would wager more willing.

Now the buddy, who has started smoking with his older neighborhood pals, is not suffering any illness or other ill effects from cigarettes. My son is asked to try a smoke. At first, he recoils; after all, his grandfather is sick from smoking. But repeated exposure to his pal enjoying smokes—just like the older kids, is beginning to wear on him. Besides, the older kids are fantastic on the skateboard AND chicks dig them—regardless of the fact that they smoke.

Eventually, my son tries a cigarette. His life does not end. In fact, he gets a neat little buzz, and a certain girl thinks he is cool. Later that day, he lands a skateboard trick he has been working on for months. He has another smoke—the second is easier than the first. Once again, the stigma that Dad placed on a certain activity is proven to be incorrect. He smoked he didn't die—his buddy was right—his father lied to him. Once again—Dad's credibility is low. Now, everything Dad ever told him might be called into question. There is a reason to doubt everything Dad ever said, and reason to listen to his friends.

Maybe sex is next—God, it's over, if it is. I had a therapist tell me one time after speaking to my son about sex—that once a young boy experiences sex, there is no turning back. I'd be better trying to put toothpaste back in the tube or make water run uphill, than to try to get a kid to stop chasing sex, after having experienced it the first time. My son had sex fairly early. He got away with it—it was a fantastic experience for him; his lover didn't get pregnant, and he didn't get any diseases. Once again—after such an experience—the credibility of the parent is way down, and the peer group grows in influence and credibility.

Somewhere in this phase of progress—the child detaches from the parents from a guidance or mentorship point of view. The separation is quite distinct, and, at this point, the parents are in a serious situation. The child's situation is precarious. Especially, if all of these milestones have been completed with little or no consequences, such as illness or injury.

Things can move fairly rapidly from here. Depending on the social group the child is a part of and the culture of the school he goes to, a kid can get weed, pills, and booze with little difficulty. I don't know exactly what the progression was for my son. But I will assume that he easily transitioned to smoking weed. He was a young pothead—other kids his age would ask him to help them get weed later in their development. This helped him get into dealing—and dealing was nice because it gave him access to money and a certain important status among his peers.

He tried Xanax early in his freshman year. Despite getting caught, he was not deterred from continuing pills. Xanax quickly turned to occasional Vicodin, and from there the path to heroin was blazed.

I don't know that I am an advocate of gateway drugs, where I understand a gateway drug to lead a user to a higher potency or bigger high. But I do believe in a progression of willingness. And provided that each stage of the progression is relatively successful—willingness to try the next level is higher, and the probability of an experiment is higher. Naturally, all this is taking place in a real-life laboratory where he can watch his older friends and more aggressive peers try everything, and then, based on their results, determine what his level of risk might be. There is no way that a kid goes straight to sticking a needle of heroin in his arm. It is foolish to think otherwise.

Pain Killers to Heroin. A Matter of Money. A Matter of Desperation

In the book, I discussed a bit about Jack's progression toward heroin. Though I don't know the exact details, I do know a little.

Prescription pain pills were easy to get in the high school he attended. At one time, I was told they were sold and distributed in the hallway like candy. The price per pill, and I don't know which pill, was allegedly between $40 and $80. The kids who were using would go to any length to get the money to buy pills. Eventually, selling everything they could get their hands on, regardless of who owned the property.

Between fourteen and sixteen, Jack was using prescription pain pills (not prescribed to him). Then he suffered a major fracture to his collarbone and was prescribed painkillers. From this point on, there was no turning back for him. He needed to be on pills, Suboxone, or ultimately heroin.

I remember vividly at one point when he was still in high school, but older than eighteen, he had a complete emotional breakdown. He just started sobbing; it was worse than any crying I had ever seen. He came over to me and just put his arms around me and cried on my shoulder. I was stunned. I didn't know what it was about then. We sent him to the family doctor, who might have put him on Suboxone. Because he was eighteen, we did not have access to his medical records, and the doctor would not discuss the case with us. Had I known a little earlier, I might have been able to stop the progression before he got to heroin. According to Jack, he used heroin from the time he was eighteen until the morning of his relapse.

Remember 80 percent of all heroin addicts started as pill poppers, and 4 percent of the pill-popper population become heroin addicts.

Appendix 2

The Valedictorian and the Addict

Prior to 2006, I would have considered myself to be a "common" member of the community. Nothing extreme ever happened at our house, or in our family, that would have been considered unreasonable or strange. We prayed before dinner, went to church on Sunday, knew who our kids hung out with, and continuously monitored their behavior.

Our kids were only punished if they lied to us, and they knew in advance what the penalty was for dishonesty. The punishments were not extraordinary; they didn't have too much, or too little, of anything, relative to social norms at the time.

My family had not suffered any form of what would be considered a tragedy. Neither had my extended family. Everything was perfectly normal in our world. We weren't perfect, by any means. We made mistakes, many of them. But we always did the best we could with how we understood any given situation at that time. We loved one another, we loved our kids, and our sole purpose was to give them a great life. We did.

When Jack was in middle school, I did believe that messed-up kids were due to messed-up parents. I also believed that there was a strong likelihood that if one kid in a family was messed-up, the rest of the kids would be too. If Jack wanted to hang out with another fifth-grade kid, we would want to know about the kid's siblings and parents. If there were an older sibling in the family who was in trouble, or even had the slightest hint of a troubled reputation, we would not permit Jack to hang out with that fifth grader.

Did the fifth-grade kid do anything to be shunned from my kid's life? No. He was perfectly innocent, but somehow his older sibling got messed-up, and his parents failed to prevent it. In my mind, none of them could be trusted to ensure that my kid would not be exposed to some form of this dysfunction.

I did not know the siblings. I did not know the parents. All I knew was there was potential danger, and it was less risky to just say no to the relationship. I did not see anything wrong with this way of thinking, and neither did most parents in our small social circle.

But I was wrong!

In the past eleven years, I have learned two important lessons that I hope you can learn, if you haven't already. The first is that a fifth-grade kid will develop into his own person. His outcome, just like his formation, is completely independent of his siblings.

Further, the failure of a child is not a reflection on bad parenting. There are cases where kids are abused and mistreated, and some of them have difficulty being normal, but many of them excel at life, despite their extreme circumstances as children. Other kids are raised perfectly, *by the book*, in model homes and families and don't turn out so well.

Most families are normal, and most parents do their best to love and support their children growing up. Some kids from these families don't turn out ok, but most do. The point is how a child turns out is not to the parent's credit, or the parent's blame.

Consider my favorite poem on the subject, by Kahlil Gibran[40]:

"On Children"

Your children are not your children.
They are the sons and daughters of Life's longing for itself.
They come through you but not from you,
And though they are with you yet they belong not to you.

You may give them your love but not your thoughts,
For they have their own thoughts.
You may house their bodies but not their souls,
For their souls dwell in the house of tomorrow,
which you cannot visit, not even in your dreams.
You may strive to be like them,
but seek not to make them like you.
For life goes not backward nor tarries with yesterday.

You are the bows from which your children
as living arrows are sent forth.
The archer sees the mark upon the path of the infinite,
and He bends you with His might
that His arrows may go swift and far.
Let your bending in the archer's hand be for gladness;
For even as He loves the arrow that flies,
so He loves also the bow that is stable.

---

[40] Gibran, Kahlil. *The Prophet*. New York: Alfred Knopf, 1923.

Children come through their parents; they do not come from their parents. In my case, there are four children. One of them is addicted. Many people outside the recovery community will point to his mother or me as the cause of his addiction and dysfunction. *Just like I used to do.*

We have three daughters. The oldest was in the top 5 percent of her high school class and attended a university ranked among the nation's top 30. The second daughter was valedictorian of her graduating class and could have gone to any university of her choosing. The youngest is also quite successful, despite the past three years of extreme difficulty in our family. All three girls are multiple varsity letter winners, socially balanced, and not addicted.

Two of them are dedicated to their faith in Jesus and spend enormous amounts of time and effort helping other people find Jesus. This activity is certainly not due to their mother or me. I'm impressed with all three of them, especially after the past three years. However, no one on the outside gives us credit for our girl's success. The girls get all the credit, as they should. My point is this—parents get the blame, unfairly, for a wayward child, but not the credit for ultra-successful kids. It seems to me that there is a problem with this logic. If the parents didn't bring about success, how did they bring about addiction?

The answer is, of course, they didn't. If you join Al-Anon, as suggested, you will learn and accept the following truths:

- You did not *cause* it.
- You cannot *control* it.
- You cannot *cure* it.

Once you come to accept these truths, you can begin the journey to peace and serenity in your life, even if you are still living and dying with a heroin addict.

Appendix 3

Is My Kid on Opiates?

Telltales, Tells

Appearance	Behavior	Physical Health	Environment
Pinpoint pupils	Nodding off	Dry mouth	Lighters
Sleepy eyes	Manipulative	Track marks	Candles
Runny nose	Legal issues	Dry skin	Spoons
Bloody nose	Money issues	Itching	Belts
Dirty	Lying	Scratching	Rubber tubing
Unkempt	Secretive	Constipated	Glass pipes
Poor complexion	Manipulative	Nauseous	Metal pipes
Hair loss	Aggressive	Vomiting	Aluminum foil
Yawning	Erratic moods	Loss of appetite	Syringes
Shallow breathing	Withdrawn	Rapid weight	Powder residue
Long sleeves	Depressed	changes	Sticky residue
Lost, droopy eyes	Disoriented	Sneezing	Laxatives
Open mouth	Drowsy	Tremors	Missing alcohol
Closed eyes	Frequent changes	Colds, flu, ill	Missing money
Dropped head	Dazed, confused	Cramps	Missing
No changing	Slurred speech	Diarrhea	prescriptions
clothes	Slow speech	In/out of	Missing valuables
	Low, soft tone	consciousness	Burn marks
	Sudden energy	Collapsed veins	Blood stains
	change	Miscarriage	Baggies
	Mental sluggishness	Infectious diseases	Balloons
	Poor at school	HIV	Cotton balls
	Alienated	Hepatitis C	Cut cigarette filters
	Anxious	Blood infections	Locked doors
	Sudden isolation		Straws
	Altered sleep habits		Pen parts
	Disengaged		
	Selfish		
	Self-centered		
	Change in routine		
	Changing personality		
	Change in peers		
	Irritability		
	Low motivation		
	No family interest		
	No hobby interest		
	Drug priority		
	Using slang		

Appendix 4

Your Other Children

If there is a heroin addict in your life, you know the pain that is inflicted on you. Fear, guilt, and anger seem to surround you always. Sometimes you feel that there is no way out, no escape from the painful reality of living and dying with a heroin addict.

Imagine being a child trying to live with you. Growing up with a normal parent is hard. Growing up with a parent who is emotionally distracted by the addiction of a sibling is nearly impossible. If the addict still lives at home, dealing with the ongoing conflicts and near tragedy makes growing up a living hell.

There is so much work to be done in saving a heroin addict's life and healing personally that we might forget about the other lives around us. We become so consumed by recovery that our normal responsibilities as parents, spouses/partners, and employees usually take a back seat.

It might be years before you see how all this affects other young ones at home. You would be foolish to believe that those young minds and hearts are not extremely affected by what they see and hear. They don't know how to process their issues any better than you do. They try their best to not take your attention away from the life-saving and recovery efforts you face, but they need you. They need way more of you than they will ever let on, and they need more than they would if there wasn't an active heroin addict in the house.

If there are children enduring the presence of a heroin addict in your life, you must be proactive and get them support at your earliest opportunity. Do not make the mistake of assuming they are ok or that no signs of distress mean no distress. There is no way a child can witness the effects of heroin in the home and not be impacted deeply. Fear, guilt, anger, envy, and resentment—all the emotions you feel—they feel too. They are most especially frightened that you are suffering, sad, and fearful. Regardless of age, children, from preschool through their early twenties, are ill-equipped to deal with heroin addiction in the family.

It is a terrible spot to be in. They need you more than ever, at a time when you are less available than ever. It is likely that you are not well prepared to help them adequately. The purpose of this appendix is to make sure that you are aware of this problem. That despite how your other children behave, you must realize they need help and they need it now.

My suggestions here are thin. As always, I would rely on the advice available from relationships you are developing at Al-Anon. Families that have survived this epidemic have far better advice than anything you could pay for.

With that said, private individual counseling and family therapy are reasonable steps. Supportive family therapy, without the addict, might be quite helpful in getting the other children to open up. Some of the kids might not be candid in front of their siblings; they might require private counseling. It might also be necessary that the children have an opportunity to discuss their concerns about you. They might have deep fears or resentments regarding your handling of the addiction. They need to get that information out, so it can be processed openly.

As stated in the main text of this book, the rehab facility you choose might offer some services, but if the facility is providing mental health services to your addict, it might have a conflict of interest in helping you and your family.

It would also be a good suggestion for you to help your children develop relationships with other members of your extended family. Your brothers, sisters, and parents can be valuable resources helping siblings of addicts recover.

Whatever you decide, do not ignore the young people. They are impacted and deeply so. You must account for them when planning the recovery process.

Appendix 5

Parents of Addicts

Heroin addicts are usually an extremely intelligent, clever, and manipulative group of people. They know how to get what they want, and what they want is more important to them than anything else in their lives, including life itself. When they are manipulating a situation to their advantage, they don't wear a sign around their neck stating that they are being manipulative. Their manipulation strategy will consist of telling you what you want to hear. It will be executed in a way that you will readily accept. It's always disguised; it often seems as if their plan is in your best interest. You might even sense that you are being manipulated, but the plan seems so good that you need to support it. This is where you are part of the disease. You are ensnared in the web of heroin's seduction as much as the addict is.

When you're being manipulated by your heroin addict, so is your spouse/partner, often, in a diametrically opposed way. The addict leads you in one direction, while leading your spouse/partner in the other. He loves to create space between you and your partner. He finds leverage there, power in the space he creates.

It's much easier for him to get what he needs when his parents are divided. The wedge he drives between his parents is strongly based on emotion. It's based on love, guilt, resentment, and blame. If the parents are not openly discussing every individual encounter with the addict, then the addict is going to win. There can be absolutely no secrets between parents when it comes to their addicted child.

Parents must remain united *as parents*. The father cannot be Dad without Mom, and the mother cannot be Mom without Dad. You must operate with your spouse/partner, as a single entity called parents. The path to recovery is much shorter when the addict has fewer options to extend his deceit and manipulation. So long as one parent offers a path, the active addiction will continue, and the deterioration of the couple's marriage/partnership will accelerate.

Often times the parents will cycle back and forth in sympathy for the addict. For a time, Dad will be the path. When Dad gets screwed, Mom will sympathize with the addict, and she becomes the path. Then Mom gets screwed. Dad is back. The addict always has a path. But if Mom and Dad unite as a single unit—it is much more difficult for him to find one.

If you are married, do not allow your marriage to be caught in a no-win situation. Commit to each other that the marriage comes first. Agree that the best chance your addict has for survival is from committed parents. Parents who are committed to each other first, to their children second, and to the addict third. This is the only way.

Marriage or couples counseling is a great way to vent in a safe and supportive environment. Learn how to communicate your most difficult feelings of fear and blame to each other while in the care of a professional. Times are going to be turbulent, and you will both need the best from the other. What is happening in your family is so outside the bounds of known parenting skills that you need help. Get help. Get prepared. Work together to help your addict and save your marriage.

Appendix 6

Friends

Your friends will not understand about your child's addiction. This is the thing about heroin addiction you might never understand.

You have a certain group of friends and professional colleagues who you share a good deal of your time with—at home and at work. In this case, I am not considering your best friends or your lifelong friends. The friends I refer to here are friends and neighbors who you spend most of your time with. There are two phases in these relationships—one before you knew you were the parent of a heroin addict, and one after you knew.

Once you realize you are the parent of a heroin addict, everything about you changes when it comes to relationships. Before you tell anyone, you're already ashamed, embarrassed, and humiliated. You desperately need to talk and be supported—just like a parent of any terminally ill patient. This is what you are—the parent of a terminally ill patient, but because this is an addiction and not cancer—you live for some time in secrecy.

When you withhold vital information from your friends who care for you, they will notice. They will become aware that something is wrong with you, that you are not yourself, and you're keeping something from them. Of course, you're not ready to tell them, because this too humiliating, so you let them know that everything is fine, just fine. They know you're hiding something, so they wait. They probably begin to wonder why they are kept in the dark, thinking perhaps everyone else knows your secret except them. Then, of course, they feel guilty, maybe they did something wrong and didn't deserve your trust and confidence. The feeling of guilt probably shifts in time to one of resentment. They don't understand why you can't tell them what's wrong, at least not until you tell them what's wrong.

In time, maybe a month, maybe a year, you will eventually let your friends know what has happened in your home. You probably feel that you might be shunned from your social groups for being the parent of a heroin addict. But, at this point, you've already withdrawn quite a bit socially, and don't really care too much if you are shunned. You just want to come clean with what's been bothering you.

Ideally, the reaction from your friends would be similar to the reaction you would get if you let them know your child had some deadly disease, like cancer. The fact is your child does have a deadly disease, but often the reaction that you get is not what you might expect. It's more like having a highly contagious disease, like leprosy. There is sympathy and concern for everyone involved, but generally, families become self-protective and defensive about drug addictions. I can't say that I blame them. There are many social problems associated with narcotics that are not part of most diseases, like cancer.

Another issue with deadly addictions is that they never go away—until death. Once an addict, always an addict. There will always be fear that addicts could relapse, regardless of how much recovery time they have. This is a pressing problem for you, the parents of the addict, because there is no timeline, there is no X-ray or MRI that shows an imminent death or miraculous remission. This total, constant uncertainty makes your life a guessing game. It would be great if your friends could support you through this time—but they usually cannot.

From their point of view, you have a life issue, and you should deal with it and move on. They understand life issues, such as cancer, miscarriage, or the death of your parents. Unless they are the parent of a heroin addict, they can never truly know how to support you or how to behave around you. They will never understand that you live in constant fear—always wondering when and how your addict is going to die.

I think from the normal person's perspective, heroin addiction needs to be accepted, dealt with, and moved on. They don't realize that there is no escape from the life you live. This is why Al-Anon is so important; it offers a place for you to go and be with friends who completely understand your situation.

It Is Like Caring for an Alzheimer's Patient

From a family member's perspective, there aren't many common illnesses that can be compared to heroin addiction. It's not fair to anyone to compare, but I want to offer something that some people might be able to relate to. My grandmother suffered from Alzheimer's. She didn't live long with the disease, but we learned and experienced quite a bit in a short time, at least enough to sympathize completely with any family dealing with it now. It's a terrible thing to watch.

I don't wish to offend anyone going through the ordeal of Alzheimer's, but there are some similarities to heroin addiction that are relatable. One idea is that when an addict is active—his behavior and personality are so foreign to the family—it is like living with a stranger. The family loves a person they don't get to experience. While the addict is active, the son, daughter, or sibling who is so loved and remembered by family members is gone. If the family is lucky—the person they know and love might return at some point during recovery. Unfortunately, the addict might leave again when a relapse occurs.

Another similarity is the endless no-way-out nature of the disease. Parents, spouses, or partners of heroin addicts cannot escape the snares of heroin's trap. When the addict is clean, we fear for relapse, when active we dread overdose or a bottoming event. Try as we might, there is no way to not care for and love the addict, but there is no escape whatsoever from the mental and emotional drama imposed by the disease.

Another common attribute is watching the life of a loved one decay as the disease progresses. Left uncorrected by treatment, a heroin addict will decay away to nothing before our eyes, and all we can do is watch.

The final parallel is the confusing behavior exhibited by the addict, especially when active. Erratic and inconsistent behavior can drive a parent or spouse/partner crazy. We never know, day-to-day or minute-to-minute, which personality we might witness.

So from a loved one's point of view, Alzheimer's and heroin addiction have similarities in some limited respects. It takes a special person to provide unconditional love to a person afflicted with either disease.

If and when your addict dies—your friends will not know exactly how to behave, they have no frame of reference, and they certainly don't want to hurt you any more than you have already been hurt; so, you might not get meals delivered to the house or baskets of sympathy cards.

Death due to drug addiction is an unknown phenomenon. Our society does not know how to deal well with it. The main thing is to not have high expectations for your friends when it comes to supporting you through these difficult times; however, remember they are all still good people. They just don't know how to treat you the right way. Like you, they might have a certain amount of fear.

Appendix 7

My Recurring Nightmares

Answering the Door

Sometimes the doorbell rings, sometimes there is a knock, sometimes I just know to go to the door.

I am always in bed and always afraid when my feet touch the floor. From experience, I know I shouldn't go to the door. But my mind questions my sanity.

It is safe to answer the door, man, go answer it. There is no danger in this neighborhood; you live under a streetlight for Chrissake.

I wander to the stairs. It doesn't matter anymore if I turn the light on or not. It never seems to make a difference if it's on or off.

I get to the front door and always have the same thoughts—*Should I turn on the outside light?* Experience has proven whether I turn the light on or not makes no difference; it's still always the same.

I leave it off.

I open the door, and there is the barrel of a black revolver pointed straight at my chest. It can't be more than a foot from my body.

I look at the person pointing the gun at me. Only for an instant, I see there is no face. Inside the hoodie, there is only darkness. White, black, male, female, I don't know. It's all so fast.

The instantaneous flash of orange light forces my eyes shut. My chest collapses against my spinal column. My breath is gone, as I hear the gunshot. I am falling backward toward the floor. Before I hit the floor, my last thought is *Wait! This is real?*

The Darkroom

It is so dark.

I cannot see anything. I might not have eyes. I cannot tell, because it is so dark. The air is heavy and thick. It feels as though I am underwater, there's so much pressure on my body. Breathing is difficult. I'm so afraid.

It is so dark I cannot determine if I am inside or outside. I only know that wherever I am, I am afraid, and I need to get out of here, wherever here is. If I don't find a way out, I am going to suffer and die. But I am already suffering, and I realize that dying is a way out—maybe the only way. But this is no way to die. Only suffering about suffering and dying is occurring.

I try to move. But I am afraid to move. I do not know which direction to go. And I do not know where I am going. Where are the edges to this darkness? Am I in a room with walls? Will I find a wall?

If I walk too far, or not at all, will I step off a cliff? Are there walls or are there cliffs?

I am so scared, I'm trembling. I do not have a way out. Any direction might take me farther from the exit. Any step I take can lead me over the cliff.

There is no way out. I am stuck here. Paralyzed in the dark. Tears drip from my chin. Suffering. More and more wishing for death to relieve me from this place, but there is no way to bring death about.

I can't leave, I can't die; I can only suffer.

Panic sets in. I struggle for breath.

I try to cry out for help, but there's no sound. The pressure builds; the pain in my body is unbearable.

My ears pop. I'm being crushed.

The end is near . . .

Am I conscious? Did I pass out? Did I die? . . .

It is so dark.

I cannot see anything. I might not have eyes. I cannot tell, because it is so dark. The air is heavy and thick. It feels as though I am underwater, there's so much pressure on my body. Breathing is difficult. I'm so afraid.

The Three Year Old

I arrived at the scene of the accident. The brilliant, blue, flashing LED lights of the five police cars were lighting up the night sky while making it impossible to see anything clearly. I can make out my son's car. It's totaled again. How many totaled cars is that now? I'll have to count. I wondered where he was; he's walked away from multiple car accidents and drug overdoses. Even though by the look of his car, he should be dead. A normal man would be dead. But I expect him to show up and tell me how this is not his fault, because it's never his fault.

The lights are making me dizzy, as I am stopped by a police officer. He takes me by the arm to the area that is quarantined from passersby. It is like a medical triage area. There are a lot of people getting attention. There are a couple of body bags that look to be in use. Because there is so much going on, the thought of death did not cross my mind yet. I scan the area for Jack—I don't see him.

I look, or try to look, in the police cars, figuring he's probably in the back of one. The lights are too bright.

An older man comes around from the back of one of the fire engines. He looks at me and introduces himself as the Cobb County medical examiner.

Very dispassionately, he tells me that Jack is dead. He tells me that he was likely dead before the accident. That he overdosed on heroin and sped into the intersection crashing into crossing traffic.

Just then, a battered woman rushes up to me. Her head is cut open, and despite the bandages, she is still bleeding.

"She's dead, you son of a bitch. She's dead, because your son is a junkie. You raised a junkie, and he killed my precious three-year-old baby girl. I hope you burn in hell! I hope your whole family burns in hell."

Glossary

Terms You Might Need to Know

These include street terms, urban terms, medical terms, and medicines.

Abuse: Using a substance for other than its intended purpose.

Acquirer: A middleman.

Addiction: A chronic, relapsing disease, characterized by compulsive drug seeking and use accompanied by changes in the brain.

Adulteration: Diluting, cutting, stepping-on a drug.

Agonist: A chemical compound that mimics the action of a natural neurotransmitter.

Antagonist: A drug that binds to the same nerve cell receptor as the natural neurotransmitter but does not activate the receptor, instead blocking the effects of another drug.

Artillery: Syringe.

Back up: Pull-back.

Bag: A hit, usually between 1/10 and 1/8 gram; $15 to $30.

Balloon: One hit of heroin; often delivered in a balloon to allow swallowing in the event of arrest.

Benzodiazepines: A class of tranquilizers.

Bundle: Multiple hits.

Buprenorphine: A narcotic agonist-antagonist for the treatment of opioid addiction that relieves drug cravings without producing the "high" or dangerous side effects of other opioids.

Business: What junkies and dealers do to obtain, distribute, and use heroin.

Chasing the dragon: Smoking heroin.

China White: White powder heroin.

Chip: Nonaddictive drug use.

Chipper: A casual drug user.

CNS: Central nervous system.

Cocktail: A blend of various drugs.

Cold shot: Heroin dissolved in cold water.

Connection: Dealer.

Cooker: Spoon.

Cop: To obtain drugs.

Craving: An uncontrollable desire for drugs.

Cut: Dilute.

Detoxification: A process of allowing the body to rid itself of a drug while managing the symptoms of withdrawal; often the first step in a drug treatment program.

Done: Methadone.

Dysphoria: Feelings of unease during withdrawal.

Endorphins: Compounds produced by the body that are used to regulate pain and create a sense of well-being. They are similar and act in the same ways as opioids.

Fentanyl: A potent synthetic opioid, 100 times more powerful than morphine.

Fit: Syringe.

Front: A loan.

Gimmick: Syringe.

Half-life: The amount of time it takes for half a drug in the body to be removed.

Hit: Dose.

Hydrocodone: A codeine derivative that is roughly six times as potent.

Hypodermic: Syringe.

IV: Intravenous.

Jones: To desire heroin.

Joypopper: Chipper.

Kick: To stop using or withdraw from a drug.

Kicking down: Using less than your normal dose of heroin to reduce your tolerance.

Kit: Works.

Mainline: Intravenous injection.

Mark: A person who is easily tricked or cheated.

Methadone: A synthetic, long-acting opiate agonist medication with a long half-life.

Mixed agonist-antagonist: An agonist-antagonist.

Naloxone: An opioid receptor antagonist that rapidly binds to opioid receptors, blocking heroin from activating them. An appropriate dose of naloxone acts in less than two minutes and completely eliminates all signs of opioid intoxication to reverse an opioid overdose.

Naltrexone: An opioid antagonist medication that can only be used after a patient has completed detoxification. Naltrexone is not addictive or sedating and does not result in physical dependence; however, poor patient compliance has limited its effectiveness. A long-acting form of naltrexone called Vivitrol is injected once per month, eliminating the need for daily dosing, improving patient compliance.

Narcan: Naloxone.

Neonatal abstinence syndrome (NAS): NAS occurs when heroin from the mother passes through the placenta into the baby's bloodstream during pregnancy, allowing the baby to become addicted along with the mother. NAS requires hospitalization and treatment with medication (often a morphine taper) to relieve symptoms until the baby adjusts to becoming opioid-free.

OD: Overdose.

One and One: Heroin and cocaine sold together in a single bag.

Opiates: Technically, morphine, codeine, and any drugs derived from them. It is often used to refer to any substance with opium-like effects.

Opioid use disorder: A problematic pattern of opioid drug use, leading to clinically significant impairment or distress that includes cognitive, behavioral, and physiological symptoms as defined by the *Diagnostic and Statistical Manual of Mental Disorders, 5th edition* (DSM-5) criteria. Diagnosis of an opioid use disorder can be mild, moderate, or severe, depending on the number of symptoms a person experiences. Tolerance or withdrawal symptoms that occur during medically supervised treatment are specifically excluded from an opioid use disorder diagnosis.

Opioid: A natural or synthetic psychoactive chemical that binds to opioid receptors in the brain and body. Natural opioids include morphine and heroin (derived from the opium poppy) and opioids produced by the human body (endorphins); semi-synthetic or synthetic opioids include analgesics, such as oxycodone, hydrocodone, and fentanyl.

Opioids: Synthetic, opium-like drugs.

Opium: The dried juice from an unripe seed pod of the flower *Papaver somniferum*. The word "opium" is thrown around loosely, but the definition is specific.

Outfit: Syringe.

Oxycodone: A semi-synthetic morphine derivative, about half as potent.

Oxymorphone: A semi-synthetic morphine derivative, about ten times as potent.

Paraphernalia: Works.

Partial agonist: A substance that binds to and activates the same nerve cell receptor as a natural neurotransmitter but produces a diminished biological response.

Percocet: Oxycodone mixed with acetaminophen.

Percodan: Oxycodone mixed with aspirin.

Physical dependence: An adaptive physiological state that occurs with regular drug use and results in a withdrawal syndrome when drug use is stopped; usually occurs with tolerance.

Pull-Back: Pulling the syringe plunger back so that the syringe will fill with blood if the needle is inside a vein.

Pusher: Drug dealer.

Relapse: A deterioration after improvement. The addict starts using again.

Rig: Syringe.

Roll: When a vein moves to the side as it is being injected.

Roxicodone: Unadulterated oxycodone.

Run: A period of constant use.

Rush: A surge of euphoric pleasure that rapidly follows administration of a drug.

Score: To acquire drugs.

Script: Prescription.

Sedative: A drug that depresses the central nervous system and causes drowsiness.

Shoot Up: Inject.

Skin Pop: Subcutaneous (under skin) injection.

Slam: To inject, especially intravenously.

Sniff: To inhale a liquid or solid through the nose.

Snort: To inhale a liquid or solid through the nose.

Speedball: Heroin and cocaine mixed.

Step On: Dilute/cut.

Straight: A nondrug-using person.

Strung Out: Addicted to heroin.

Sublimaze: Fentanyl.

Syringe slang: Fit, gimmick, hypodermic, outfit, rig, works.

Tie: Tourniquet.

Tolerance: The capacity of the body to become less responsive to a substance with repeated use; the necessity to ingest more of a drug on subsequent episodes to achieve the same effect.

Tolerance: A condition in which higher doses of a drug are required to produce the same effect as during initial use; often leads to physical dependence.

Tracks: Repeated needle entry scars along a vein.

Vicodin: A prescription medication widely used for moderate pain, which contains hydrocodone and acetaminophen.

Withdrawal: A variety of symptoms that occur after use of an addictive drug is reduced or stopped.

Works: A syringe.

About the Author

Robert L. Hobbs Jr. was born in Youngstown, Ohio, to Robert Sr. and Alice L. McLaughlin. He was raised along with six brothers in Ohio's finest village—McDonald. Robert Sr. was an electrician at the US Steel McDonald Works, until its closing in 1979, while Alice was busy raising a young family of active boys. The late 1970s and early 1980s were difficult on blue-collar families in the Steel Valley but provided the Hobbs boys with a strong work ethic and a never-quit attitude.

Robert Jr., known as Bobby growing up, earned his way through college by joining the Ohio Army National Guard as a member of the military police. He graduated cum laude from Ohio University in 1988 with a bachelor of science degree in electrical engineering. After a short time at General Motors Packard Electric Division, he joined the Naval Nuclear Propulsion Program as an employee of the General Electric Company, where he advanced through increasing levels of qualification and responsibility. Following the 1996 completion of a master of business administration degree at Rensselaer Polytechnic Institute (Troy, New York), he moved to the metro Atlanta, Georgia, area, where he still resides with his wife, Wendy, whom he met growing up in Ohio.

Bob has worked as an executive in several software companies that developed products for the broadband, Internet telephony, cellular telephone, and satellite telephone industries. He is currently a certified professional coach, a strategic interventionist, and a Pose Method of Running technique specialist. He is focused on coaching executives in crisis, set-backs to comebacks, and parents and loved ones dealing with addicted family members.

Connect with Me

Web Page
www.heroinlivinganddying.com

Coaching Web Page—The Sandalwood Wellness Center
www.sandalwoodwellness.com

Facebook Page
https://www.facebook.com/bob.hobbs.399

Twitter
www.twitter.com/roberthobbs31

Google+
google.com/+roberthobbs31

LinkedIn
www.linkedin.com/in/roberthobbs31

Instagram
www.instagram.com/roberthobbs31